8.95

Sex and Class in Women's History

History Workshop Series

General Editor

Raphael Samuel, *Ruskin College, Oxford*

Already published

Village Life and Labour
Miners, Quarrymen and Saltworkers
People's History and Socialist Theory
Rothschild Buildings: Life in an East End
    Tenement Block, 1887-1920
East End Underworld: II. Chapters
    in the Life of Arthur Harding
Culture, Ideology and Politics

Routledge & Kegan Paul
London, Boston, Melbourne and Henley

edited by

Judith L. Newton
La Salle College, Philadelphia

Mary P. Ryan
University of California, Irvine

and

Judith R. Walkowitz
Rutgers University

Sex and Class in Women's History

First published in 1983
by Routledge & Kegan Paul plc
39 Store Street, London WC1E 7DD,
9 Park Street, Boston, Mass. 02108, USA,
296 Beaconsfield Parade, Middle Park,
Melbourne 3206, Australia, and
Broadway House, Newtown Road,
Henley-on-Thames, Oxon RG9 1EN
Set in Great Britain in IBM Press Roman by
Columns, Reading
Printed by The Thetford Press Ltd, Thetford
Introduction, selection and editorial matter © copyright
Feminist Studies, *1983*
All other matter © Routledge & Kegan Paul plc, 1983

Library of Congress Cataloging in Publication Data
Main entry under title:

Sex and class in women's history.
(History workshop series)
1. Feminism – History – Addresses, essays, lectures.
2. Sexism – History – Addresses, essays, lectures.
3. Social classes – History – Addresses, essays, lectures.
I. Newton, Judith Lowder. II. Ryan, Mary P. III. Walkowitz,
Judith R. IV. Series.
HG1154.S457 1983   305.4'2'09   82-25006

ISBN 0-7100-9529-5

IN MEMORY OF JOAN KELLY

Contents

Foreword

Sex and Class in Women's History is the first volume of essays in women's history to be published in the History Workshop Series. The essays all initially appeared in *Feminist Studies*, an American journal too little known and read in Britain, despite the fact that it has published many seminal articles on British and European, as well as American, women's history. This volume therefore is doubly welcome to the series both in its own right, as a collection of important (and, in some cases, already very influential) essays, and as a way of emphasizing the Anglo-American connection within feminist historical scholarship.

Recent years have seen a virtual explosion in the research and writing of feminist history, particularly in Western Europe, North America and Australia, although it has been by no means confined to these regions. This quantitative development has been accompanied by such important qualitative changes – in the types of questions asked, the methodologies employed, the scope and sophistication of analytical approaches adopted – that feminist history has now clearly moved on to the frontiers of progressive historical writing. This volume reflects those developments. Indeed many of the articles in it were born as contributions to a major international conference in women's history, at which the theoretical and political agendas of feminist historians were discussed with a vigour and urgency possible only where scholarship is infused with social aims. Both the vigour and the urgency remain audible in the essays collected in this book, essays which set the tone for the many more volumes of feminist history which we anticipate publishing in the History Workshop Series.

Barbara Taylor (*History Workshop Journal*)

Editors' Introduction

JUDITH L. NEWTON, MARY P. RYAN and JUDITH R.
WALKOWITZ

This volume collects under one cover a series of essays on
women's history which were originally published in the journal
Feminist Studies.[1] Focusing for the most part on women in
nineteenth-century Britain and America and including work by
contemporary scholars in both countries, this collection takes its
place in a long history of Anglo-American debate. It was in the
1600s, after all, that Anne Hutchinson migrated from Britain to
New England full of the dissenting religious ideas which inspired
women on both sides of the Atlantic. In the next century, Mary
Wollstonecraft's *Vindication of the Rights of Woman* was printed,
debated, celebrated and ridiculed in the United States as well as in
England. It was a journey to London by Elizabeth Cady Stanton
and Lucretia Mott, for the World Anti-Slavery Convention of
1840, which reputedly kindled the idea of calling the first
women's rights convention, held eight years later in Seneca Falls,
New York. And from that point forward there was a heavy traffic
of feminists between English and American ports.

This heritage of connection, which continues today in the shape
of international conferences, publications and debates, invites us
to consider our similarities and to confront our differences. As
British and American scholars we share more than a commitment
to the study of women's history. We share several ideological
positions characteristic of the second wave of feminism in the
West. We tend to agree that the task of women's history is more
than to commandeer a few female public figures to be given
positions of honor in the historical record. Instead, we employ
gender as a category of historical analysis, and in so doing, we try
to determine and to understand the systematic ways in which sex
differences have cut through society and culture and in the process
have conferred inequality upon women. After half a decade of
research, moreover, we have moved beyond a one dimensional
emphasis upon the oppression and victimization of women and

have also come to recognize and explore the lines along which women have shaped their own history and that of men.[2]

Within this framework of agreement, however, there have been important differences between English and Americans — marked disparities in the themes we have favored, the concepts we have employed, and the modes of explanation we have chosen; differences which have their roots in distinctive political, social, economic, and intellectual conditions. If as feminist historians we have all viewed sex-based divisions as central to processes of social transformation, British historians have tended to place more emphasis on class than their American counterparts. Class lines have always appeared more rigid and exact in Britain than in America, and class consciousness in Britain has therefore been more acute — a fact naturally reflected in the work of feminist historians. Many feminist historians in Britain, moreover, have emerged from a socialist and labor-oriented tradition which assigns a key place to the study of class relationships, and this strong inheritance of labor history has marked much feminist historical research.

Labor historians, of course, have a great deal to offer scholars of women's history, both in Britain and America. Labor historians have used and given legitimation to non-traditional historical sources such as documents drawn from popular culture or oral testimony, which are important for the study of female experience. The exploration of prepolitical forms of resistance, as they grow out of traditional rituals and social practices, has led historians like E.P. Thompson to see women and children as political actors and has helped establish a subtle conception of resistance which has been crucial to the study of women's power.[3] But labor history, both British and American, has tended none the less to impede the study of gender in so far as it has been informed by male bias, a bias which has expressed itself, as Anna Davin suggests, not only in a lack of attention to the untraditional sources of women's history but in a reluctance to acknowledge that such sources exist. Their definitions of labor, moreover, have led historians within this tradition to focus on the wage labor done by men and until recently to ignore the unwaged (or even waged) labor of women. Finally, labor history has also tended to accept the sexual division of labor as a given rather than to see it as an object of study or a category of analysis.[4]

Yet questions about gender are "crucial for any proper analysis of the very subjects with which labor history should be concerned."[5] As many feminists have pointed out, the sexual division of labor is basic to an understanding of the way in which capitalism has maintained itself, for it has allowed capitalism to divide the work force, to secure lower wages, to maintain a reserve army of inexpensive labor, and to ensure cheap maintenance and reproduction of the labor force.[6] Feminist historians, moreover, have demonstrated, in many different ways, that gender divisions have weakened and debilitated a mass working-class movement by separating working-class women from working-class men.[7] In this volume, for example, Barbara Taylor and Christine Stansell explore some of the specific ways in which gender has been an antagonistic element in working-class life, Stansell finding sexual antagonism reflected in the failure of labor to support suffrage and Taylor locating similar antagonism in the recognition of working-class feminists that "the men are as bad as their masters."[8] A theory of gender and of male domination, then, is central to the study of capitalism itself – and it is crucial to the study of women. For women have not only worked for capital, they have worked for men, and the implication of this dual oppression is that the end of capitalism does not spell the end of sexual hierarchy.[9]

It is in developing a theory of gender, and of women's culture, that American historians of women have made their distinctive contribution, and like the British emphasis on class the American focus on gender has grown directly out of the scholarly tradition in which historians of women have been trained. Labor history, for example, although it has experienced an American renaissance in the last generation, has not been as central to American historiography as to English.[10] American historians of women, therefore, had to find more eclectic paths into women's past, the first historians simply going in search of female subjects within the terrain of their own specialties – in politics, letters, culture, institutions and social movements. This approach proved most successful in those areas of American life where female subjects were most easily discernible and socially distinct, in literature about femininity, for example, or in all-female institutions like women's colleges and settlement houses. By 1975 this brand of scholarship had produced a wealth of literature about women,[11] although it was a literature in which women too often appeared as discrete, apparently autonomous subjects of history.

The shift from writing about women to engaging in the self-conscious study of gender has been a slow process and is still incomplete. It is a process, moreover, which occurred in a distinctly political as well as historiographic context. The rudiments of gender analysis, for example, appeared early in the 1970s in the politics and theories of radical feminists, who saw something called sex, sex-class, or sex caste as the most fundamental, most oppressive social division.[12] Radical feminists also sponsored a separatist movement, called for a self-sufficient women's community and celebrated a distinctively female culture. This heightened consciousness of gender and this move towards the establishment of segregated female institutions soon found academic expression in the rapid growth of women's studies. Today women's studies is an established discipline in colleges and universities across the country. It is the theme of several journals, the basis of a national professional association, and the foundation of innumerable scholarly congresses, one of which, the Berkshire Conference on Women's History, draws well over a thousand participants.[13] It is the success of women's studies programs, journals and conferences which prompts British historians of women to marvel at the scale and institutional solidity of American scholarship about women and which often reaffirms for American historians of women a belief in the collective strength of women in history and in the significance of gender as a fundamental social division.

The pointed focus on gender which is reflected in the American contributions to this volume evolved within this female politics and these female institutions. Indeed, it came directly out of radical feminism which demanded a women-centred history – a history seen through the eyes of women and validated by women's values.[14] This perspective, moreover, fostered another important contribution on the part of American historians of women, the identification of a relatively autonomous social and sexual world signified by terms such as homosocial bonds, women's networks and women's culture.[15] Still, if many American historians of women have tended to focus on the resources of a relatively autonomous female world, they have also become increasingly concerned to establish its boundaries and to determine when, to what degree, and with what patterns of domination women's experience intersects with a male universe.[16] It is this analytic problem which has often prompted American historians of women to turn not only to Marx but to other disciplines such as anthropology. It is in addressing this problem that feminist scholars have made concepts such as the sex/gender system and the "public" as opposed to the "private" central to the language of their work.[17]

To talk of a British focus on class, therefore, and of an American focus on gender is to make our categories too exact. Not only do socialist and radical feminist tendencies inform the work of women's historians in both countries, but British and American historians of women are becoming more alike. As the essays in this volume suggest, scholars in both countries are beginning to adopt what Joan Kelly calls "the doubled vision of feminist theory," the view that it is the simultaneous operation of relations of class and of sex/gender that perpetuate both patriarchy and capitalism. It is, perhaps, this dual vision of feminist theory which can resolve those conflicts between radical-feminist and socialist-feminist, feminist and Marxist, American and British which result from attempts to reduce sex oppression to class interests, on the one hand, and to see the relation of the sexes as always and ever the same, regardless of race, class or society, on the other.

Of course, to adopt this doubled vision is to question other traditional distinctions as well. In particular, it is to question neat divisions between relations seen as "private" and relations seen as belonging to a purely "public" sphere. This challenge to traditional divisions, for example, informs much recent work on the family. In this volume, "Examining Family History" by Rayna Rapp, Ellen Ross and Renate Bridenthal argues that the very notion of family as a "natural unit" existing in separation from the total social formation is a legacy of that nineteenth-century bourgeois ideology which initially separated male and female life into a public and a private sphere. Family relations may be experienced as private, but ideology "penetrates our most intimate social relations and conditions our acceptance of or resistance to dominant values in the larger society." Indeed, belief in the family acts as a kind of ideological shock absorber "which keeps people functioning and which diminishes the tensions often generated by economic processes."[18]

Like the family, sexuality has also become a locus for making connections between what have been seen as separate spheres.[19] Sexuality, that is, is being explored not as a natural essence but as a socially constructed practice, a set of relations, and as relations which interact with those of class and production.[20] In work on nineteenth-century Britain and America, in particular, sexuality is often regarded as central rather than peripheral to social change, for the transformation of work and community in the Victorian era intersected at various points with a reorganization of gender, family and sex, and collective struggles over the relations of work and class were often accompanied by collective struggles over the relations of sexuality and gender. These subtle connections, of course, are often difficult to explore for, according to Gayle Rubin, "sexuality in Western societies" is so mystified that "the wars over it are often fought at oblique angles, aimed at phoney targets, conducted with misplaced passions, and are highly intensely symbolic."[21]

In this volume, Leonore Davidoff's study of "Class and Gender in Victorian England" demystifies a symbolic drama to suggest how individual, seemingly private, erotic behavior might be subtly informed by and indirectly reflect more collective sexual practices. It also suggests several ways in which sexual practice, both on the individual and collective levels, may have enforced hierarchies of gender and of class, for in the last half of the century the efforts of middle-class men to maintain positions of power within society and within their own households merged with their efforts to control sexuality itself — their own, that of middle-class women, and that of the working class. That working-class women and men, for example, as well as native blacks, were seen as more sexual than white men of the middle class, functioned to justify their subordinate class position. In similar fashion, the ideological construction of middle-class women as pure and passionless, and thus as creatures needing protection, indirectly justified their continuing subordination to men. Sexual ideologies and sexual practices, that is, stood in mutually reinforcing relation with hierarchies of gender and of class, relations which were acted out in private scripts and in more public dramas.

Maria Ramas, in her work on "Freud's Dora, Dora's Hysteria: The Negation of a Woman's Rebellion," also explores this intersection of public and private roles. Freud's analysis of Ida

Bauer, according to Ramas, was immersed in current sexual codes. By insisting that Ida really loved Herr K and not his wife and by constructing Ida's rejection of Herr K as abnormal, Freud restricted female sexual practice to heterosexuality and equated feminine behavior with submission. Freud, in turn, along with other medical experts, was to reaffirm these patriarchal ideologies by raising them to the level of scientific fact. Indeed, as several studies of reproduction have pointed out, public debate over sexuality became dominated by male professional experts by the end of the century.[22] It is in this context of domination, however, that Ida's troubled resistance to ideology and to Freud — partially expressed in her continuing rejection of Herr K and in her lesbian attachment to his wife — might be seen as the emblem of a later counter-struggle. For if nineteenth-century patriarchal and capitalist societies had the power to enforce heterosexuality and to define homosexuality as sick, these impositions of identity were ultimately to provoke lesbian and gay self-naming and self-identification in the next century.[23]

The history of Dora should remind us that women have characteristically entered into sexual struggles as something more than the passive recipients of sexual codes. Indeed, it was in coming to terms with women's resistance to oppression that historians of women began to abandon their earlier focus on victimization in order to reconceptualize the very nature and locus of power. While continuing to maintain that power is exercised by specific historical agents with access to different levels and different sources of power, they have also come to see power less as one group's "consolidated and homogeneous domination over others" than as something "which circulates" or functions "in the form of a chain."[24] In this volume, for example, John Gillis's study of "Servants, Sexual Relations, and the Risks of Illegitimacy in London, 1801-1900" cites statistics on the number of illegitimate births among higher-class servants which might imply at first a simple tale of working-class women seduced and abandoned, but Gillis's analysis of the local and specific situation of these women suggests something more complex. Their sexual arrangements, however oppressive, were also negotiated. It was in part their internalization of upper-class values, the values dominant in the households where they served, that prompted them to have liaisons with higher-class working men who were unusually mobile. It was their desire for upper-class respectability that prompted them to carry on courtships with decorous secrecy, a secrecy that often left them without witnesses to call when they wished to sue errant fathers for the support of a child.

Black women in American afford particularly eloquent studies
of the complex relation between oppression and resistance,
powerlessness and power. From the slave quarters of the
nineteenth century to the ghettoes of the 1980s, poor black
women have inhabited the lowest ranks of American society and
have had access to the most marginal forms of economic and
political power. And yet the very tenacity and strength with which
such women have survived oppression presents feminists with
powerful images of black womanhood. To label such women
"matriarchs," however, as many American social scientists, and
even some black activists, have done, is to disregard totally their
subordinate position relative to black as well as to white men.[25]
The myth of matriarchy obscures the complicated knot of
relations between race and gender in America, a knot which
historians of women have hardly begun to trace.[26] Suzanne
Lebsock's study of free black women at the turn of the century
takes up this tangle of connections to provide a provocative case
study of how racial oppression might coexist with relationships
which are at least *relatively* egalitarian between black women and
black men.

Women, of course, have exerted power not just as individuals
but as collectivities. In "The Power of Women's Networks," for
example, Mary Ryan suggests how the largely white middle-class
women of the Female Reform Society in the 1830s and 1840s in
New York exerted communal power by regulating sexual behavior.
In the process — by devising sexual codes and practices which
would distinguish the urban middle class from their artisan and
farming parents — these women played a central role in the
transformation of class and ideology, and they opened a "new
social space" through which their sex could maneuver for power.
It was through this voluntary organization, that is, that women
exerted influence outside the home and applied pressure to men in
public spheres, thereby muting the barriers between the public
world of men and the private world of women and enhancing the
power of middle-class white women within their communities.
Later in the century and across the Atlantic the middle-class
women of the Ladies National Association also intervened in the
sexual arrangements of their community. By attacking state
regulation of prostitution these women opposed the police, the
parliament, the military, and the medical establishment who
administered the Contagious Diseases Acts. They both challenged
male centers of power and defended the interests of their sex.[27]

If women have exerted power, however, it is important to
acknowledge that the power they have exerted has not always

been progressive. If the moral reformers of New York managed to enhance, at least momentarily, the power of white middle-class women in their community, they also constructed a sexual morality which, by emphasizing the purity of women, further confined them to the home and was therefore particularly repressive to their sex.[28] If the British Ladies National Association began as a libertarian struggle against state-sanctioned male vice, it eventually helped spawn an attack on non-marital and non-reproductive sexuality in the shape of repressive crusades against prostitution, pornography, and homosexuality.[29] Ultimately the reformist energies of both groups functioned to limit women's sexuality and to support the divisions of nineteenth-century capitalist states. This subversion of reformist energy, moreover, although it must be explained in part by loss of authority to male professional experts, is also to be explained by the continued adherence of female reformers to an ideology of women's separate sphere. Both reform movements, for example, emphasized the moral supremacy and sexual purity of women; both conceived of women as spiritual creatures to be protected by males. The very terms in which they conceived of sexual reforms tended to endorse traditional inequities between female and male.

Similar contradictions informed female collectivities in poor communities. In studies of working-class neighborhood life, an area largely neglected by labor historians, we see that working-class culture and consciousness were often expressed and articulated through female networks. Female neighbors not only shared space and services, they created a matrilocal and female-centered community life in which the role of the mother may have become more central. And yet, like women in middle-class female societies, these women did not reorganize gender within the working class or even challenge its inequities. It was the mothers of Salford, Plymouth and Bethnal Green who established standards of female behavior which were constrictive to their daughters and who demarcated social divisions in their communities on the basis of gender and age.[30]

This contradiction in the exercise of women's historical agency — that women both wielded power and that their power was not always progressive — raises questions about where effective female resistance begins. Carroll Smith-Rosenberg has suggested that homosocial bonds, emotionally intense and erotic friendships between women in the nineteenth century, created a sphere of womanhood that transcended the boundaries of the individual home and that often expanded into dense networks of female ties and loyalties.[31] Women's networks, in turn, became formalized into voluntary reform groups and charitable institutions which celebrated female values and served a female clientele. But the adherence of women's networks and societies to a limiting ideology of woman's proper sphere suggests that feminism was not a natural outgrowth of female culture even though it might emerge from it in certain political conditions.[32] In this volume, Barbara Taylor suggests that popular working-class feminism had its base both in the prior existence of working-class socialism and in the prior existence of feminism on the part of self-educated "odd women" of the middle class. Working-class feminism, moreover, only emerged from this base during a crisis in the sexual division of labor which was provoked both by heightened sex as well as class consciousness. It was from a complex interaction between sex and class issues, therefore, that working-class feminism was to grow.

The interrelation of gender and class in the history of feminist movements suggests the need for a vision that combines an account of gender and an account of class relations. It is this kind of vision which Christine Stansell calls for in her review of two books on suffrage, *One Hand Tied Behind Us* by the British historians Jill Liddington and Jill Norris and *Feminism and Suffrage* by the American Ellen DuBois. According to Stansell, Liddington and Norris, as historians writing from a laborist tradition, have a firm sense of how working-class women acted as historical agents of change, but they give limited attention to gender and to patriarchy as a system cutting across class lines. Thus, they neglect both the negative role of sex antagonism in the failure of working-class men to support women's suffrage and the positive role of cross-class alliances between feminists from the working and the middle classes. At the same time, Stansell suggests, American historians have tended to emphasize women's networks and women's culture as the automatic base of women's political movements and to pay little attention to class divisions among women (an imbalance which she feels is redressed in DuBois's study). What Stansell argues for, in effect, is that dual vision to which we have already referred, a vision which examines the operations of both sex/gender relations and the relations of race and class.

The engagement of this dual vision is particularly important for the study of Victorian culture in which a transformation of work and community was bound up with the reorganization of gender and of sex. The study of gender, for example, is particularly crucial to an understanding of nineteenth-century life, for although every known culture has employed gender as a fundamental principle of organizing social life, nineteenth-century England and America seemed to be particularly bold about dividing up social space itself between female and male. In the early preindustrial world men and women went about their sex-linked activities within a common household and in a world where biological distinctions such as age and kinship organized a variety of social tasks. With industrial capitalism, however, the genders seemed to be separated into bi-polar domains, although for middle-class white women that domain was more expansive than the home, extending to a network of voluntary associations and to a women-centered politics.[33]

But even white women of the middle class did not inhabit an entirely sex-segregated universe. Heterosexual relations and marriage still determined much of their status and defined many of their social relations, and the same is true for women laboring outside the home. It is imperative, therefore, that historians of women also chart the points at which male and female spheres intersect and with what consequences. Similarly, movements for sexual and labor reform in the late nineteenth century brought males and females together in common cause. We need to know more about the internecine sexual politics of these movements. We need to examine carefully how the boundaries of gender cross and cross again the lines of class.

This doubled vision, moreover, may also help us clarify the present. For as in mid-nineteenth-century Britain and America, a conservative ideology about women is being reconsolidated, not only as a means of keeping women in their place, but as a means of strengthening a class-stratified economic order at a time of crisis. In this country, the renewed effort to persecute lesbians and gays, to enforce racism, to restore male control of women's bodies and of the family as a whole may be seen as part of a more general attempt by corporate powers to dismantle the welfare state, to redirect funds for social needs into the private sector, and to reprivatize what had been made public through the historical struggles of women, minorities, and the working class.[34]

Thus once again the relations of class and race, gender and sexuality entangle. But as Joan Kelly suggests, those relations may be in sufficient conflict for us to see now how relations of production, reproduction and consumption operate to support a patriarchal order. In being able to see, we may be empowered to act. In drawing upon our heritage of feminism, agency and connection we may move beyond the construction of a doubled vision to an exercise of collective power.

NOTES

[1] *Feminist Sudies*, which receives administrative support from the Women's Studies Program at the University of Maryland, appears three times a year. It was first published in 1972. Manuscripts and correspondence should be directed to the Managing Editor, *Feminist Studies*, c/o the Women's Studies Program, University of Maryland, College Park, Md. 20742.

[2] On the shift from victimization to historical agency see Gerda Lerner, "Approaches to the Study of Women in American History" and "Placing Women in History: A 1975 Perspective," in *Liberating Women's History: Theoretical and Critical Essays*, ed. Berenice A. Carroll (Urbana, Illinois: University of Illinois Press, 1976), pp. 349-56, 357-67; Hilda Smith, "Feminism and the Methodology of Women's History," ibid., pp. 368-84; Sheila Ryan Johansson, " 'Herstory' as History: A New Field or Another Fad?" ibid., pp. 400-30.

[3] See, for example, E.P. Thompson, "The Moral Economy of the English Crowd in the Eighteenth Century," *Past and Present* 50 (1971), 71-136, and *The Making of The English Working Class*, rev. edn (Harmondsworth: Penguin Books, 1968), chapters 10 and 12. See also Dorothy Thompson, "Women and Nineteenth-Century Radical Politics: A Lost Dimension," in *The Rights and Wrongs of Women*, ed. Juliet Mitchell and Ann Oakley (Harmondsworth: Penguin Books, 1976), pp. 112-38.

[4] Anna Davin, "Feminism and Labour History," in *People's History and Socialist Theory*, ed. Raphael Samuel (London: Routledge & Kegan Paul, 1981), pp. 176-87.

[5] Davin, "Feminism and Labour History," p. 178.

[6] See, for example, Sally Alexander and Barbara Taylor, "In Defense of Patriarchy," *New Statesman* 99:161; Davin, "Feminism and Labour History"; Laura Owen, "The Welfare of Women in Labouring Families: England, 1860-1950," *Feminist Studies* 1, no. 3-4 (Winter/Spring 1973), 107-25; Nancy Grey Osterud, "Women's Work and the Putting-Out System. The Hosiery Industry in Nineteenth-Century Leicestershire," paper delivered at the Berkshire Conference on the History of Women, June 1981; Rosalind Petchesky, "Dissolving the Hyphen: A Report on Marxist-Feminist Groups 1-5," in *Capitalist Patriarchy and the Case for Socialist Feminism*, ed. Zillah Eisenstein (New York: Monthly Review Press, 1979), pp. 373-89.

[7] See, for example, Alice Kessler Harris, "Where are the Organized Women Workers?", *Feminist Studies* 3 (Fall 1975), 92-110; Oren, "The Welfare of Women in Labouring Families"; Jacqueline Jones, " 'My Mother Was Much of a Woman': Black Women, Work, and the Family Under Slavery," *Feminist Studies* 8 (Summer 1982, 235-69); Nancy Gabin, " 'They Have Placed a Penalty on Womanhood': The Protest Actions of Women Auto Workers in Detroit-area UAW Locals, 1945-47," *Feminist Studies* (Summer 1982), 373-98; Martha May, "The Historical Problem of the Family Wage: The Ford Motor Company and the Five Dollar Day," ibid.; Ruth Milkman, "The Sexual Division of Labor: The Auto Industry During World War II," ibid.; Joan Smith, "The Way We Were: Women and Work, a Review Essay," ibid.; Sally Alexander, "Women's Work in Nineteenth-Century London: A Study of the Years 1820-1850," in *The Rights and Wrongs of Women*, pp. 59-111; Mary McIntosh and Michele Barrett, "The Family Wage: Some Problems for Socialists and Feminists," *Capital and Class* II (Summer 1980), 51-72.

[8] Barbara Taylor, " 'The Men are as Bad as Their Masters . . .': Socialism, Feminism, and Sexual Antagonism in the London Tailoring Trade."

[9] Work by radical feminists such as Adrienne Rich has forced socialist-feminists to theorize about the construction of heterosexuality. See, for example, Rich's "Compulsory Heterosexuality and Lesbian Experience," *Signs* 5 (Summer 1980), 631-60. For theoretical work on capitalism and gender see the following, among others:

Heidi Hartmann, "Capitalism, Patriarchy, and Job Segregation by Sex," in *Capitalist Patriarchy*, ed. Eisenstein, pp. 206-47; Gayle Rubin, "The Traffic in Women: Notes on the 'Political Economy' of Sex," in *Toward an Anthropology of Women*, ed. Rayna R. Reiter (New York: Monthly Review Press, 1975), pp. 157-210. For historical work which incorporates both a theory of capitalism and gender see, for example, Mary Ann Clawsen, "Early Modern Fraternalism and the Patriarchal Family," *Feminist Studies* 6 (Summer 1980), 368-91; Natalie Davis, "Women in the Crafts in Sixteenth-Century Lyons," *Feminist Studies* 8 (Spring 1982), 47-80.

[10] For recent labor history which has been helpful to feminist historians, see work by David Brody, Allen Dawley, Herbert Gutman, Bruce Laurie, and David Montgomery.

[11] For examples of this approach see Eleanor Flexner, *Century of Struggle: The Women's Rights Movement in the United States* (Cambridge, Mass: Harvard University Press, Bellknap Press, 1976); Gerda Lerner, *The Grimké Sisters from South Carolina: Rebels Against Slavery* (Boston: Houghton Mifflin, 1967); William O'Neill, *Everyone Was Brave: The Rise and Fall of Feminism in America* (Chicago: Quadrangle Books, 1969); Barbara Welter, "The Cult of True Womanhood 1820-1860," *American Quarterly* 18 (Summer 1966), 151-74.

[12] See, for example, Ti-Grace Atkinson, *Amazon Odyssey* (New York: Links Books, 1974); Shulamith Firestone, *The Dialectic of Sex: the Case for Feminist Revolution* (New York: Bantam Books, 1971); Kate Millett, *Sexual Politics* (Garden City, New York: Doubleday, 1970).

[13] There are, for example, over 300 Women's Studies programs in American colleges and universities.

[14] For a discussion of women-centered history see Gerda Lerner, *The Majority Finds its Past: Placing Women in History* (New York: Oxford University Press, 1979).

[15] See, for example, Carroll Smith-Rosenberg, "The Female World of Love and Ritual: Relations Between Women in Nineteenth-Century America," *Signs* 1 (Autumn 1975), 1-29. For a debate on women's culture see Ellen DuBois, Mari Jo Buhle, Temma Kaplan, Gerda Lerner, and Carroll Smith-Rosenberg, "Politics and Culture in Women's History: A Symposium," *Feminist Studies* 6 (Spring 1980), 26-64.

[16] But even as American historians of women have focused on the limitations of a female world and even as they have addressed questions about race, class and ethnicity, it has been with a focus on gender as their primary subject and category of analysis. See, for example, Thomas Dublin, *Women At Work: The Transformation of Work and Community in Lowell Massachusetts 1826-1860* (New York: Columbia University Press, 1979); Elizabeth Pleck, "A Mother's Wages: Income Earning Among Married Italian and Black Women, 1896-1911," in *The American Family in Social-Historical Perspective*, ed. Michael Gordon (New York: St. Martin's Press, 1978), pp. 490-510; Suzanne Lebsock, "Free Black Women and the Question of Matriarchy: Petersburg, Virginia," this volume.

[17] Anthropological studies which have been particularly helpful to historians of women include Michelle Zimbalist Rosaldo, "Woman, Culture, and Society: A Theoretical Overview," in *Woman, Culture, and Society*, ed. Michelle Zimbalist Rosaldo and Louise Lamphere (Stanford: Stanford University Press, 1974), pp. 17-42; see also Rosaldo's "The Use and Abuse of Anthropology: Reflections on Feminism and Cross-Cultural Understanding," *Signs* 5 (Spring 1980), 389-417; Rayna R. Reiter, "Men and Women in the South of France: Public and Private Domains," in *Toward An Anthropology of Women*, pp. 252-82. The term "sex/gender" is used by Gayle Rubin in her important synthetic article "The Traffic in Women."

[18] Rayna Rapp, Ellen Ross, Renate Bridenthal, "Examining Family History."

[19] Recent historical discussions of sexuality which may be of use to feminists include those of Edward Bristow, *Vice and Vigilence: Purity Movements in Britain Since 1700* (Totowa, New York: Rowman & Littlefield, 1977); Nancy F. Cott, "Passionlessness: An

Interpretation of Victorian Sexual Ideology, 1790-1850," *Signs* 4 (1978), 129-236; Lillian Faderman, *Surpassing the Love of Men: Romantic Friendship and Love Between Women from The Renaissance to The Present* (New York: William Morrow, 1981); Linda Gordon, *Woman's Body, Woman's Right: A Social History of Birth Control in America* (Harmondsworth: Penguin Books, 1977); Deborah Gorham, "The Maiden Tribute of Modern Babylon Reexamined: Child Prostitution and the Idea of Childhood in Late Victorian England," *Victorian Studies* 21 (Spring 1978), 358-69; Sheila Jeffreys, "The Spinster and Her Enemies and the Last Wave of Feminism," *Scarlet Women* 13 (July 1981); Paul McHugh, *Prostitution and Victorian Social Reform* (London, 1980); Angus McLaren, *Birth Control in Nineteenth Century England* (New York: Holmes & Meier, 1978); Mary Ryan, *Cradle of the Middle Class: The Families of Oneida County New York, 1790-1865* (Cambridge: Cambridge University Press, 1981); Carroll Smith-Rosenberg, "Sex as Symbol in Victorian Purity: An Ethnohistorical Analysis of Jacksonian America," *American Journal of Sociology* 84 (1978), 212-47; Martha Vicinus, "Sexuality and Power: A Review of Current Work in the History of Sexuality," *Feminist Studies* 8 (Spring 1982); Judith Walkowitz, *Prostitution and Victorian Society: Women, Class, and the State* (Cambridge: Cambridge University Press, 1980).

[20] See, for example, Robert A. Padgug, "Sexual Matters: On Conceptualizing Sexuality in History," *Radical History Review* 20 (Spring/Summer 1979), 3-24; Joseph Interrante and Carol Lasser, "Victims of the Very Songs They Sing: A Critique of Recent Work on Patriarchal Culture and the Social Construction of Gender," ibid., 25-40; Jeffrey Weeks, "Movements on Affirmation: Sexual Meanings and Homosexual Identities," ibid., 164-79; Michele Barrett, "Femininity, Masculinity, and Sexual Practice," in *Women's Oppression Today: Problems in Marxist Feminist Analysis* (London: Verso Editions, 1980); Jeffrey Weeks, *"Prostitution and Victorian Society: Women, Class, and the State* by Judith R. Walkowitz," *History Today* 31 (April 1981), 52-3.

[21] Gayle Rubin, unpublished essay.

[22] See, for example, Anna Davin, "Imperialism and Motherhood," *History Workshop Journal* no. 5 (Spring 1978), 9-65; Jean Donnison, *Midwives and Medical Men: A History of Inter-professional Rivalries and Women's Rights* (New York: Schocken Books, 1977); Jacques Donzelot, *The Policing of Families*, trans. Robert Hurley (New York: Pantheon Books, 1979); Lillian Faderman, *Surpassing the Love of Men*; Linda Gordon, *Woman's Body*; John S. Haller and Robin M. Haller, *The Physician and Sexuality in Victorian America* (Urbana: University of Illinois Press, 1974); Jane Lewis, *Politics of Motherhood: Child and Maternal Welfare in England, 1900-1939* (London: Croom Helm, 19XX); Judy Barrett Litoff, *American Midwives: 1860 to the Present* (Westport, Conn: Greenwood Press, 1978); James C. Mohr, *Abortion in America: The Origins and Evolution of a National Policy 1800-1900* (New York: Oxford University Press, 1978); Jeffrey Weeks, *Sex, Politics and Society* (London: Longman, 1981).

[23] For discussions of this counter-struggle see Faderman, *Surpassing the Love of Men*; Smith-Rosenberg and Esther Newton, "The Mythic Lesbian and the 'New Woman': Power, Sexuality, and Legitimacy" (paper delivered at the Berkshire Conference of Women Historians, Vassar, 16 June 1981); Jeffrey Weeks, *Coming Out: Homosexual Politics in Britain from the Nineteenth Century to the Present* (London: Quartet Books, 1977), and *Sex, Politics and Society*.

[24] Michel Foucault, *Power/Knowledge: Select Interviews and other Writings 1972-77*, ed. Colin Gordon (New York: Pantheon Books, 1977), p. 98.

[25] See Daniel Moynihan, "The Negro Family: The Case for National Action" (Washington DC, 1965).

[26] See, for example, Angela Y. Davis, *Women, Race, and Class* (New York: Random House, 1982); Claudia Dale Goldin, "Female Labor Force Participation: The Origin of

Black and White Differences, 1870-1880," *Journal of Economic History* 37 (March 1977), 87-108; Suzanne Lebsock, "Free Black Women" this volume.

[27] Walkowitz, *Prostitution*, chapters 6 and 7.

[28] In a culture, however, where women were often the victims of sexual coercion and were then blamed for crimes committed against them, in a culture where it was difficult even to conceive of female sexual agency as long as women lacked agency in other vital areas, most female activists in the nineteenth century could and did regard the doctrine of female passionlessness and male sexual self-control as a significant advance over traditional assumptions about a dangerous and active female sexuality. Whatever its drawbacks, this sexual strategy made it possible for women to act as historical agents and to challenge the traditional sexual prerogatives of men.

[29] See David Pivar, *Purity Crusade: Sexual Morality and Sexual Control, 1868-1900* (Westport, Conn: Greenwood Press, 1973); Judith Walkowitz, "Male Vice: Feminist Virtue and the Politics of Prostitution in Nineteenth-Century Britain," *History Workshop Journal* (Spring 1983, forthcoming). There was also, of course, a minority of sexual radicals who concerned themselves with women's sexual pleasure: Stella Brown, Olive Schreiner, Victoria Woodhull, Margaret Sanger, Emma Goldman and Crystal Eastman among others.

[30] See, for example, Robert Roberts, *The Classic Slum: Salford Life in the First Quarter of the Century* (Manchester: Manchester University Press, 1971); Ellen Ross, "The Anatomy of Married Life in Working-Class London," *Feminist Studies* 8 (Winter 1983, forthcoming) and "Survival Networks: Domestic Sharing in an East London Neighborhood 1870-1914," unpublished paper.

[31] Smith-Rosenberg, "The Female World."

[32] See Susan Porter Benson, "Business Heads and Sympathizing Hearts: The Women of the Providence Employment Society," *Journal of Social History* 12 (Winter 1978), 302-12; Karen Blair, *The Clubwoman as Feminist: True Womanhood Redefined, 1868-1914* (New York: Holmes & Meier, 1980); Barbara Leslie Epstein, *The Politics of Domesticity: Women, Evangelism, and Temperance in Nineteenth-Century America* (Middleton, Conn: Wesleyan University Press, 1981).

[33] Although the nineteenth century did separate men's and women's spheres in many ways, it was also a period when, for the first time, gender boundaries and divisions were challenged. In this sense the age was progressive as well as reactionary for women.

[34] See Judith Lowder Newton, "Preface," in *Women, Power and Subversion: Social Strategies in British Fiction 1778-1860* (Athens, Ga.: University of Georgia Press, 1981), p. xix. See also, Rosalind Pollack Petchesky, "Antiabortion, Antifeminism, and The Rise of The New Right," *Feminist Studies* 7 (Summer 1981), 206-46.

"Hannah Cullwick, scrubbing." Photograph by A. J. Munby. By permission of the Master and Fellows, Trinity College Cambridge, England.

1   Class and Gender in Victorian England

LEONORE DAVIDOFF

> Her strong, bare, sinewy arms and rugged hands
> Blacken'd with labour; and her peasant dress
> Rude, coarse in texture, yet most picturesque,
> And suited to her station and her ways;
> All these, transfigured by that sentiment
> of lowly contrast to the man she served,
> Grew dignified with beauty and herself
> A noble working woman, not ashamed
> Of what her work had made her
>
> A grace, a glow of quick intelligence
> And ardour, such as only Nature gives
> And only gives through Man. . . .
>
> *Ann Morgan's Love: A Pedestrian Poem*
> A. J. Munby, 1896

SYMBOLISM AND REALITY: The Creation of a World View

In investigating the connections between class, gender, and sexuality a detailed study of one case can be a useful check on either prescriptive literature or listings of household and family structure.[1] This paper attempts to show how the themes of fantasy and the manipulation of symbols in one such study can throw light on the dynamics of a whole society. But first it is necessary to look at the meaning of class and gender divisions at a more general level and at the mechanisms by which they were created.[2]

The nineteenth century was the time when traditional social boundaries were being eclipsed by the rapid development of a market economy and the creation of a "class" society. All social relationships including gender divisions were affected by these changes. During this period, class designations came to carry gender overtones. The status characteristics associated with *gentility*, for example, differed for men and women; and the concepts *manhood* and *womanhood* which are peculiar to the nineteenth century have very different resonances. (It was on the basis of claims to *manhood* that the independent respectable workingman petitioned for both a living wage and the right of entry to full citizenship through the franchise.)

What makes the analysis of the interaction of class and gender so difficult, however, is that the same forces which produced a world view dividing the society between masculine and feminine, working class and middle (upper) class, urban and rural, also separated physicality, e.g., bodily functions in general and sexuality in particular, from the public gaze. This is an example of the privatization we have come to associate with the development of industrial capitalism and was part of a changing view of men's and women's positions in the cosmos and of their relation to Nature.

The world view of Victorian society which has been handed down to us was mostly the creation of those persons in positions of power who had the resources as well as the need to propagate their central position. Within this world view, those categories of people who are furthest away from the centers of decision making are ranked accordingly; and they are also visualized in images that emphasize their powerlessness and degradation as well as their potentially threatening and polluting effects on those persons closer to the center who exploit their labor and their persons. Middle-class Victorians, as middle-class persons in many other societies, expressed this powerlessness by associating peripheral groups with physiological origins.[3] This association was then used in a circular fashion to lock such people into menial positions for life.

The unskilled, uncreative occupations whose incumbents order very little, handle brute matter as brute matter, express little that is vital and do not penetrate intellectually into the nature of anything, rank very low. The occupations whose incumbents handle only the detritus of man's existence and do so only by manipulating it directly come lowest.[4]

It should be remembered, however, that it is not the tasks themselves that degrade; it is the power of the dominant groups which defines what tasks are to be considered degrading and then forces the incumbents of socially constructed categories to perform these tasks.[5]

The degradation of peripheral groups was also expressed in body images, for Victorian social commentators, including early sociologists like Herbert Spencer, often used a body metaphor in an effort to stress the organic nature of their society. This image was set in explicit contrast to both the mechanistic visions of the eighteenth century and the conflict models put forward by early Victorian radicals. According to the organic view, society was able to operate as a system because of its hierarchically ordered but interdependent parts. The adult middle-class (or aristocratic) man, representing the governing or ruling group, was seen as the Head of the social system as well as the Head of his household which was in turn a society in miniature. The Hands were the unthinking, unfeeling "doers," without characteristics of sex, age, or other identity. (The implication of the word "Hands" for workers is mercilessly castigated by Dickens in his novel *Hard Times.*) Because work was central to Victorian society, the implication was that middle-class men did brain work while the hands did menial work. Middle-class women represented the emotions, the Heart, or sometimes the Soul, seat of morality and tenderness. Women performed these functions as keepers of the Hearth in the Home, and here we find a body/house connection which figured widely in the Victorian world view.

The final section of this mental map was not as often or as openly expressed, for middle-class Victorians shrank from naming their own bodily functions. Still, Victorians visualized the "Nether Regions" of society which, by their definition, were inhabited by the criminal classes, paupers, beggars and the work-shy as "stagnant pools of moral filth" comprised of the "effluvia of our wretched cities." Historians, in fact, have recently drawn attention to the disturbing equations made by commentators, such as Mayhew, between the sanitary and the human condition, to "the cloacal imagery of the social investigators [who] pursued the social 'offal' and 'moral refuse.' "[6] Prostitutes, who were seen as the potential source of both physical and moral contagion for middle-class men, were also cast into this region. Defenders of prostitution saw it as a necessary institution which acted as a giant sewer, drawing away the distasteful but inevitable waste products of male lustfulness, leaving the middle-class household and middle-class ladies pure and unsullied. None of the inhabitants of this twilight zone could ever aspire to be included in the "body politic" but had to be hidden and controlled whenever possible. Indeed, by the third quarter of the nineteenth century, there were drives to segregate certain groups by sexual designations as well as by class labels. The separating out of a criminal class was followed by the creation of a homosexual subculture and a hardening of the lines between professional and casual prostitution.[7]

In keeping with this body imagery, certain groups were seen to be closer to nature than the rational adult middle-class man who dominated educated opinion. These groups included not only women, children, servants, and many other elements in the working class, but also natives in the colonies and by extension all non-whites. Their supposed affinity with nature also helps to explain the animal analogies which were often applied to them in literary writing as well as popular sayings. The position of animals, of course, had changed during the growth of industrial capitalism. From being the central source of energy and production, the "first circle of mediation between man and nature," the relationship between man and animal became much more metaphoric; and in this latter stage two themes were always stressed: what animals and man had in common and what differentiated them.[8] ("Man" is here put forward as a generic term but quite clearly the implication is that it really referred to adult men, preferably middle-class educated men.) The belief in an organic hierarchy, finally, provided the basis for scientific theories about biological divisions which were refurbished within a Darwinian evolutionary framework.[9]

Within this framework, sexuality—particularly male sexuality— became the focus of a more generalized fear of disorder and of a continuing battle to tame natural forces.[10] The social as well as psychic importance of this focus is clear in Max Weber's analysis, which considers sexuality as a non-social, even antisocial force: ". . , the drive that most firmly binds man to the animal level. . . . Rational ascetic, alertness, self-control and methodical planning of life are threatened the most by the peculiar irrationality of the sexual act which is ultimately and uniquely unsusceptible to rational organization . . . the more rationalized the rest of society becomes, the more eroticized sexuality becomes."[11] The effort of adult middle-class men to maintain their positions of power within the society as a whole and the "little kingdoms" of their own households, as well as in regard to their own sexuality, seems to have created a kind of "psychological backlash" within their own personalities. They combined excessive fears of pollution, disloyalty, and disorder from subordinates with a desperate search for a moral order which would help to control all three, as well as the immoral forces of the market. Indeed, with the help of religion, the restraint of male sexuality came to be seen as a great feat of self-control, one of the hallmarks of middle-class gentility. But this was a gentility reserved for middle-class men. The working class and native blacks supposedly allowed their sexuality to spill out over their total lives, diverting them from the goal of achievement through work, wasting their energies and draining their vital forces. In Victorian language they displayed a lack of self-control resulting in incontinence.[12]

One well-documented solution to the problem of controlling middle-class male sexuality had been to see middle-class women (ladies), particularly within marriage (the golden chain that binds society together), as agents of salvation,[13] and with the crisis in religious faith, the image of a desexualized Madonna took on increasing saliency.[14] Madonnas, however, imply Magadalenes; and Victorian culture and social institutions provided both. A dual vision of women was already available, of course, as a legacy from classical culture, a culture inculcated through the curriculum of the grammar and public school, which emphasized hierarchical and misogynist interpretations of society.[15] The dualistic view of women was also a keystone of Christian theology, which justified the subordination of female to male on the grounds of woman's potential "carnality." Since femaleness was equated with the body, so the female must be subordinated to the male "as the flesh must be subject to spirit in the right ordering of nature."[16] Victorian women, therefore, were not only divided between working class and middle class, they were divided between "ladies" and "women," categories which signified as much gender as economic and social meaning. In viewing Victorian women it is as if we are looking at a picture through a double exposure.

Indeed, the dual vision of women, as woman and lady, becomes mixed with other polarities such as those between white and black, familiar and foreign, home and empire. In a perceptive discussion of these polarities, as expressed in literature, Cleo McNelly cites the following:

... [in] the binary opposition between here and there, home and abroad ... home represents civilization, but also order, constraint, sterility, pain and *ennui*, while native culture, the far pole of the myth, represents nature, chaos, fecundity, power and joy. The home culture is, moreover, associated always with the ability to understand by seeing, abstractly, while the other culture is associated with black, with the sense of touch, the ability to know by feeling, from within. The far pole of the tropical journey is indeed the *heart* of darkness.

At either end of this journey stand two figures, each of which has a profound mythological past: the white woman at home and her polar opposite, the black woman abroad. These figures come from a long and well-entrenched tradition in the West. The first of them, the white woman, is not only Beatrice, she is Rowena and even Mrs. Ramsay as well. At her best she is "a star to every wand'ring bark," gentle, courteous and endowed with the immortality of the gods. At her worst she is Virginia Woolf's "angel in the house," the angel of death and sterility. In either case she tends to be sexless and *familiar* in every sense of the word. She is mother, sister or wife rather than mistress or friend.

The second figure, the black woman, is her mirror image. She is the ever-present exogamous mate, the dark lady of the sonnets, savage, sexual and eternally other. At her best she is a "natural woman," sensuous, dignified and fruitful. At her worst she is a witch, representing loss of self, loss of consciousness and loss of meaning. In either case she is most emphatically *not* familiar. She is an unknown quantity, and in her strangeness lies, both her value as an object and her ability to fascinate the white man.[17]

These are stereotypes which are deliberately cast in terms of opposites. There cannot be one without the other, and politically, one of the key functions of this particular set of oppositions is to separate white women from black women and, by extension, middle-class ladies from workingwomen to insure that they relate only through men.[18] The opposition also ensures that real women are given an identity and destiny which they can only approximate and never fulfill. Above all, it is an identity cast upon them by the dominant group, for no matter what the locus of the dual image of women—art, literature, advertising, costume, song, pornography, even architecture and landscape—it is man (middle-class educated man) who is the active observer and doer. Not only women but the whole world, extending to the farthest reaches of the Empire, becomes his object. And though in fact active manipulation of such objects was often severely constrained, in fantasy, as well as in the range of activities from anthropology to photography, middle-class men appear to be engaging in a kind of voyeurism which comes out of their privileged position as actors and doers. This voyeurism, for example, is particularly evident in the preoccupation with child pornography and child prostitution, not to mention father-daughter incest,[19] which is such a strong, if underground theme in Victorian middle-class culture.

It is striking, moreover, that middle-class men's interests in rescue work, in the plight of workingwomen, as well as pornographic imagery, focused on girls and *young* women, that it was they who carried the burden of purity and pollution, and indeed of projected male sexuality. For this obsessive concern with keeping young girls in innocence, preserving the "bloom of ignorance" is built on an obvious paradox. If girls were "by nature" innocent why were they so easily aroused, why all the need for protection and suppression of sexual knowledge? As Gorham has shown, the attempt to combine the two views, of the girl child as totally pure but also as naturally wicked and corrupted gave rise to two powerful but opposed images, the child as redeemer (little Nell) and the child as evil incarnate,[20] a parallel to the dual vision of women in general.

This preoccupation with young women, of course, is directly related to the power structures of gender and class;[21] and it was reinforced by the legal system and such customary practices as the large discrepancies in age between middle-class husbands and wives, both in reality[22] and in fantasy.[23] It was not unknown, for example, for an upper middle-class man to raise a ward or poor relation with the intention of making her his wife when she reached her middle or late teens.[24] The cult of domesticity, moreover, removed married women, particularly mothers, from the sexual arena. Thus we have many images of older middle-class men in relation to young girls (sometimes middle class, sometimes illicitly working class) but almost no images of the older middle-class woman in relation to working-class men or younger men at all, except in the all-powerful, deliberately desexualized mother/son image.

It seems clear from the preceding argument that many of the preoccupations of the Victorian middle class and many of the dichotomous themes which pervaded their world view were laid down in childhood, even infancy, and that, even though the mechanisms are not yet completely understood, class as well as gender divisions were, partially at least, created in the nursery.[25] The dual vision of women, for example, has much to do with new divisions of labor in the middle-class home. From the end of the eighteenth century, a middle-class life-style had evolved which emphasized the importance of a well-ordered, and increasingly, a materially well-stocked home. While the responsibility for the management of the home and the emotional demands of husband and children were the domain of the wife and mother, there was a continued effort to shift the manual work, or at least the heavier, dirtier tasks onto domestic servants.[26] Of course this division of labor depended very much on the financial resources of the family as well as on the number of children. Nevertheless, there was increasing pressure to employ domestic servants in larger numbers and, as the century progressed, for more specialized functions.

Although in the eighteenth century, female and male servants had been equally employed, by the mid-nineteenth century the proportion of male servants had dropped substantially; and by the 1870s even the upper middle class was substituting women, partly because of expense (for other occupations such as school teaching attracted men), but also because working-class definitions of masculinity and independence made domestic service less and less palatable to young men.[27]

By the 1850s there were already 750,000 women employed as residential domestic servants, and by the 1890s this figure had reached 1,300,000. The majority of these women were young and unmarried. The evidence from servants' as well as from employers' memoirs suggests that in households where there were young children, even where only one servant was employed, she would spend a good portion of her time helping to care for them. Upper middle-class ladies in households with two or three servants were unlikely to have taken any active part in the physical care of infants or toddlers.[28] It was the nurse or maid who fed, nappied, washed, dressed, potted, put to bed, and directly disciplined the infant and small child. Within the nursery domain she had total power over her charges; yet middle-class children learned very quickly that she was their inferior and that they were both, children and servants alike, subject to a higher authority. It was very often these girls and women who first awakened sexual as well as other feelings in the child.

This was the case with Freud himself, although psychoanalysts have been remarkably uninterested in the role of nursemaids. Recently, however, the importance of the social background of the maid and her position of dependency in the household combined as it was with "derived" power over the child, has been recognized in a discussion of Freud's self-analysis and confirms many of the findings in upper middle-class memoirs and autobiographies.[29] Freud's nurse was actually a maid who had worked in the family before he was born and who had other duties in addition to looking after him. This was a much more common experience than the specialized Nanny we expect from nostalgic fiction. Freud's nurse was of Czech working-class and Catholic origin so that her employment by a bourgeois, German-Jewish family implied cultural, social, economic, and ethnic inferiority, "a potent combination to be carrying into a relationship with an infant boy."[30]

In many households, the maid in charge of the children would be very young, scarcely more than a child herself; so it is not surprising that both bribes and threats were used to keep order and to control her charges and it is likely that sexual stimulation was one of the ways nursemaids amused and quieted infants. In his analysis of Freud's case, Swann notes the parallel with the American South where white infants were nursed by black Mammies and grew up into a culture that idealized white women. "The same splitting is present, in society and psyche alike, to make the idealisation possible":[31] "White women are lovely but not carnally lovable; they are more like the Virgin Mary. But there is the maid or mammy, the black mother figure, at once the real thing and a substitute."[32]

The extent of the splitting would obviously depend on the re-sources of the family, e.g., space available, number of children, number of servants. It became extreme in the wealthiest house-holds and was a particular ideal of the English upper class whose trained Nannies were famous the world over. In her memories of this division of labor, an upper middle-class woman of the 1890s said: "To me she was the perfect mother. I would not have liked her to dose me, bathe me, comfort me or hold my head when I was sick. These intimate functions were performed by Nanny or by Annie our nurserymaid. . . . I did not like mother even to see me in the bath."[33] Ideally the mother in this type of household would direct the intellectual and particularly the religious and moral up-bringing of her children. She would see them only either in the nursery when it was set in order for her visit or when they were taken to see her, specially washed and dressed at the appointed "children's hour." Whether the nurse was loved, hated, or simply endured, this split remained.

R. L. Stevenson wrote of his beloved Nanny: "My second Moth-er, my first wife/The Angel of my Infant life."[34] Yet servants also dealt with the underside of household life, and their work was seen to be dirty and menial. They were thus more intimate and earthy than middle-class adults who were debarred from many activities because of taboos, manners, and etiquette. Children soon learned that servants talked differently, walked differently, even smelled differently. Memories, for example, are evoked of a maid's hands which smelled of dishwater when dressing a child, or of the fusty smell of servants' bedrooms. A lady in her sixties still remembered the maids' stories about their courting escapades, stories whispered in an atmosphere redolent of the exciting mingled smell of "hair oil, pantchouili and body odour."[35]

Victorians of the middle class, in contrast, were affected by a drive for personal cleanliness and sanitary reform which began early in the nineteenth century. Some middle-class Victorians even suffered from a type of obsession such as that suggested in the re-cent account of the life of Charles Kingsley, an active sanitary re-former who was constantly preoccupied with personal cleanliness and cold baths and who could not bear to wear clothes that were dirty.[36]

Despite this drive (or possibly even in reaction to it), the naturalness, even "rankness'" of working-class people, and servants in particular, could have a subtle attraction. (In the context of class domination, of course, this attraction was as falsely romantic as the opposite fears of depravity and bestiality.) A country clergyman's sons remembers the illiterate charwoman who lived in a cottage at the foot of his house, a woman he regarded as his "second mother": "She was a woman always poor, always comfortable, always free, rich and racy in her mind and in her speech, pagan and fearing neither God nor devil."[37]   Middle-class children liked to slip down into the kitchen and laugh and play with the servants, cadge scraps of forbidden adult food, and listen to less inhibited conversation than they usually heard; and the direct accessibility of servants, who were not governed by the etiquette rituals of middle-class front door conventions, continued to have a particular appeal to many middle-class adults who remembered with pleasure visits to the homes of servants when they were children: "A cottage with an open door, not closed till day is done."[38]   Indeed, the fascination with the alien, often forbidden but exciting, world of the servants is a common theme in middle-class memoirs:

In the maid's room I read romances . . . bound volumes which lay concealed beneath Karolines underclothes in the bottom drawer. Without the exchange of a word, we both knew that I would not have been allowed to read them if I had asked my mother. And indeed, I read them with something of a bad conscience but it was more than that . . . there was something in these romances which made one think of tainted water that has been forgotten in a carafe; of all the foul and unwholesome smells whereby the town became familiar to my senses.[39]

This fascination with the forbidden world of the working class had obvious sexual overtones. Herman Hesse, for example, described in his novel *Demian* (1913, written immediately after his psychoanalysis), how, at least for boys, attraction to working-class life took on an explicitly sexual character. Hesse is speaking of his hero as a pubescent boy, who sees the world in terms of dark and light forces: the light being the bourgeois world of parents, sisters, law and order; while the dark world, the world of his awakening sexual desires, inextricably draws him to the maidservant. The equation of working class, sexuality, disorder, and guilt has has been well-established. In fact, not only symbolically but physically and often with covert social sanctions, the young servant was available to the middle-class male adolescent. The first sexual experience in the long and notorious career of the protagonist of *My Secret Life* takes the form of just such an encounter (although, this incident, as he recounts it can be described more as a rape than as a seduction). And there are enough reminiscences by domestic servants to confirm the characteristic nature of these relationships.

For middle-class children, these social divisions and their erotic overtones were also reflected in a spatial view of their world—a view which started with their own bodies, extended to the houses where they lived and eventually to their village, town, or city. Just as society was often symbolized by a body metaphor, so house and body images were conflated. Within the house the child was safe and warm in the cozy nursery or sitting room with the glowing hearth at its center, an image very often associated with the mother. The servants, on the other hand, lived and worked in the dark underground parts of the house or slept in the inaccessible, often spooky attics. Their territory was the "back passages" (nursery euphemism for anus) where the working parts of the household machine were visible and where waste and rubbish were removed. Such images carried over into adulthood and help to explain the often irrationally divided and inefficient design of middle-class housing.

Thus spatial segregation was associated both with control over servants (and by extension over other members of the working class) and control over polluting aspects of the body. Control over one's own body became, in turn, associated with both the ability and the right to control and dominate others. The natural extension of this bodily domination was, of course, legitimate physical punishment; the right to beat or strike a servant was only removed in the 1860s[40] while the legitimacy of wifebeating, not to mention physical punishment of children, remained unchallenged long into the twentieth century.

Middle-class children not only learned that certain social spaces belonged to certain social groups, they also learned to use their bodies to express class and gender boundaries. Little ladies and gentlemen did not sit on steps; they stood absolutely straight; they did not whistle, scuff, or slouch. By imitating middle-class adults they learned habits of command through silent body language, through the way they looked at people, through tone of voice as well as accent.

Servants in return, showed deference in the way they used their bodies, a point also observed by the children of the house. Servants stood when spoken to and kept their eyes cast down, they moved out of a room backwards, curtsied to their betters, and were generally expected to efface themselves; doing their work and moving about the house so as not to be visible or audible to their employers. In an extreme case they were made to turn their faces to the wall when the employer passed by.[41] One instruction book for young servants devotes a whole section to *Standing and Moving* and shows the extra burden which the need to express deference placed on the already heavily worked servingmaid class:

I was once in the nursery bedroom when Anna came in panting with a can of water. As I spoke to her she sank down on a chair saying "Excuse me, ma'am, I am so tired," but I could not excuse her. She acted very rudely. It would have been but a small effort to stand for a few moments, however tired she might be and girls who are not capable of such an effort are not fit for service.[42]

In the street, servants, male or female, walked a few paces behind their master or mistress. They walked on the outside of the pavement if escorting a lady in a rough or dirty street, just as a middle-class man would have, to act as her protector.

Servants also contributed to the growing child's mental map of their social geography outside the home: "The servants of the house made windows for us into the outside world."[43] After all, one of the primary tasks of servants in even lower middle-class homes was to take the children out for walks and the small child's first view of the neighborhood may have been very much through servants' eyes. Many of these children were first- or second-generation suburban dwellers as the middle class started to move away from the city centers where factories poured out both wealth and filth. Servants passed back and forth between the "good," clean, orderly but dull suburbs and the "bad," dirty, disorganized but exciting center. A schoolmaster's daughter living in a south London suburb expressed this feeling in her attitude towards Deptford, the dockland home of the general servant girl who had charge of her: "This name meant for me unimaginable squalor. I was never taken there; somehow I was brought up to think of it as dark, dirty, common, low. Yet I hugged a secret fascination with the very idea of it."[44]

Without claiming some sort of implicit functionalism it is still possible to observe that the housing, the life-style, and the child-rearing practices of the middle class helped to create and maintain a structure of authority and a personality suited to the group which was instrumental in running the business, of governing, and reaping, the rewards of Victorian society. This is not to deny that the structures so created did not produce major contradictions both at the individual and group level, especially in the realm of sexuality.[45]

Freud, for example, believed that it was almost impossible for the "love of civilized man" to avoid the split between affection and sexuality because of the need to avoid direct erotic attractions to the mother (incest). For him the whole sphere of love remained divided into sacred and profane (animal) love: "Where they love they do not desire and where they desire they cannot love." For him it is this which underlies the double standard, including the tendency of men in the highest classes to choose a woman of a lower class as a permanent mistress or even a wife, in the need for a debased object, since the "sexual act is seen as something degrading which defiles and pollutes not only the body.'[46] This theory takes for granted the existence of women of the lower class and, therefore, does not need to explain the stage at which they enter the individual drama or any active role that they might play. Ultimately, as with most nineteenth-century thought, it rests on a conception of society in which hierarchical divisions of both class and gender are natural. The relationship of master to servant, of men to women, that is, was seen as natural and organic in contrast to the newer and much more threatening relation of employer and workman.

Natural in this context has two related meanings: the relationship was taken for granted; it was a given. It was also part of nature as opposed to the civilized, the man-made, which was unnatural. Some sensitive men struggled against a world view which posed such polar opposites and especially which split the world into masculine and feminine, or into lady and woman. Edward Carpenter, E. M. Forster, and William Morris, for example, in their lives and in their writing, have given us a glimpse of the anguished efforts needed to break through the constraints, conscious and unconscious, which it produced. The minor poet and man of letters who is the subject of this study, A. J. Munby, also senses this dilemma posed by the dual vision of women as the following passage from his diary, written in his characteristically sententious style, illustrates. He is visiting with friends in an old house in Kent.

It became necessary for me to retire for a space; but the men-servants had gone to bed, and amongst the intricate passages [sic] of the old house I could nowhere find the spot I wanted. So, encountering in the hall the waiting maid, a ruddy domestic damousel, I had no recourse but to ask her the way. An unpleasant process! With much hesitation and awkwardness I strove by delicate circulocations to hint to her my needs: but the girl's rude mind could not comprehend them—she looked at me with respectful wonder, and at last I was obliged to say bluntly "could you tell me, where is the water closet?" She would blush, I half thought and stammer, and I should regret having said it. Not at all! it was only the reflex of one's own training that made one think so.

[The maid takes him to the door of the water closet]
Significant of several things. Not certainly of vulgarity or any culpable coarseness, rather of a rude simplicity and innocence of shame. We are brought up

to ignore these ultimate necessities of nature, and to be animals only by stealth: but your housemaid has had quite a different schooling in knowing that such things exist, sees no harm in speaking of what she knows.[47]

ARTHUR J. MUNBY AND HANNAH CULLWICK: A Double Portrait[48]

It is one thing to identify a world view and its possible sources, but another to analyze the way in which it was incorporated into everyday life: "People are living in the middle of their cosmology, down in amongst it; they are energetically manipulating it, evading its implications in their own lives if they can, but using it for hitting each other and forcing one another to conform to something they have in mind."[49]

While one should be fully aware of the power of symbols and images, it would be a mistake to see these phenomena purely in symbolic terms. Fear of pollution and obsession with dirt and degradation had a very real basis. Victorian cities were filthy with soot, smoke, mud, and appalling muck heaps lying in the streets; and cholera was a very real threat to life. Indeed, the effort to enforce sanitary reform had to start with the middle class before moving on to controlling the habits of the working class.[50] Similarly, the images of women as domestic beings produced feedback which restricted their lives to the extent that many of them *were* insipid, underexercised, narrow-minded and neurasthenic.

In the record left by two obscure Victorians, however, it is possible to catch glimpses of the world view I have outlined and of the way these divisions operated in practice since one of the pair was male and upper middle class and the other was female, not only of a working-class but also of a rural background and a domestic servant. She was one of the great army of working-class women who did, in fact, spend a good deal of their lives in direct face-to-face contact with the middle class. (Both in reality and fantasy it was young female servants who bore the direct personal brunt of class interaction. Independent workingmen could protect their manhood by remaining within social contexts of their own kind and it was they who were the first to confront employers as members of a *class*.) A detailed examination of such a relationship can show that the private lives, even obsessions of two individuals, far from being simply psychological quirks or even aberrations, flowed directly from the social situation of these two typical individuals.

The main source for understanding that relationship is the private diary, letters, drawings, and photographs of a minor poet and writer, A. J. Munby, and the companion diary of his disciple, servant, and eventually his wife, Hannah Cullwick. By Munby's instructions the diaries were locked up until 1950 by which time, as he had foreseen, the shock and degradation of such a story would have died away. Munby's diary, which he kept regularly from 1859 to 1898 with scattered entries after that date, runs to millions of words. In addition, there are about 800 letters as well as dozens of drawings and photographs. (Because of his special interest in working women, the collection has already become known as a valuable source for historians.) It is interesting to note that although the content of the diary is so unusual, the form is conventional for its period.[51]

A. J. Munby's avocation (and private obsession) in making encounters with, observing and collecting information on, working girls and women was not as unusual as it may appear at first sight. The passion for collecting information on and statistics about the working class, particularly working-class women, has a streak of voyeurism which can be sensed behind the work of a journalist such as Mayhew, as well as in the detailed accounting of moral depravity in the pages of staid publications such as the *Journal of the Royal Statistical Society*. This voyeurism also appears in both the lives and writings of men like George Gissing and Somerset Maugham. "Rescue" work among fallen women or simply the compulsion to nocturnal wanderings in search of conversation with "women of the streets," which figure in the lives of men like Gladstone, have some close affinity to the sexual scoring and collecting described at length in the notorious diary, *My Secret Life*.[52] ("Walter," the anonymous author, came from much the same background as Munby, was also born in the mid-1820s, and also had an obscure job in the civil service which allowed him the same time and freedom of action for his pursuits.) While "Walter" was concerned with strictly sexual encounters, Munby was collecting examples of women at work; but the pattern of wandering from place to place in search of encounters, the emotional urgency and the sense of culmination with each "find" lies below the surface of both diaries whose form is similar.

Unlike Mayhew or Booth, Munby's observations were not commissioned by any official body nor were they intended to answer public questions or even written for publication. Rather, as with sexual diaries such as *My Secret Life* or the diary of the homosexual, A. J. Symonds, Munby seems to have been using the diary to construct a meaningful identity by using themes from his culture— both those that were explicitly admired and those that were forbidden—and reinterpreting them to fit his own psychic structure. It is only in his poetry that he expressed some of his views to the public, if in a somewhat muted form (see Appendix).

Arthur Joseph Munby was born in 1828, the eldest child of a
York solicitor and the daughter of a wealthy clergyman. He had
been brought up from infancy by a nurse called Hannah Carter
who remained the faithful servant of the family for twenty-eight
years. Six younger siblings were born in the span of ten years and
his mother, not surprisingly, was delicate to the point of spending
much of her time lying on a sofa, weak in health and with a tendency to become hysterical. Munby always viewed her with exceptional awe and love. He described her as charmingly "old fash-
ioned," with a "fair delicate face and golden-auburn hair and
dainty figure." He remembered her best for her pious, gentle way,
as one who "believed as devoutly in my father as he believed in
God and Christ." Her whole being was in the affections, "her
husband first and her children next . . . her love was so tremulous
and tender, and her health so delicate always, that each of us felt
it might kill her, if he went into the army or navy, for instance,
or went away very far or very long."[53] With such a mother, no
disturbing or distasteful subjects could ever have been broached.
Sexuality, much less any bodily functions, would have been completely taboo.

The family had an assured social position and Munby, although
having a provincial and country childhood, received a traditional
middle-class boy's education first at a local private school supplemented by private tutoring from a local clergyman and then at
Cambridge. Unfortunately we know little more than this about
his early life. He became a barrister despite his distaste for the law,
probably in deference to his father and his position as eldest son.
However, he did not practice law but moved to London where he
lived "in chambers," e.g., in a set of rooms within one of the Inns
of Court. Here he remained for the rest of his life, partly supported
financially by his father. At the age of thirty-one, he found a position with the Ecclesiastical Commission, work he disliked for the
most part but felt obliged to take in order to have some financial
independence. Despite his middle-class Victorian belief in work,
therefore, in his own life, work was always a burden and a distrac-
tion.

In his lifetime, A. J. Munby was known only in a small circle.
He passed his life as an undistinguished but respectable civil servant, teacher, amateur poet and artist, who was on the fringes of
both the Pre-Raphaelite and Christian Socialist circles, particularly
through his teaching for the Working Men's College. His real interest lay in his self-created avocation, the observation and collection of the lives of workingwomen. Although he was in no way a
radical, he did occasionally protest at moves to keep women out of

manual work even to the extent of heading a delegation to parliament on behalf of the collier girls of Wigan.[54]

For the most part, however, he enjoyed the modest comforts of a professional bachelor, strolling through London to look on at the building of the Embankment; to dinner at his Club; or to play writing games at the Pen and Pencil Society; to a late supper in a friend's rooms in London's Inn where politics, art, and writing were discussed; meandering home at 4 a.m. amid Covent Garden porters; watching, talking to anyone in the street, walking anywhere with perfect ease. His diary thus emphasizes the freedom of action enjoyed by a middle-class man, even on a small but assured income, in contrast to the lack of freedom imposed on middle-class women.

His first love was for what he persisted in calling "peasant" or "country wenches." He idealized the rural and the out-of-doors, which may be a partial explanation for his fascination with a ruddy countenance and suntanned skin. This rural nostalgia, of course, was widespread among the recently urbanized Victorian middle class.[55] In his country wanderings Munby sought out farm girls; the "flither girls" of the North East coastal region who made their living by being lowered over the edges of cliffs to collect sea bird's eggs and limpets; and, above all, the "pit brow lasses" who worked in the coalfields sifting cinders and hauling carts at the pit surface. They not only worked outside in a primarily man's world but they were covered in coal dust and at least in Wigan, wore trousers.

In the city he favored women in outdoor occupations: flower sellers, milkmaids, and prostitutes. He was particularly interested in circus women and acrobats and made a large collection of photographs of these performers.[56] Although he sought out entertainment places used by female clerks and shop assistants, these girls were approaching too near to the lady to really attract him: "Commend me to the honest roughness of a solid maid of all work rather than to the hybrid fine ladyism of Miss Swann and Edgar"[57] (a large clothing store in the West End). It was not work or even financial independence per se which he found so fascinating in women, but menial work. In common with many other upper middle-class Victorians, not absolutely sure of their own position, he disliked those who tried to rise above themselves. In a typical passage describing one of his country rambles he contrasts his "ruddy farm servants and true peasant women" with the upper servants he saw at North Repps Hall, "lean, pale-faced insolent looking hussies in would-be lady's clothes."[58]

Munby's attitude illustrates the appeal of working-class openness which we have observed as a theme laid down in childhood:

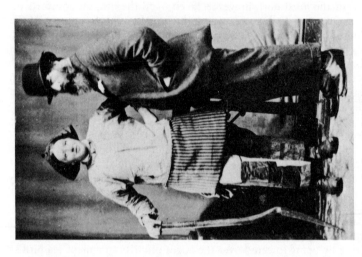

Symbolism and reality: Watercolor sketch by A. J. Munby of himself and a colliery girl; photograph of same (photographer unknown). Both reproduced from Derek Hudson, Munby: *Man of Two Worlds: The Life and Diaries of A. J. Munby 1828-1910* (London: Abacus, 1974). By permission of the Master and Fellows, Trinity College Cambridge, England.

Nothing is more striking than the contrast of behaviour which even courteous gentlemen exhibit in dealing with a lady or a quasi-lady and in dealing with a servant or other labouring woman. To the lady, you are all deference and smiles: you smooth your phrases and put away all allusions to things coarse or common, you do things for her, you would not hear of her doing things for you. To the servant, you are civil, indeed, but you speak plainly and frankly to her about things which may not be mentioned to a lady; you call her by her Christian name though you never saw her before and expect her to call you Sir in return; you order her about and expect or allow her to fetch and carry for you as indeed it is her calling to do so.[59]

Deep down in the great shifting mass of the people, their own histories and names have for them nothing private or sacred. . . . They are accustomed to be close questioned about themselves by mistresses and to be called "Anne" or "May" by anyone who chooses to address them. To be asked bluntly "What is your name?" or "How old are you" by a stranger, does not seem to them at all offensive or impertinent.[60]

Munby does not acknowledge that this quality he so much admires was at least partly a result of his position as a dominating middle-class man, who for sixpence could feel a girl's palm and for a shilling could take her to a photographer to have her picture taken in whatever pose he chose to put her. It was economic necessity combined with the service role, which made his "wenches" so available. It is noticeable that Munby seldom tried to approach a Lancashire mill girl or even a London factory worker.

Because of this position of economic and social power we know a considerable amount about the middle-class, particularly male, world view. We know very little about the way working-class children, particularly domestic servants, were molded by the social structure into which they were born. This makes Hannah Cullwick's diary, with its detailed record of childhood memories, conditions of work and work performed, wages, hours, recreations, relationships among fellow servants, and many other details, a unique and precious document. However, it must be remembered that she was writing it for Munby's eyes alone, a further way in which he could dominate and even "create" her life. Thus, the diary has to be interpreted with caution. Still, through a reconstruction of her relationship to Munby, as interpreted by both of them, it may be possible to gain some insight into the construction and acceptance of deferential interaction based on both class and gender, an interaction which female servants must have carried back into the working class when they married and had children.

Hannah Cullwick was born in 1833 and raised in Shropshire, but through her work as a servant she came to London when she was in her late teens. Except for her relationship to Munby her life was typical of literally millions of women of the period. Hannah started in service when she was eight years old, which was not atypical for the 1830s. Her rural background is important as an element in her acceptance of the status quo because there were no alternatives to some form of personal service for her or her family. Her father had been both a farm servant and worked in a gentlemen's stables. Her maternal grandmother had been in service before marriage and returned to residential service after she was widowed. Her mother had been a lady's maid and companion to the Lady at the Hall near their village of Shiffnal. This lady became Hannah's godmother' and had wished Hannah, as the eldest child, to be named after her, Anna Maria Dorothea, but Hannah's mother thought that this was too pretentious for one of her station. Hannah's first memory is of a visit to their cottage by the butler from the Hall when she was five years old. He came with gifts of a Bible for Hannah and a print dress for her Mother, and he summoned them to come up to the Hall: "I remember it because it seemed so grand to me and i polished my shoes as well as ever i could and i trotted up by Mother as fast as possible o' purpose to see my godmother who was a *lady*."[61]   The little Hannah curtisied as her mother had taught her and the lady kissed her, gave her cake and wine and a toy. Later, this all-powerful and beneficent lady sent her special clothes and paid her fees for the Charity School which Hannah attended from the age of five to eight, the only formal schooling she ever had.

Her first employer was a farmer who was a friend of her mother's. Here her position was much like that of an extra daughter, but one who had certain special duties to perform. The family was kind to her; she was taught to cook and sew; the farmer took her fishing and opened a savings account for her. This kind of gradual introduction to the authority system of service in which discipline was enforced first through the mother and then often through female teachers, relations, or friends is one of the factors which made it possible to maintain the institution of domestic service for so long and make it seem so "natural" even to those who were subordinated and who gained very little in real terms from their positions.[62]

By the time she was fourteen, Hannah had left the farmer's family which could no longer afford her higher wages. After a short spell as a "pot" girl at the local Red Lion pub (a position of which neither her mother nor the farmer and his family approved), she was sent to the Vicarage at Ryton to be nurserymaid under a Nanny to eight children. This position meant a heavy load of cleaning, fires to be made, bath water to be carried up and down, as well as children to look after. She had only been there a month when fever struck her home village. Her mother wrote her of her father's death but no one told her of her mother's death a fortnight later until a neighbor happened to call by the Vicarage. Although it was only three miles away from her home, Hannah was not allowed to go, even to see what had happened to her younger brothers and sisters (a ban possibly laid down because of the fear of infection but also to maintain discipline.) Whatever the cause of the prohibition, Hannah was devastated. Her goal of earning money to send to her mother which had made her situation bearable was suddenly gone: "i *thought* it *was* no use tho i ax'ed to go and all my strength seemed gone." She was ordered to go back to the schoolroom to start work immediately.[63]

The total power of the employing class over her existence was again brought home to Hannah, then about fifteen, in her next place of third under-housemaid in an aristocratic household. She had been very proud to be taken on in this position and enjoyed working in the beautiful surroundings, learning how to make a bed and "do out" the long gallery and great rooms. One sunny day, she and the second under-housemaid were outside cleaning the sixteen copper kettles used daily by the household: "Maria and me was cleaning our kettles in the yard and *playing* over it, for we was young things; and My Lady, see'd us out o' the nursery window and sent the housekeeper to give us warning."[64] Hannah's pleas were useless and she was sacked on the spot. She then had to take a job as scullery maid in another large household nearby: "i couldn't help crying when i come to clean the stew pan and great spits and dripping pan and live only in a rough out-house next the kitchen," a shed with no window which she could only reach through the coal hole.[65]

Hannah learned at a very early age that her world was made up of powerful middle-class and upper-class people and that only her strength to labor gave her a footing in that world. She was particularly vulnerable having been orphaned early but this was by no means an unusual state at this period. In any case, servant memoirs emphasize that their own families, almost always under pressure for income and house room, could do little for them. There was also the question of sexual power. In the course of her service in country houses, visiting gentlemen as well as menservants, tried to "make a pass" at Hannah. In one instance when she has been offered a ride home in a carriage with one of these gentlemen, she was set down with him "in a lonely spot" to walk the rest of the way home. He tried to kiss her and she threatened him: "if you

offer to touch me again I'll do something you won't like, so you
go your way and i'll go mine."[66]   Like many working-class girls
she learned early in life that strength of body and personality were
her chief resources for both work and self-protection.[67]

Like so many girls, particularly of rural origin, Hannah accepted
her position (not for nothing did employers prefer girls fresh from
the countryside, "uncorrupted" by urban life). She tried to gain
a sense of dignity and worth both in the work she did and through
the love she craved. With Munby she achieved that sense of work
and love although it was on his terms and ultimately at a very high
price. Running throughout her diary, however, there is a sense
that the system as it stood had cheated her, that the pious plati-
tudes about the dignity of service were not believed in even by
middle-class employers. Over the years, the tone of her diary
subtly changes as her life experience and education through Munby
widened her horizons. In one of the very last entries she made,
after she had been married for about nine months, and thirty-five
years after her first experience of residential domestic service
Hannah wrote:

I went out to service too soon—before I really understood the meaning of it—
and at the Charity School i was taught to curtsey to the ladies and gentlemen
and it seem'd to come natural to me to think them *entirely* over the lower
class and if it was our place to bow and be at their bidding and I've never
got out o' that feeling somehow.[68]

IMAGES, GAMES, AND TRANSFORMATIONS

In 1854, when A. J. Munby was twenty-five he met Hannah Cullwick, aged twenty-one, on a London street. In his usual manner
he struck up a conversation with her. She combined all the qualities he prized most highly: she was from a country background;
strong and robust but good-looking; a maid-of-all-work, but excep-
tually intelligent and lively. From then on she was the center of
his emotional life as he was for hers. For nineteen years until their
marriage they were involved with each other, although during all
that time he remained a nominal bachelor living at 6 Fig Tree
Court, the Temple, and she living in various residential servant
situations. It is not clear from the sources we have whether their's
was, in conventional terms, a sexual relationship and there are
some indications that Munby may have been impotent. In any
case, there were no children nor indications that Hannah ever
thought she was pregnant, a situation which might have totally
altered their relationship.[69]   Munby and Hannah finally married

"Hannah carrying slop pails." Photograph by A. J. Munby. By permission of the Master and Fellows, Trinity College Cambridge, England.

in 1873 when he was forty-four and she was thirty-nine. She lived with him for just over four years as his servant, not openly as his wife. After a period of increasing tension in their relationship, she returned to her people in Shropshire and lived for the rest of her life in a cottage provided for her by Munby where he visited her regularly. Her relatives and friends accepted him; while his middle-class circle, with the exception of two of his closest friends, never knew of her existence.

Soon after their relationship began, they started a series of games and playacting in which they used the differences between them to emphasize their love and devotion. They were intensely aware of the impression that they made on other people. In public, Hannah would act the perfect servant, demurely walking behind Munby, carrying his heavy luggage, calling him Sir and meekly obeying his orders. He would act especially "masterful," give her ostentatious tips, and send her off to do his bidding. Later they would meet in his rooms and giggle like children over the incident reveling in the "if they only knew" aspect of their situation. This is, of course, not an unknown phenomenon:

On occasions, individuals will come together and find that they share each other's bizarre fantasies. The fantasy ceases to be a personal mental resource to be drawn upon intermittently during the course of everyday life; now it can be elaborated with the help of another and may shift into the centre of our lives. The classical description of this phenomenon is *folie à deux*: a situation in which two individuals actively cultivate their extreme fantasy to the point at which scripts may be assembled.[70]

The point about Hannah and Munby's "scripts" is that they were written around the theme of class and gender differences played out through games of mastery and submission.

In following these themes through the diaries, it becomes clear that Munby's inversion of the usual Victorian stereotypes suggests the possibility of transformations, of passing back and forth from one "side" to another at will. Black becomes white, degradation becomes love, masculine becomes feminine, working class becomes genteel. All this happens at the will of the middle-class male protagonist who creates the situation and engineers the transformation. Through the use of his position as an upper middle-class man, Munby was able to find a partner and carry through into reality at least some of these fantasies. Hannah, although much more clear-sighted about the reality of her own situation, was driven by her economic and emotional needs to willingly act as this partner. She was, indeed, very jealous of his interest in one or two of his charity cases, particularly the "girl without the nose" but seems to have been quite accepting of his friendship with women of his own class.

Most of the themes which preoccupied Munby, and to a lesser extent Hannah, clustered around the question of dominance and subordination, strength and weakness, autonomy and dependence. The dichotomies and contrasts allied to these subjects are characteristic of much Victorian culture: respectable/not respectable, lady/woman, pure/impure, clean/dirty (and by extension white/black), indoor/outdoor, fairness/suntanned or ruddy (blushing was thought to be a sign of sexual arousal in middle-class women), clothed/uncovered skin, and above all, of course, feminine/masculine. Many of these themes are related either directly or indirectly to the major Victorian preoccupation with *work*: what was it, who did it, where did they do it. This produced another set of contrasts: work/leisure, work/home, manual work/brain work.

Connected to both sets of contrasts and in keeping with the body imagery we have already mentioned, *hands* take on a special significance and play a central role in both class and gender imagery, e.g., "the language of gloves." They also carry an explicitly sexual connotation for Munby, and one would guess, for many other Victorians as well.[71] White, dainty hands indicated gentility as well as femininity. They were symbolic of inner breeding but also of life-style. George Augustus Sala who was a contemporary and friend of Munby's, a man-about-town and commentator on the social scene (as well as a connoisseur and collector of erotica) wrote a novel in which the middle-class hero rescues a "fallen woman" who turns out to be a lady by birth. He has literally pulled her out of a horse trough and takes her to a cafe where he listens to her story: "As she spoke she laid her right hand on the filthy table cloth. The woman's hand was, considering her stature, small, but the fingers were long and tapering, the nails, although grimy, filbert-shaped. Otherwise it was a handsome hand, and very very white."[72]

When Munby tried to persuade Hannah to dress as a gentlewoman he wanted her to wear gloves, but she resisted saying "they baffle my hands so." He quotes this statement approvingly, however, for contrary to what had usually been considered attractive, Munby is fascinated by, even addicted to looking at, touching (at times cutting the skin from) large, rough, red, work-hardened hands of workinggirls. With monotonous repetition Munby's diary entries and poems dwell on the motif of hands, their color, shape, and texture:

> For she is still a working wench
> and sits with hands still bare[73]

Hannah deliberately rubbed the bars of grates and cleaned knives with her bare hands, despite the unpleasant feeling, in order to harden them in a paean of love for Munby, expressed through work.

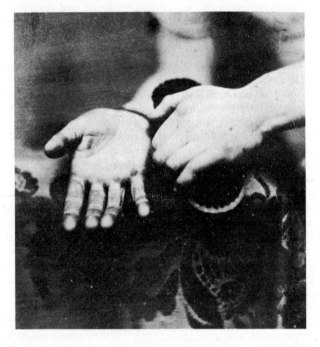

"Hands." Photograph by A. J. Munby. By permission of the Master and Fellows, Trinity College Cambridge, England.

A similar, although slightly less compelling preoccupation of Munby's was with women who either had large masculine-looking feet or who wore heavy boots; in fact Hannah often wore his old boots. He writes approvingly of a colliery girl: "Her ponderous boots with iron on the sole, shod like a horses hoofs." Here Munby connects this image with one of his favorite animal analogies. Small, dainty feet and hands, of course, were the pride of middle-class Victorian women and figure widely in descriptions of feminine attractiveness, a physical characteristic evoked in characters from Dora, the wife in *David Copperfield*, to Meg in *Little Women*, or Rosamund in *Middlemarch*. This concern extended to doubts about workingwomen who did not conform to the expected distinction. In 1862, a private factory welfare officer for a silk firm wrote "I immediately remarked the small delicately formed hands of the weavers, and I have seen the smallness to be, in a domestic point of view, a great disadvantage to women in that condition of life. . . ."[74]

The animal/human analogy which Munby used for his colliery girl pervades his diary. It indicates lowliness and degradation, but also a brute strength and dumb loyalty expressed through love and service. In his poetry, girls and women are compared to cows, horses, dogs, and in the case of the "ebony slave girl" (who eats on all fours out of a bowl on the ground), even an elephant. Note that all these are examples of domesticated animals who have been "trained" and "broken in" by man. This analogy is, as we have seen, by no means unique to Munby. The comparison of the "handling" of women to horses has a long history in literature about the relations between the sexes.[75] In some writers, middle-class women may appear as "spirited fillies," but for Munby the domesticated animal evocation is more often expressed in a fond-ness for watching women standing and working in lowly positions. He was a firm believer in the importance of curtsying, for example; and he finds the young milkwoman he saw stooping to take up her new yoke looking "proud as a young cart horse." He imposes the same image on a servant washing the kitchen floor in a country inn: "I spoke to her first, she did not understand me: but leaning on her hands which were spread upon the wet brick pavement like forefeet . . . she scrubbed away busily under tables and dresser, folks stepping over her whenever they came in her way."[76] Fasci-nation with love expressed through drudgery, dirt, defilement, and even disfigurement reaches its height (or depth) in a poem which no publisher would accept. It combines all these themes with one of Munby's favorite locations, a coal mining area. In this poem his heroine works underground and is eventually hideously disfigured in a mine explosion. (Coal miners had a general fascination for Victorians. They were the troglodytes who produced the power on which the whole edifice of comfortable middle-class life rested but they were hidden away under the ground.) Munby's imaginary pit lass:

> . . . thinks it sweet to walk all day upon her hands and feet.
> With a full wain behind! To rejoice in being a quadruped?
> To give her voice for such degradation?
> Let her go, disgusting creature!
> Ah! You little know the ways of women and the rights of love.[77]

The special importance of dirt or blackness for servants should be obvious. They spent a great deal of their lives maintaining clean-

liness in middle-class homes. Their most important job was to remove dirt and waste: to dust; empty slop pails and chamber pots;
peel fruit and vegetables; pluck fowl; sweep and scrub floors, walls,
and windows; remove ash and cinders; black lead grates; wash
clothes and linen.[78]

The equation of servants with dirt and pollution, however, and
the equation of dirt with blackness had particular overtones in mid-
Victorian England, as some of the literary symoblism cited has already indicated. In Western culture blackness has always carried
strong symbolic meaning: "being the antagonist of white which
is God, it becomes the symbol of personified evil."[79] From the
sixteenth century onwards, this symbolism was enlarged by its
associations with the Dark Continent and the slavery of black
peoples.[80] As Jordan points out, embedded in the concept of
blackness was its direct opposite—whiteness: "Every white will
have its black." White and black connotated purity and filthiness,
virginity and sin, virtue and baseness, beauty and ugliness. From
the Elizabethans onwards, whiteness had been the color of perfect
human beauty, especially female beauty, implying the desirability
of a fair rose and white complexion.[81] It should not come as a
shock, therefore, that Hannah's pet name for Munby was Massa,
that is, what they took to be the Negro slave's word for Master.
Three years after they met she began to wear a leather strap around
her wrist and a chained collar with lock around her neck to which
Munby held the key. He particularly enjoyed seeing her face and
arms blackened—in his phrase "in her dirt."

Again, these associations were commonplace in the Victorian
era. In the classic children's book, *The Water Babies*, written by
Munby's friend and contemporary, Charles Kingsley, the climactic
scene shows Tom, chimney sweep boy, leaping out from the chimney covered in soot, "looking like a little black gorilla," into the
spotless white bedroom of Ellie, the golden-haired middle-class
child. Tom has to be purified by dying and becoming a water
baby, that is, washed clean and returned to a nonsexual infant
innocence before he can join Ellie in heaven.[82]

Natives, particularly African slaves, were also associated with
nakedness and by implication were heavily sexualized in contrast
to buttoned-up, controlled Englishmen. Showing oneself uncovered and dirty in public was thus considered especially degrading.
In their memoirs, several servants emphasized the humiliation they
felt at having to kneel (thus showing legs and petticoats) to scrub
the front doorsteps and paths every morning, open to the stares of
passersby, the whistles and importunings of men and boys. The
symbolic meaning of cleaning in public helps to explain the use

"Hannah as a slave." Photograph by A. J. Munby. By permission of the Master and Fellows, Trinity College Cambridge, England.

of "step girls" by those who could not afford any other domestic
services. Hannah reported that the mistress she served in summer
when there were lodgers and visitors in the house "told me she
would try to do with no servants in winter—only for the errands
and for cleaning the front door steps—she says 'i *cannot* do them—
and i felt sorry for her—i can do them and always do everywhere
i like, but she seem'd to think it degrading and of course it would
be to her." She added, "it wants nerve to stand or kneel in the
street before everybody—feeling that you're despised and degraded
before them all."[83]

It is only by understanding these symbolic meanings that the
fantasy games which Hannah and Munby played can be apprecia-
ted:

I got up early, for Massa was coming at ½ past eight to see me clean the steps
and do the *sign* of my 'lowness' like i did awhile ago . . . and i wanted to be
black from doing' the grate as well . . . i did the dining room fire—got my
arms blacked and wiped my mouth and nose across with my black hand . . .
I washed the doorsteps and flags and when I saw Massa coming I got the door
mat out and shook it well in the road and then i laid it on the causeway (side-
walk) & knelt on all fours and swept it well o' both sides wi the hand brush
& last of all i knelt an wiped my face on the dirty mat in front of all the folks
what pass'd by and Massa was looking on from a few doors up . . . & then i
rubbed my face on it & put my lips again it & i thought now i was one o' the
lowest drudges as could be—but Massa loved me & i love my work, both for
its and also Massa's sake & i felt so happy.[84]

The power to create or transform another human being and in
so doing to reaffirm upper middle-class masculine identity provided, as we have seen, the compelling attraction of rescue work
as well as the rationale for the phenomenon of the child bride. In
"Susan: A Poem of Degrees," 1893, it is Munby, thinly disguised
as the hero, who speaks of creating "the new Pygmalion":

> He look'd at her: a Juno covered in coal,
> With lustrous eyes and firm devoted soul;
> Goddess within, beneficent and brave,
> Yet outwardly a negress and a slave

She flings herself at his feet. He raises her up (a favorite phrase in
"rescue work") and "kisses her foul lips" until they "again grew
ruddy from their black eclipse." There are, indeed, several photographs in the Munby collection of collier girls in their filthy, masculine pit clothes with the same girl neatly dressed in her Sunday best,
looking like any other respectable working-class woman in crino-
line, bonnet, and shawl. Hannah was also photographed as slave,

"Hannah, scrubbing steps." Photograph by A. J. Munby. By permission of the Master and Fellows, Trinity College Cambridge, England.

drudge, neat serving maid, middle-class lady and "angel." After their marriage she would work in the basement kitchen in Fig Tree Court all day but sit with him, "dainty in black silk" in the evening. "Is she not a servant during the day, and a lady in the evening? and fulfils either part so well, that for the time being she seems incapable of the other."[85]

For Munby, as we have seen, one of the most important transformations was the crossing of sex lines. The more sharply that gender was differentiated in dress, looks, voice, walk, coloring, and size, the more intriguing and exciting passing through or reversing these boundaries could be. Victorian writing, costume, and visual imagery constantly emphasizes the largeness, hardness, and muscularity of men as opposed to the small fragility and roundness of middle-class women. The Victorians took every opportunity to emphasize and create differences between the sexes just as they did between the working-class woman and middle-class lady. Or in Munby's phrase the shoulders of the girl farm servant, who he compares to a young guardsman, are three foot broad and "square, massive, muscular, made for work, just as those sloping white ones of a drawing room were made for show."

Munby was fascinated by working girls and actresses who dressed in men's clothes. He often had pictures of himself taken with the pit girls in their working dress and in the diary compares himself, his stature, his hands, and feet with theirs.[86] In several places, Munby compares his size with that of Hannah. We know that she was 5'7½" tall and weighed nearly as much as he did, 11½ stones (161 lbs). At various times he measured her biceps and the size is given variously as thirteen, fourteen and once even eighteen inches round. Hannah in her diary too, glories in her strength and size relative to "Massa." Her hands are too big to wear his gloves. "i can heave my Master easy and carry him as if he was a child, nearly."[87] She was even photographed by Munby with hair cut short and dressed in men's clothes. (She also recorded in her diary in various places that she wrestled a calling tradesman and floored a young, male fellow servant, neither of whom were amused.) The sex reversal theme, then, just as the class transformation theme figures in their fantasy games. In one of his dialect poems Munby wrote:

> Look at mah Master, then an' look at me
> Wi' his fine fingers an' his dainty ways
> He's like a lady—an Ah often thinks
> He *is* a laady, when Ah waits on him—
> An me a common mon'[88]

"Hannah as neat serving maid."

"Hannah as middle-class lady."

"Hannah as 'angel.'"

"Hannah dressed as a man."

Photographs by A. J. Munby. By permission of the Master and Fellows, Trinity College
Cambridge, England.

Again, women dressing as men, especially as "gentlemen" was a
favorite music hall turn and a common frolic below stairs reported
in servants and children's memoirs.[89]

The other major theme in these reversal games was the city/
country division. Munby liked to see Hannah not only with bare
arms and rough hands, but also wearing old-fashioned short frocks
and peasant bonnets or picturesque white caps. He loved her
"countrified" speech and kept lists of dialect words she used; he
delighted in her rural simplicty juxtaposed to the sophistication
of the drawing rooms where he met middle-class women. As we
know, many of his contemporaries were also trying to rediscover
country customs, dialect, and song in the beginnings of the "folk
culture" movement popularized by people such as Cecil Sharpe.
Pre-Raphaelite painters, too, took as a motif the warm red and
brown skin tones of rural figures, often dressed in folk costume.

Although Hannah was a country woman by origin, the long
years in London had cut her off from a genuinely rural culture.
Although she could switch to her Shropshire dialect at will, she
also had learned some French from Munby and German from a
fellow servant. Her diaries, especially the later ones, are vividly
written if not perfect in spelling and grammar. Munby himself
introduced her to many classical authors and liked to discuss them
with her. She enjoyed suprising him with her ability to do household accounts and add up column of figures. She copied manuscripts for him, wrote letters, and even checked references. Yet,
to please him, she made a French peasant's bonnet from a picture
he had shown her and continued to wear it despite ridicule from
fellow servants.

Some of their games and activities had a strong mother (nurse/
child) theme. Sometimes *he* sat on *her* lap: "Massa sits on me,
feet and all on my knees—at first he thought i couldn't bear him,
but i said 'oh i can, so ever since then i expect to nurse him after
dinner." She would then usually fetch a basin of water and kneel
down to wash his feet.[90] One of their favorite activities in the
Shropshire cottage was to bathe each other. Hannah, of course,
had fetched and heated the water and prepared everything before-
hand. She would rub his back and wash him, an office which he
says only a mother or wife (or nurse) could perform. After his
bath, she would get into the tub using the same water and he would
wash her back. Indeed at one point he specifically says of Hannah:
"Let me be refreshed by a mother's love *and* by that of one so
different."

Not all their games were so benign. Over the years Munby had
taught Hannah to value her lowliness. He cut out of his diary those

"Hannah as a rural maiden." Photograph by A. J. Munby. By permission of the Master and Fellows, Trinity College Cambridge, England.

passages which explicitly explain what this "training" in love
through degradation was, but it most certainly included kissing
his feet and licking the mud off his boots. (In *My Secret Life*
when the hero is still in his teens, he was inflamed with lust when
the maidservant had to kneel to take off his boots, a standard part
of a maidservant's duties.)

As in the ritual "sign" of lowliness previously described, with
Munby and Hannah, both bodily and spatial symbolism was exaggerated. We have already noted his use of animal analogies
and fascination with women in a kneeling position. Hannah would
lurk in the basement of Fig Tree Court, she would revel in going
into the backs of coal holes and water closets to clean them out,
she would climb up the chimney to clean it (twice in the nude)
and would curl up inside it, "like a dog" and covered with soot.
She deliberately would allow lodgers to walk over her while she
scrubbed on hands and knees. While she was kneeling to hammer
down a new carpet, a lady kicked her and she was glad for she
could put it in her diary to show Munby.[91]

Nine years after they had first met and their relationship was
firmly established, Hannah had a dream which she recorded in her
diary. She dreams she is at "Massa's." She is on the floor and he
is showing her a book; a gentleman walked in and looked astonished.
She asks Munby what to do. He says lie still but she creeps around
the table "and lay curl'd up like a dog under the window" and
"Massa talking to the gentleman and he didn't seem to notice me
nor hardly to know i was a girl [note she was 30 years old] laying
there and i was glad of that."[92]

In the two-room cottage in Shropshire where Hannah went to
live, the parlor was kept solely for Munby. In this room his desk
and writing equipment, the symbols of his work and attachment
to the wider world, took pride of place. This scene is laid in one
of Munby's barely disguised verses describing their relationship:

> His parlour an' mah kitchen is as near
> To one another, an' an mooch unlike
> As him an' me is . . .
>
> The kitchen's *my* home, Sir, an always was
> An always will be.[93]

Their compromise situation of master/husband and servant/wife
was literally reproduced in space.

CONTRADICTIONS

It seems evident that Hannah tried, and to an extent, succeeded in accepting and believing in Munby's equation of dirt, lowliness, even degradation with love and inner worth. On the other hand, she admits that most servants, herself included before her "training," would have wanted to rise above scullery work or a maid-of-all-work position if they could. She too had internalized conceptions of respectability, order, and cleanliness. It was, after all, partly her task to create that order. After the incident where she rubbed her face in the dirt and kissed the mat on the pavement in front of Munby, she records her feelings: "i was glad i'd done it, but i felt so overcome somehow with the feeling of love and degradation—been in the street like that—so low and so dirty—yet liking the work so and especially for Massa's sake that it was some time afore i could feel calm."[94]

Her training in degradation was a lesson with contradictory repercussions. At one time she took a place as a "skivvy" in a lodging house in the Strand to be nearer Fig Tree Court. This kind of service was the lowest in status and the most onerous in heavy, dirty work required; it was often done by girls who had been brought up in the workhouse. It was winter and the frost had cracked Hannah's hands into open chilblains which had become ingrained with soot (a very common and painful complaint of both domestic servants and working-class housewives whose hands were constantly in water). One day she slipped out to visit Munby hoping to please him to be seen thus "in her dirt" but even Munby was appalled. In another place she was left to "clean down" a large house that had not only its full complement of London grime and soot aided by three coal fires in the house, but also a railroad running at the bottom of the garden. The family had gone away on holiday while the cleaning was being done (the usual practice) and Hannah invited Munby to come and visit her: "i wanted him to see what a big gloomy dirty house this i have to live in, and what a deal o' work was left for me to do all by myself, and i felt *so* dirty and miserable too, for after all too much dirt & too much work is sickening, & i was not surprised to see Massa look disgusted."[95]

As early as 1860, Munby himself began to realize the ramifications of his scheme. When he was on a visit to Hannah, then a maid-of-all-work in a dreary suburb, he noticed how five years of "scrubbing & cleaning, of sun & wind out of doors and kitchen fires within" have coarsened Hannah's looks: "And she was pleased with the change—*pleased* that she is now so much rougher and

coarser—because it pleases me, she thinks. Truly, every smear and
stain of coarseness on her poor neglected face comes of love. And
now, it is high time that all this discipline should cease, but I have
no means of ending it! To be a smart parlour maid, or even lady's
maid are distinctions far above her reach: she would smile incredu-
lous if I proposed them. Che sera, sera."[96]

In 1864 when Hannah was working as a maid-of-all-work in a
prosperous tradesman's household, she was told to remove the wrist
strap she wore as a badge of servitude to Munby. She refused and
was sacked on the grounds that it made her too dirty to wait on
table. The constant need to wash and change from work clothes
to a clean apron at any minute to be summoned upstairs or answer
the door was a complaint of both Hannah and many other domestic
servants. The effort to maintain a clean frontstage and working
backstage was an extra burden on servants when there was only
one employed. After she had lost her job, Hannah wrote bitterly:
"i felt a bit hurt to be told i was too dirty, when my dirt was all
got with making things clean for them." This is her satisfaction,
the work that her strength and skill can accomplish:

How shamed ladies'd be to have hands and arms like mine and how weak
they'd be to do my work and how shocked to touch the dirty things even
what i black my whole hands with every day—yet such things must be done
and the lady's'd be the first to cry out if they was to find nobody to do it
for 'em—so the lowest work i think is honourable in itself and the poor drudge
is honourable too providing her mind isn't coarse and low as her work, both
cause its useful and for be'en content with the station she is placed in.[97]

Once Hannah even made the dangerous connection between this
strength and the constraints of her deference and dependency. In
a tiff with an employer, occasioned by her visits to Munby, she
noted: "i told Massa how it was to feel a great big wench & strong
as i am, as could crush a weak thing like Miss Margaret is with one
hand (though of course i *wouldn't* & she must know that)—for her
to *trifle* with me about going out when i'd got leave to—& *play*
with me as if i was a child" (Hannah was 38 years old at this time).
Hannah was resentful at Munby's taking the lady's part and not
helping her. She claims she wasn't rude, only "spoke up plain"
but "humble as i *ought* to be to them above me." It was not a
pleasant evening she spent with Munby after this incident "but i
could see he didn't exactly *dislike* me for showing *spirit*."[98]

Here was one of the paradoxes of their relationship. Hannah
was in many ways a more independent agent than Munby as she
had supported herself from the age of eight while he was financially
and in many ways still emotionally and socially dependent on his

parents. Yet for all her strength and independence, Hannah's position forced her into a childish dependency on Munby. Both referred to her moods and outbursts as "being naughty." When she is
put in an intolerable situation by her employer, Munby gives her
a double message; backing up the authority of the employer yet
obviously enjoying her show of spirit especially as he knew that
he had ultimate loyalty over her life through love:

> Obeying other folks' commands
> Although she was my own[99]

Munby especially delighted to subtly attack middle-class women
through Hannah; his love was stronger than their legitimate authority. In "Queen Kara" he says:

> From Nature's sanctum: whose degree is sure
> And even a slave obeying finds reward
> That Woman still should mould herself to Man
> And not to Woman. Masculine regard
> Is hers by right for blessing or for ban.[100]

He believes that Hannah, like all young servants while outward-
ly respectful, regards "the ladies as her natural enemies" but the
gentlemen as her allies. This is very like the childhood alliance
of children and servants against the moral authority of the mother.
Munby was incapable of realizing that while Hannah was subservi-
ent and hardworked by all middle-class employers, the women varied just as much as the men. The ex-governess for whom Hannah
worked in Margate was particularly kind and uncondescending,
talking to her at length, teaching her about astronomy and loaning
her books.

The same psychological shallowness is evident in Munby's reaction to any illness or even fatigue on Hannah's part. On these occasions, in contrast to his attitude to his mother's perpetual illnesses,
he both panics and becomes angry with her like a child depending
on an all-powerful, never-exhausted mother figure if she shows any
sign of weakness:

And again my Massa, why shd you be put out cause I had the lumbago & them
sweats & languid feelings—I shall not like telling you if anything's the matter
if it puts you out o'sorts, as you say—I know you'll say it's love & all that, but
i know how *soon* you *wince*, & are really put out if all doesn't go to your liking, & if you was a married man with a family & delicate wife & kep a lot a
servants you'd often ha' things to vex I can tell you. . . .[101]

In the year before they were married, Hannah was working for
an eccentric maiden lady who lived alone. She often made Hannah

get up in the middle of the night and search the house from coal cellar to dust hole in the yard for "wicked men." Munby scolded Hannah for exposing herself to yet more colds and rheumatic pains for she had been ill on and off for some months:

I told Massa how i'd got a cold from it. he was angry with me for running the risk but i said "if my missis orders me to do a thing i must *do* it" & i said "If it costs one's life we ought to do it, else what's a servant good for?" Massa said "Yes you *shd* obey your missis of course but shouldn't you obey *me* first?" So i said "Yes Massa & if you'd bin there & told me *not* to go in the coal hole i wouldn't."[102]

In addition to these psychological contradictions, there was an economic problem. With her skill, experience, and intelligence, Hannah could have earned upwards of twenty pounds a year as an upper servant. She did try a place as cook with a kitchenmaid under her at twenty-two pounds but she soon gave it up and didn't try again: "indeed it was only nonsense for me after being used to the lowest only and Massa teaching me to love rough dirty work . . . i dislike the thought of being over anybody and ordering things not only cause i'd rather do the work myself but for fear anyone should think me set up and proud . . . for freedom and true lowliness there's nothing like being a maid of all work."[103]

Hannah, by her own admission, was very glad to turn her financial affairs totally over to Munby whom she trusted implicitly. It is probable that part of this financial dependency was the product of her blocked ambition and her acceptance of her lowliness. In February 1871, on Munby's advice, she withdrew £100 of her savings (a very substantial amount by working-class standards of the period—Munby himself only started his job at £160 a year). She was given the money in sovereigns and notes but she records in her diary that she didn't even count it: "it seem'd such a lot & confused me, for though i like saving and being careful, i hate going to the bank or having anything to do with money affairs, so i feel glad to get rid of it as long as its safe, & glad that Massa doesn't mind managing it for me, for i certainly would do nothing with it myself."[104]

Nevertheless, Hannah's relationship to Munby in his persona as *gentleman* was extremely important to her. She claimed several times that she had "seen his face in the tea-cups" before she met him; in other words that she was psychologically attuned to finding someone of higher status as proof of her own self-worth. She muses in her diary at various points about whether she could have ever fallen in love with a man of her own rank and comes to the conclusion that it is doubtful. Yet, as with women of any class, without marriage, the final mark of her dependent status was the lack of a home of her own. Unmarried female servants no matter what their age, were always considered "girls." The mythology of the middle class maintained that these women would be taken care of as Munby took care of his old nurse, Hannah Carter, by giving her a pension in her old age. (Munby himself published a collection of *Epitaphs and Obituaries of Faithful Servants* in 1891, material culled mostly from tombstones found in his wanderings.) The Royal Commission on the Poor Law enquiry at the turn of the century confirmed that, for those domestic servants who were single and had never had a home of their own, a much more common fate was for them to seek indoor relief in the workhouse when they could no longer work.[105] Hannah felt this gap in her life increasingly as her relationship with Munby drew her further away from her childhood roots in Shropshire. Some of the entries in her diary show her often desperately "homesick." The cottage she finally had in Shropshire partly made up for this and made her resigned to living apart from Munby.

Munby too was torn by the contradictions implicit in his relationship with Hannah. He resented what he felt to be her underestimation of what he had sacrificed in remaining loyal to her. Most importantly, he didn't see, as most employers of servants didn't see, the physical and mental burden of the work load a servant such as Hannah was expected to carry. Despite the vivid, detailed description of her daily work that Hannah provided in her diary, and his own observations of working women, Munby, who had never worked with anything heavier than a pen in his life, romanticized manual work. He delighted in the fact that Hannah spent her Sunday afternoons off with him doing his housework, getting his tea, washing his feet. She also took his laundry, mending, and sewing away to do in her spare time.

After they were married, Hannah not only did all the housework, shopping, and cooking for Munby; but because she was nominally the housekeeper for the whole building at Fig Tree Court, she worked for the other tenants as well. Writing of this period, Munby exults half-jokingly in his diary: "She emptied slops, she drew water, and brought up the full can and pail, she dug coals and carried up the full scuttle; which things she does daily without any help from her Brutal Husband."[106]

Although he taught working women Latin at the Working Women's College, Munby believed that the working girl should remain simple. In his poetry he sneers at the "listless pale imitations" of gentility into which such girls develop who strive to become educated. Rather, their education should consist of "Nature, Labour

and Life." While thoroughly appreciating Hannah's inborn refine-
ment and obvious intelligence, he lists her best characteristics as
"Devout purity, homely household skill, love of nature, strength,
humility and artless simplicity." A careful reading of Hannah's
diaries, however, conveys the impression of an extremely efficient
administrator as well as hard worker with a wide knowledge of the
social nuances of her several worlds and a shrewd skill at manipulating her employers within the limits of her service relationship.

Munby's "not seeing" Hannah's distress and physical exhaustion
was part of the natural relationship of the servant/wife. After they
were married, he did, indeed, consider that he owned all her loyalties and legally, of course, he gained control of her income and savings. After their marriage Hannah at last took off the wrist strap,
collar, and chain which she had secretly worn all the years of their
courtship.

He was found of quoting Ruskin's words to her: "that the best
of all service is unpaid because it is done for love." In a poem written after her death in 1909 in which Munby openly acknowledged
their relationship, he calls Hannah "my faithful servant wife" and
he equates love and labor as one and the same thing:

> Happy in her humble calling
> Happy on her hands and knees
> Nothing checks her—nothing daunts her,
> Til her daily work is done;
>
> And she does it not for merit but to prove
> That no labour is too low to be
> The language of her love[109]

In *Ann Morgan's Love* he repeats his favorite theme that a woman's true love will be expressed through loyalty and labor:

> Of sacrifice, of self-abandonment
> Of pure devoted, unregarded toil
> For him to whom she gives herself: for *me*

In many ways, Hannah was, in fact, a creature of his fantasy. He
could not face the fact that she was a real human being with wishes
and needs of her own. After they were married for a short time,
Munby persuaded Hannah to dress and live as a lady and openly
become his wife. It worked very briefly while they were on their
wedding trip in France and for the odd week or two in hired rooms
in the country. But after their return to Fig Tree Court, Hannah
refused to continue and Munby, with secret relief, allowed her to
remain as his housekeeper. His fascination with the pretending and

transformation game made this enjoyable at first and they could now at least live in the same house.

Munby was obviously afraid of his father's wrath and the effect on his frail, unworldly mother if he revealed the truth about his marriage. And yet after his parents' death, he seemed to become even more ambivalent about the relationship. The games were beginning to lose their charm as Hannah gained more understanding of middle-class life at close quarters, and the "strange trials" and nineteen years of waiting had left their mark on both of them. Hannah clung more than ever to her servant identity as her one claim to independence, but to Munby it seemed rather that she had learned the lesson of lowliness only too well.

In middle-class Victorian terms, A. J. Munby failed to become a full social adult for he never set up and supported a household complete with wife, children, and servants. His relations with women of his own class were mostly formal, his secret despising of their weakness was compensated by extreme chivalry and courtesy in his dealings with them in person.[108] His diary reveals that he felt much more at ease in the company of his male companions. He was especially hostile to any claims made by what he considered to be feminist women. He considered that they had neither the attractions of his "rustic maidens" nor the acknowledged, fragile femininity of their own class; rather they were unsexed beings who were viciously determined to take away real men's vocations and he remained opposed to women's suffrage all his life.[109]

Clearly, Munby was no radical in the sphere of sexual politics. Once at a party in Campden Hill he made a special effort to speak at length to a young lady with whom a close friend and contemporary was deeply in love. (He and Munby were in their early forties at the time.) "A lively good natured very pretty girl of nineteen: voila tout! Yet there is something noble in that worship of beauty and girlish weakness which makes a brave high-minded man fall down before such an object in despite of his own judgement."[110]

Munby himself had twice become involved with young middle-class women and even thought of proposing marriage, but before long he withdrew. The impression from the diary is that he was never seriously emotionally drawn to any of those from his own class. In any case, marriage to a middle-class woman would have meant his obtaining a level of income and life-style which Munby could not and would not do.

It may have been, as in the case of many other middle-class men who turned to working-class girls (or men) for their emotional life, that the split image was too great for him to maintain in a traditional marriage.[111] Nevertheless, this inability also sharpened his awareness of the contradictions in his society. He was attracted to Hannah and the women like her, degraded and dirty for his sake, but also for the independent spirit of her life in refusing to be a "lady" and thus losing that independence. Munby said of service that "it may blunt the home affections." but it gave a "sturdy independence, self-reliance and shrewdness" to the character. He quotes approvingly from one of his servant informers, "I know if I don't take care of myself, nobody else'll take care of me."[112]

Despite his, to us, repellent fascinations with certain symbolic themes: the equation of dirt and degradation with female strength and love; the comparison of women to brute beasts, of both to black slaves; and the identification of all these inferior breeds as agents of a threatening but compelling Nature, Munby did recognize, if only dimly, a fundamental contradiction of Victorian society. The sheltered lives that middle-class ladies were ideally supposed to lead depended directly on the labor of working-class girls and women, who through their services created the material conditions necessary to maintain a middle-class life-style for men and women alike.[113]

He went further than expressing his concern about this contradiction in more normal activities like the moral reform of individual women or the "rescue" of symbolically important, but marginal, groups such as child prostitutes. He wanted to see working women remain independent and in charge of their own destiny through economic and social control of their own lives. The tragedy was, of course, that his championship of this cause remained at the individual level, and stopped short at the significant barrier of manual work.

CONCLUSIONS

A detailed study of such a source as the Munby collection brings alive the connection between social structure and personality. The pervasiveness of both class and gender categories, which it illustrates, stems from the effect of often unconscious, highly charged, emotional expectations laid down in childhood, which in many cases appear in the form of subliminal images. The mutual preoccupations of Munby and Hannah with boundaries and their experience of crossing these boundaries in both fantasy and reality can tell us a great deal about the way the fabric of Victorian society was created and maintained.

Hannah's experience of both sides of the class barrier, in particular, while emphasizing the monotony and sheer drudgery of domestic work, provides insights into the constraints as well as privileges of middle-class women. Hannah obviously valued the social, physical, and spatial freedom of movement open to a servant but denied to any woman who had pretensions to gentility. In her experiments with ladies' clothing and life-style she demonstrates in a very human way the constraints which such apparently trivial factors meant in daily life. On her wedding journey to France, she had changed her short servant's skirt and jacket to dress as a lady, complete with felt hat with a feather and veil, "a grey frock with frill round my neck, and white cuffs and grey kid gloves, and carrying my striped sun shade—all different to anything i had got used to, that one day in the train i got almost ill tempered at being so muffled up, and i felt i'd much liefer feel my hands free as they used to be."[114]

When set against background knowledge of the period, the omissions in the diaries can also be as revealing as what is recorded. Munby, for example, scarcely ever mentions working-class men in detail, even those he taught at the Working Men's College. If he does, they are noted without emotion, as figures in the landscape or occasionally as part of Hannah's circle: her brother, uncle, or fellow servants. He seems to have concentrated almost exclusively on women although heavily "masculinized" women. Yet it is known at this period that cross-class homosexual relations exercised both intense attraction as well as fear for many men of Munby's background and education.[115] Working-class youth, as well as girls, could represent the natural and uncorrupted domain. Edward Carpenter expressing his love for the poor and uneducated "thick-thighed, hot, coarse-fleshed young brick layer, with the strip around his waist" uses language very reminiscent of Munby's.[116] The lure of the unknown appears especially strong in the image of the dusky native boy so easily available to colonial soldiers, administrators, and adventurers.

This view at times comes close to a vision of the working class as representing "true" masculinity, the power of manual work. Such a force would revitalize the effete, over-urbanized, even feminized, middle class; but at the same time, it is equated with fear of the threatening working class mob. Munby, as well as reformers of many varieties and even radicals, tried to use personal (sexual) relationships to bring the classes closer together, to bridge the artificial gap between human beings—consider E. M. Forster's cry of "only connect." Yet cross-class relationships always displayed a certain ambivalence for they were ultimately based on power and exploitation; first and foremost the power of money, but also the education and life-style, while within heterosexual relations these powers were augmented by the rights traditionally due to the man.

A. J. Munby had a dim sense of this ambivalence for he had spent his whole life in trying to come to terms with the dilemma of class and gender while at the same time making full use of the prerogatives of his status as an upper middle-class man. He expressed his unease in a passage from his diary where he focuses, as so often, on the metaphor of *hands*.

In 1860 he was dining with some of his men friends at a country inn. One of his favorite types of "country wench" with big, red hands and bare arms waited at table and Munby mused:

Are the relations of the sexes really inverted when three men sit at table, with hands delicate and jewelled, and a woman stands behind and waits, offering the dishes with so large coarse a hand that makes her master's look almost lady-like: And is it the proper thing, that the *women* should sit as at a ball supper, drawing the gloves from their dainty fingers, and waited on by *men* whose hands that seemed so ladylike by comparison with Molly's, look sinewy and labourious by the side of Blanche's tender tips? If *this* is right for one class is that for the other? In short, what, in the Equation of Life, is the respective value of the terms *sex* and *station*."[117]

In the course of studying this one relationship in depth it has become evident that the separation of spheres for women and men which had begun as an attempt to solve the contradictions created by the pursuit of economic power and rationality through the market, had itself created intense contradictions for the individual men who reaped its benefits. At the same time, it also becomes clear that the interconnection of these hierarchical divisions could blight innumerable lives of those who were made most vulnerable by that system, particularly young working-class women.

APPENDIX

From A. J. Munby, *Benois: Poems*, 1852

THE SEXES

O, you are fair—you have soft turtle-eyes,
   Not flush'd with vulgar passion, clouded not
With stains of folly,—whose transparent lymph
   No shadows dull, no fretful eddies blot:

Your souls are precious oratories, closed
   And curtain'd in from all things not divine;
Where smoothest sounds enrich the loving air,
   And moons alone and silver cressets shine.

You dwell in peace among your pleasant hours—
   You hear no echoes from the far-off strife;
You lift your shining eyes, and all the place
   Feels happier—feels the magic of your life.

But we—for us in the thick thronging days
   No shrine, no bower, no oasis appears;
No path is left whereby we might have climb'd
   Back for a moment to the better years:

We have forgotten all—we hear not now
   Our mothers' teachings,—see not in the land
Its ancient beauties,—look on you as dreams
   Too fair to love, too high to understand:

We are uncover'd—the rank, stagnant air
   Infects our breath—our curdled souls endure
A press of crawling horrors—and vile sounds
   Hiss in our dull ears: how can we be pure?

TWO HANDS

I

This is her hand, her cool and fragrant hand:
   Long lissome fingers, soft as the south wind;
   A roseleaf palm, which Love's own kiss would find
Sweet as the rose; and many a thin blue strand
Vein'd in the white, our homage to command.
   All grace of form and colour has combined
   To give us this fair index of a mind
Pure as her hands, and not less nobly plann'd.

Ah, tender toys, so slight, so flexible!
   Can they too share the strenuous work of life,
And help their owner to do long and well
   The duties of a woman and a wife;
Or, may they brook no labour more severe
Than just to charm the eye and soothe the ear?

II

This is her hand, her large and rugged hand:
   Strong nervous fingers, stiff with homely toil,
   Yet capable; for labour cannot spoil
Their native vigour, nor their swift command
Of household tools, indoors or on the land.
   What if rough work must harden and must soil
   Her massive palms? They are but as a foil
To that sweet face which all can understand.

Yes, all enjoy the beauty of her face;
   But few perceive the pathos and the power
Of those broad hands, or feel that inner grace
   Of which they are the symbol and the flower:
The grace of lowly help; of duty done
Unselfishly, for all—for anyone.

NOTES

I would like to thank Angela John, Pat Bradford, Ann Kallenberg, Jean L'Esperance, Helen Hirsch, Jeff Weeks, Steff Pixner and members of the University of Essex Research Seminar for help and suggestions in preparing this paper.

[1] Throughout this paper, I shall be using *gender* to refer to the socially constructed categories, masculinity and femininity, while *sex* refers to the biological categories, male and female. See Ann Oakley, *Sex, Gender and Society* (London: Temple Smith, 1972).

[2] Anthropologists have made use of this approach far more often than historians. E.g., "Gender is very much made use of in Hagen to talk about things other than men and women, and the fact that it is so used has a feed back effect on how the sexes are perceived. . . . The logic inherent in the way such notions are set up must be understood in relation to general values in the society." (M. Strathern, "The Achievement of Sex: Paradoxes in Hagen Gender Thinking," in *Yearbook of Symbolic Anthropology*, ed. E. Schwimmer [Montreal: McGill-Queen's University Press, 1978], p. 171.)

[3] Mary Douglas, *Natural Symbols: Explorations in Cosmology* (Harmondsworth: Pelican Books, 1973).

[4] Edward Shils, "Charisma, Order and Status," in *Center and Periphery: Essays in Macrosociology* (Chicago: University of Chicago Press, 1975), p. 269.

[5] C. Delphy, "Proto-Feminism and anti-feminism," in *The Main Enemy: A Materialist Analysis of Women's Oppression* (London: Women's Research and Resources Centre, 1977).

[6] Geoffrey Pearson, *The Deviant Imagination: Psychiatry, Social Work and Social Change* (London: MacMillan, 1975), p. 162; Michael Steig, "Dicken's Excremental Vision," *Victorian Studies* 13 (March 1970): 339-54; Gertrude Himmelfarb, "Mayhew's Poor: A Problem of Identity," *Victorian Studies* 14 (March 1971): 307-20. See also H. Hallam, "Report of the Council of the Statistical Society of London from a Committee of its Fellows appointed to make an investigation into the state of the poorer classes," *Journal of the Statistical Society of London*, August 1848, p. 193: ". . . since the population (St. George's in the East) is, to some extent the drainage from the grades next above them we should rather hope to find a cure by cutting off the supply of degradation than by attempting to reform and elevate it in the lowest depths to which it can sink."

[7] Jeffrey Weeks, *Coming Out: Homosexual Politics in Britain from the Nineteenth Century to the Present* (London: Quartet Books, 1977); Judith Walkowitz, "The Making of an Outcast Group: Prostitutes and Working Women," in *The Widening Sphere*, ed. Martha Vicinus (Bloomington, Indiana: University of Indiana Press, 1977).

[8] John Berger, "Animals as Metaphor," *New Society*, 10 March 1977, pp. 504-5. The idea that women are both part of but outside "society" is a point of view still expressed in discussions of sexual divisions. It has recently been the center of a debate: nature/culture = female/male. See Edwin Ardener, "Belief and the Problem of Women," in *Perceiving Women*, ed. Shirley Ardener (London: Dent, 1977); and a critique, Nicole-Claude Mathieu, "Man-Culture and Woman-Nature," *Women's Studies International Quarterly* 1 (Spring 1978): 55-65.

[9] Examination of physical features such as skull capacity and other "evidence amassed from the very beginning tended to relegate the female, with the Negro, to a subordinate position," John S. Haller and Robin M. Haller, *The Physician and Sexuality in Victorian America* (Urbana, Illinois: University of Illinois Press, 1974), p. 48.

[10] Yet we as observers should know that the way sexuality and particularly rituals surrounding sex are used can tell us something not so much about sex per se as about the society. Mary Douglas, *Implicit Meanings: Essays in Anthropology* (London: Routledge, 1975).

[11] Max Weber, "Religious Ethics and the World: Sexuality and Art," *Economy and Society*, trans. Guenther Roth and Claus Wittich (Glencoe, Illinois: Free Press, 1968), 3: 603.

[12] G. J. Barker-Benfield, *The Horrors of the Half-Known Life: Male Attitudes toward Woman and Sexuality in 19th Century America* (New York: Harper & Row, 1976); and Peter Cominos, "Late Victorian Sexual Respectability and the Social System," *International Review of Social History* 3 (1963).

[13] Carroll Smith-Rosenberg, "Sex as Symbol in Victorian Purity: An Ethnohistorical Analysis of Jacksonian America," in *Turning Points: Historical and Sociological Essays on the Family*, eds. John Demos and Sarane S. Boocock, *American Journal of Sociology* 84, supplement (Chicago: University of Chicago Press, 1978).

[14] Eric Trudgill, *Madonnas and Magdalanes: The Origins and Development of Victorian Sexual Attitudes* (London: Heinmann, 1976).

[15] Sarah Pomeroy, *Goddesses, Whores, Wives and Slaves: Women in Classical Antiquity* (New York: Schocken Books, 1976).

[16] Rosemary Ruether, "Misogynism and Virginal Feminism in the Fathers of the Church," in *Religion and Sexism: Images of Women in the Jewish and Christian Tradition*, ed. R. Ruether (New York: Simon & Schuster, 1974).

[17] Cleo McNelly, "Nature, Women and Claude Lévi-Strauss: A Reading of Tristes Tropiques as Myth," *Massachusetts Review* 16 (Winter 1975): 10-11.

[18] Ibid., p. 11.

[19] Anthony Wohl, "Sex and the Single Room: Incest among the Victorian Working Class," in *The Victorian Family: Structures and Stresses*, ed. A. Wohl (London: Croom Helm, 1978).

[20] Deborah Gorham, "The 'Maiden Tribute of Modern Babylon' Re-examined: Child Prostitution and the Idea of Childhood in Late Victorian England," *Victorian Studies* (Spring 1978); Eric Trudgill, *Madonnas and Magdalanes*.

[21] Stephen Marcus, *The Other Victorians: A Study of Sexuality and Pornography in Mid-19th Century England* (New York: Bantam Books, 1971).

[22] Charles Ansell, *On the Rate of Mortality at Early Periods of Life, the Age of Marriage & Other Statistics of Families in the Upper and Professional Classes* (London: C. and E. Layton, 1874).

[23] C. Carey, *Wee Wifie* (London and New York: F. M. Lupton, 1869).

[24] Betty Askwith, *Two Victorian Families* (London: Chatto and Windus, 1971).

[25] Theresa McBride, " 'As the Twig is Bent': The Victorian Nanny," in *The Victorian Family: Structures and Stresses*, ed. Anthony Wohl (London: Croom Helm, 1978); James Bossard, "Domestic Servants and Child Development," *The Sociology of Child Development* (New York: Harper & Row, 1954).

[26] Leonore Davidoff, "The Rationalization of Housework," in *Exploitation in Work and Marriage*, eds. Diana Barker and Sheila Allen (London: Longman's, 1976).

[27] Leonore Davidoff, "Mastered for Life: Servant and Wife in Victorian Edwardian England," *Journal of Social History* 7 (Summer 1974): 406-28.

[28] J. Gathorne Hardy, *The Rise and Fall of the Victorian Nanny* (London: Hodder and Stoughton, 1972).

[29] McBride, " 'As the Twig is Bent' "; and Leonore Davidoff, "Forbidden Territories: Children, Servants and the Victorian House," unpublished lecture delivered to the Victorian Society, Spring 1978.

[30] J. Swann, "*Mater* and Nannie: Freud's Two Mothers and the Discovery of the Oedipus Complex," *American Imago: A Psychoanalytic Journal for Culture, Science and the Arts* (Spring 1974); and Kenneth A. Grigg, "All Roads Lead to Rome: The Role of the Nursemaid in Freud's Dreams," *Journal of the American Psychoanalytic Association* 21 (1973): 108-12ö.

[31] Eugene Genovese, *Roll Jordan Roll: The World the Slaves Made* (New York: Pantheon Books, 1974), pp. 354, 361.

[32] Calvin C. Hernton, *Sex and Racism* (London: Andre Deutsch, 1973).

In his section on "The Sexual Gain," John Dollard discussed the illicit but acknowledged sexual exploitation of black women by white men in the American South. In a period when black and white cultures varied it is possible that diet etc. produced body odours which differed but it is also possible that the difference was perceived as greater than it really was. In any case it has obvious similarity to the case I am discussing. "It may be that just those odours which are revolting when one is in a conventional mood may be exciting in the sexual mood." See John Dollard, "The Sexual Gain," in *Caste and Class in A Southern Town* (New York: Doubleday Anchor Books, 1949), p. 144.

The complexity and importance of this taboo subject is brought out by Clara Thompson's point that female sexuality was directly associated with uncleanness and especially odour. Any evidence of bodily secretion or odour betrayed them and thus sex itself becomes evidence of lower-class origins which may be related to the question of menstruation. See Clara Thompson, "Some Effects of the Derogatory Attitude towards Female Sexuality," in *Psychoanalysis and Women,* ed. Jean Baker Miller (Harmondsworth: Penguin Books, 1974).

[33] Mary Lutyens, *To Be Young: Some Chapters of Autobiography* (London: Rupert Hart-Davis, 1959), p. 15.

[34] Robert Louis Stevenson, *Collected Poems,* ed. Janet Adam Smith (London: Rupert Hart-Davis, 1951), p. 361.

[35] Ursula Bloom, *"Mrs. Bunthrope's Respects": A Chronicle of Cooks* (London: Hutchinson, 1963), p. 42.

[36] Susan Chitty, *The Beast and the Monk: A Life of Charles Kingsley* (London: Hodder & Stoughton, 1974).

[37] Geoffrey Grigson, *The Crest on the Silver: An Autobiography* (London: The Cresset Press, 1950), p. 51.

[38] Arthur J. Munby, "Dichter und Baverin," *Relicta* (London: Bertram Dobell, 1909); Leonore Davidoff, *The Best Circles: Society Etiquette and the Season* (London: Croom Helm, 1973).

[39] Alrik Gustavson, *Six Scandinavian Novelists* (Minneapolis: University of Minnesota Press, 1966), p. 292.

[40] Legal protection for servants from being physically punished was only provided as part of the Offenses Against the Person Act of 1861 and complaints had to be made to two J.Ps. J. D. Caswell, *The Law of Domestic Service* (London: Grant Richards Ltd., 1913).

[41] Ronald Blythe, *Akenfield: Portrait of an English Village* (London: Delta Books, 1971).

[42] M. Motherly, *The Servant's Behaviour Book: Hints on Manners and Dress for Maid Servants* (London: Bell and Daldy, 1859), p. 49.

"Humility is expressed in all postures which involve bowing, crouching or lowering the body." (M. Argyle, *Bodily Communication* [London: Metheun & Co., 1976], p. 284).

[43] Stephen Tallents, *Man and Boy* (London: Faber & Faber, 1943), p. 10; Sigrid Undset, *The Longest Years,* trans. A. G. Charter (London: Cassell & Co., 1935).

[44] Jennifer Wayne, *Brown Bread and Butter in the Basement: a "twenties childhood"* (London: Gollancz, 1975), p. 43.

[45] Cominos, "Late Victorian Sexual Respectability and the Social System."

[46] Sigmund Freud, "On the Universal Tendency to Debasement in the Sphere of Love," *On Sexuality* (Harmondsworth: Pelican Freud Library, 1977), pp. 251-54.

[47] Arthur J. Munby, *Munby Diary,* September 1860.

[48] Munby's story has been told and excerpts from his diary sensitively edited in Derek Hudson, *Munby: Man of Two Worlds: The Life and Diaries of A. J. Munby*

1828-1910 (London: Abacus, 1974); and Arthur J. Munby, *Diaries 1859-1898.* I am very indebted to Hudson's work and interpretation. All quotations from the diaries are by permission of the Master and Fellows of Trinity College, Cambridge. I have retained spelling, punctuation and underlining exactly as they appear in all excerpts. I have also followed the general convention of referring to Arthur Munby by his last name only while Hannah Cullwick is invariably called simply Hannah. Nevertheless, the status and power implications of this naming convention should not be overlooked. The adult middle-class man is given the impersonal dignity of his surname while the female servant retains the personalized, childlike use of her first name only.

See also: Arthur J. Munby, *Benois: Poems* (London: John Oliver, 1852); Arthur J. Munby, *Verses: New and Old* (London: Bell and Daldy, 1865); Arthur J. Munby, *Dorothy: A Country Story* (London: Kegan Paul & Co., 1880); Arthur J. Munby, *Vulgar Verses (by "Jones Brown")* (London: Reeves and Turner, 1891); Arthur J. Munby, *Susan, A Poem of Degrees* (London: Reeves and Turner, 1893); Arthur J. Munby, *Ann Morgan's Love: A Pedestrian Poem* (London: Reeves and Turner, 1896); Arthur J. Munby, *Poems, Chiefly Lyric and Elegiac* (London: Kegan Paul & Co., 1901); and Arthur J. Munby, *Relicta* (London: Bertram Dobell, 1909).

[49] Douglas, *Implicit Meanings: Essays in Anthropology*, p. 61.

[50] Richard L. Schoenwald, "Training Urban Man: A hypothesis about the sanitary movement," in *The Victorian City: Images and Realities*, eds. Michael Wolff and H. J. Dyos (London: Routledge, 1974), 2: 669-92.

[51] Robert A. Fothergill, *Private Chronicles: A Study of English Diaries* (London: Oxford, 1974).

[52] Anon., *My Secret Life* (New York: Grove Press, 1966).

[53] Letter from Munby, quoted in D. Hudson, *Munby: Man of Two Worlds*, p. 39.

[54] A. John, *By the Sweat of Their Brow: Women Workers at Victorian Coal Mines* (London: Croom Helm, 1980).

[55] Leonore Davidoff, Jean L'Esperance, and H. Newby, "Landscape with Figures: Home and Community in English Society," in *The Rights and Wrongs of Women*, eds. Anne Oakley and Juliet Mitchell (Harmondsworth: Penguin Books, 1976); and John Henry Raleigh, "The Novel and the City," *Victorian Studies* 11 (March 1968): 291-329.

[56] Actors and especially circus performers and travelling players, like gypsies, held a special place in the pantheon of Victorian fantasy. Their independence from the duties and constraints of work, the element of play in their lives, held a special attraction as well as moral opprobrium. See, for example, the place of the circus people in Charles Dickens's *Hard Times.*

[57] Munby, Diary, June 1859, quoted in Hudson, *Munby: Man of Two Worlds*, p. 35.

[58] Munby, Diary, 1860.

[59] A. J. Munby, Hannah's Volume 2, 1877.

[60] Munby, Diary, 1860.

[61] A. J. Munby, Hannah's Place, 1841-1872.

[62] This point has been made by Pam Taylor, Centre for Cultural Studies, Birmingham, in her study of domestic service in the inter-war period.

[63] Interestingly, it was the governess who comforted her in her sorrow. Governesses, especially retired or "broken down," were often noted by Hannah throughout her diaries. The two maiden ladies who she worked for in Margate and who were very kind to her were ex-governesses who were trying to run a boarding house. Hannah was always slightly pitying of such women, not real ladies, yet trying to live a genteel life without the resources to do so and unable to do a thing for themselves, not even sew their own clothes. Hannah's diary confirms the social and metaphorical, not to be confused with statistical, importance of the governess in the Victorian view of gender and class. See also, Leonore Davidoff, "The English Victorian Governess: A Study in Social Isolation," unpublished manuscript, 1971; M. Jeanne Peterson, "The Victorian Governess: Status Incongruence in

Family and Society," in *Suffer and Be Still: Women in the Victorian Age*, ed. Martha Vicinus (Bloomington, Indiana: University of Indiana Press, 1973).

[64] A. J. Munby, Hannah's Volumes, 1875.

[65] A. J. Munby, Hannah's Places, 1841-1872.

[66] Ibid.

[67] Cissie Fairchild makes the point that it was the physical, social and economic vulnerability of lower class women which made them susceptible to seduction by their masters (masters' sons, relatives, or friends) or to promises of marriage from their swains. See Cissie Fairchild, "Female Sexual Attitudes and the Rise of Illegitimacy: A Case Study," *Journal of Interdisciplinary History* 8 (Spring 1978): 627-67.

[68] Hannah Munby's Diary of Her Life As A Servant in the Temple, September 1873.

[69] Hudson, *Munby: Man of Two Worlds.* Personal communication, Pat Bradford, archivist, Trinity College, Cambridge, who catalogued the Munby collection.

[70] Stanley Cohen and Laurie Taylor, *Escape Attempts* (London: Allen Lane, 1976), p. 92. For the recent discovery of another case of double play acting which expresses themes of mastery and submission in a sexual context, see the case of Charles and Mary Kingsley, Susan Chitty, *The Beast and the Monk.*

[71] At the level of the individual psyche, hands were also regarded as the agents of the "dirty" work involved in masturbation, an obsessive concern of the middle class at this time. See Trudgill, *Madonnas and Magdalenes.*

"It is just as plausible to examine sexual behaviour for its capacity to express and serve non-sexual motives as the reverse": John H. Gagnon and William Simon, *Sexual Conduct: The Social Sources of Human Sexuality* (Chicago: Aldine, 1973), p. 17. Feet and hands as fetishes often screen actual relations from oneself and others. See Gertrud Lenzer, "On Masochism: A Contribution to the History of Phantasy and Its Theory," *Signs: Journal of Women in Culture, and Society* 1 (Winter 1975).

[72] G. A. Sala, *Margaret Foster: A dream within a dream* (London: T. Fisher Unwin, 1897), p. 15.

[73] A. J. Munby, *Vulgar Verses* (by "Jones Brown") (London: Reeves and Turner, 1891).

[74] Mary Merryweather, *Experience of Factory Life: Being a Record of Fourteen Years Employed at Mr. Courtauld's Factory in Halstead* (London: B. R. Parkes, 1862), p. 9.

A late Victorian health visitor noted that this perception by the rich that the poor have large hands and feet resulted in the giving of cast off clothing, particularly boots, which never fitted properly: See M. E. Loane, *The Next Street But One* (London: Edward Arnold, 1907). In fact, given differential feeding, standards of living and the effects of grinding physical work, we know that the poor would have been of smaller physique than the middle class or even regularly employed working class.

[75] See the following 17th century description of the perfect wife: "when shee submits herselfe with quietness, cheerefully, even as a well-broken horse turns at the least check of the riders bride, readily going and standing as he wishes that sits upon his back," in William Whatley, *A Bride-Bush or a Wedding Sermon*, quoted in Kathleen Davies " 'The Sacred Condition of Equality'—how original were Puritan doctrines of marriage?" *Social History* 5 (May 1977): 572. Davies goes on to say that "the metaphor of horse breaking was a favorite one."

[76] A. J. Munby, Diary, 1863.

[77] A. J. Munby, "Leonard and Elisabeth: A Subterranean Story," unpublished poem, 1896, kindness of the late Dr. A. N. L. Munby and Dr. A. John.

[78] Davidoff, "The Rationalization of Housework."

[79] Arrah B. Evarts, "Color Symbolism," *The Psychoanalytic Review* 6 (April 1919): 124-57.

[80] James Walvin, *Black and White: The Negro in English Society 1555-1945* (London: Allen Lane, Penguin Press, 1973). According to the O.E.D. definition from that per-

iod black implied "deeply stained with dirt, soiled, dirty, foul . . . having dark or deadly purposes, malignant, pertaining to or involving death, baneful, disasterous, sinister—an emotionally partisan colour, the hand maid and symbol of baseness and evil."

[81] Winthrop Jordan, *White Over Black: American Attitudes toward the Negro 1550-1812* (Chapel Hill: University of North Carolina Press, 1968).

[82] Chitty, *The Beast and the Monk.*

[83] Hannah's Diary, February 1872. Munby and Hannah have constructed these "signs of lowness" on the base of "socially valid and institutionally recommended standards of 'preference' " given by the position of Victorian domestic service. See H. Garfinkel, "Conditions of Successful Degradation Ceremonies," in *Deviance: The Interactionist Perspective*, eds. Earl Rubington and Martin Weinberg (London: Collier-MacMillan, 1973), p. 89.

[84] Hannah's Diary, April 1870.

[85] A. J. Munby, Diary, May 1873, quoted in Hudson, *Munby: Man of Two Worlds.*

[86] This is a kind of selective perception which still influences our behaviour. "If pairing were random, the woman would actually be taller than the man in 1 out of 6 couples." Judith Stiehm, "Invidious Intimacy," *Social Policy* 6 (March/April 1976): 12.

[87] A. J. Munby, Diary, 1859.

[88] A. J. Munby, *Ann Morgan's Love: A Pedestrian Poem* (London: Reeves and Turner, 1896).

[89] Edith Oliver, *Without Knowing Mr. Walkley: Personal Memories* (London: Faber and Faber, 1939).

[90] Hannah's Diary, February 1870. To "nurse" implies cuddling a baby or child on one's lap rather than the American usage which specifically means breastfeeding.

[91] Hannah's Diary, July 1864.

[92] Hannah's Diary, February 1863.

[93] A. J. Munby, *Ann Morgan's Love.*

[94] Hannah's Diary, April 1870.

[95] Hannah's Diary, July 1871.

[96] A. J. Munby, Diary, February 1860, quoted in Hudson, *Munby: Man of Two Worlds*, p. 52.

[97] Hannah Cullwick, A Maid of All Work's Diary, 1864.

[98] Hannah's Diary, May 1871.

[99] A. J. Munby, "Dichter Und Baverin," *Relicta* (London: Bertram Dobell, 1909).

[100] A. J. Munby, *Vulgar Verses*, (by "Jones Brown").

[101] Letter from Hannah to Munby, December 5, 1886, quoted in Hudson, *Munby: Man of Two Worlds*, p. 411.

[102] Hannah's Diary, April 1872.

[103] A. J. Munby, Hannah Cullwick's Account of Her Own Life, 1873.

[104] Hannah's Diary, February 1871.

[105] *Royal Commission on the Poor Law*, (Statistical Appendix, 1910, Vol. 53).

[106] A. J. Munby, Hannah's Volumes 1875. With the co-operation of the Castle Museum at York, I have been able to estimate that a standard coal scuttle, when full, weighed between 28 and 30 pounds. A large bath jug when filled with water also averaged about 30 pounds.

[107] A. J. Munby, *Relicta*, 1909.

[108] Hudson, *Munby: Man of Two Worlds.*

[109] The contradiction between the beliefs and practices of upper-middle-class men who accepted the idea of middle-class women as pure gentle creatures in need of protection from the rough and tumble of the public world have been discussed in A. Sachs and J. H. Wilson, *Sexism and the Law: A Study of Male Beliefs and Legal Bias in Britain and the United States* (London: Martin Robertson, 1978). See also Brian Harrison, *Separate Spheres: the opposition to women's suffrage in Britain* (London: Croom Helm, 1978).

[110] A. J. Munby, Diary, 1863.

[111] "The man almost always feels his respect for the woman acting as a restriction on his sexual activity, and only develops full potency when he is with a debased sexual object, and this in its turn is partly caused by the entrance of perverse components in his sexual aims, which he does not venture to satisfy with a woman he respects": Sigmund Freud, "On the Universal Tendency to Debasement in the Sphere of Love," *On Sexuality*, p. 254.

[112] A. J. Munby, Diary, 1860.

[113] Gorham, "The 'Maiden Tribute of Modern Babylon,' " p. 378.

[114] Hannah Munby's Diary of Her Life as a Servant in the Temple, August 1873.

[115] Weeks, *Coming Out*; and Jeffrey Weeks, "Inverts, Perverts and Mary Annes: Aspects of Male Prostitution in the 19th and early 20th Centuries," *Journal of Homosexuality*, Vol. 6, Nos. 1 and 2, Fall/Winter 1980-1.

[116] Weeks, *Coming Out*, p. 41.

[117] A. J. Munby, Diary, 1860.

2 Freud's Dora, Dora's Hysteria

MARIA RAMAS

> Remind me how we loved our mother's body
> our mouths drawing the first
> thin sweetness from her nipples
>
> our faces dreaming hour on hour
> in the salt smell of her lap . . .
>
> and how we thought she loved
> the strange male body first
> that took, that took, whose taking seemed the law
>
> and how she sent us weeping
> into the law. . . .
>
> Adrienne Rich[1]

   In the fall of 1900 a wealthy Austrian industrialist, Philip
Bauer, brought his eighteen-year-old daughter to Sigmund Freud
for treatment. She came reluctantly. She suffered from severe
coughing attacks that often took her voice away entirely. In
addition, she was chronically depressed and had threatened
suicide. She had long been on bad terms with her mother, but
recently she had become hostile toward her father as well. She
insisted that he break off relations with a married couple, the K's,
with whom he and his family had been close friends for years.
Philip Bauer told Freud that he suspected his daughter's changed
character and intensified nervous symptoms had some connection
with an event she insisted had occurred one summer, two years
earlier, when they had joined the K's at a lake in the Alps for a
brief vacation. Although his daughter had intended to stay with
the K's for several weeks, she insisted on accompanying him when

he departed a few days after their arrival. Shortly afterwards, she told her mother that Herr K had "had the audacity to make a proposal" to her while alone on a walk by the lake, pleading, "You know I get nothing out of my wife." She said that she had slapped his face and fled. When he met her again on the way back to the house, Herr K "begged her to forgive him and not to mention the incident." Philip Bauer had been assured by Herr K, however, that she no doubt "fancied the whole scene," most likely as a result of becoming overexcited by erotic books which Frau K said she was in the habit of reading. He was sure his daughter's "tale of the man's immoral suggestions" was "a phantasy." Taking his leave, hoping that Freud would "please try and bring her to reason," Bauer left Freud to face a young woman of "intelligent and engaging looks" and "independent judgment," one "who had grown accustomed to laugh at the efforts of doctors." Later, betraying his own phantasy, Freud called her Dora.[2]

All of this probably seems familiar. Certainly Freud's analysis of Dora, formally titled "Fragment of an Analysis of a Case of Hysteria," is one of his best known case histories.[3] It is read as literary classic, as sociology, as popular romantic fiction, and, occasionally perhaps, even as soft core pornography. The Collier paperback, currently in its fifth edition, certainly has been designed to entice a broader audience than psychoanalysts. Its back cover bears the titillating heading "Dora – her homosexual . . . love for Frau K was the strongest unconscious current in her mental life." It advertises the cast of supporting characters as "an obsessive mother, an adulterous father, her father's mistress, Frau K, and Frau K's husband, who had made amorous advances to Dora."[4]

But "Fragment of an Analysis" is not only romantic fiction. It is considered a classic analysis of the structure and genesis of hysteria and has the first or last word in almost every psychoanalytic discussion of hysteria. Although some have written addenda to Freud's case study, following up on one or another of Dora's multiple identifications, or reconsidering the case from the point of view of ego psychology, or from that of technique, or transference, the essential meaning of the analysis remains unchallenged. Dora's frigidity, so haunting to Freud and to us, is still considered a cornerstone of hysteria and its most profound symptom. And the meaning Freud attributed to it is still considered to be "truth" by psychoanalytic theory and by popular culture.[5]

Although psychoanalysts seem to have determined the full

meaning of Freud's Dora and Dora's hysteria, I would like to look at this case once again with feminist eyes.[6] My intention is not to use feminism to explain away the unconscious meaning of Dora's hysteria, or to deny psychoanalytic discoveries. I will argue, however, that Freud's analysis is only partly true — intriguing fiction and flawed analysis — because it is structured around a phantasy of femininity and female sexuality that remains misunderstood, unconscious if you will. This phantasy continues to be an essential part of psychoanalytic explanations of hysteria, forcing the recognition that psychoanalysis is not simply *the* theory of the formation of gender identity and sexuality in patriarchal society, but is profoundly ideological as well.[7]

Dora's real name was Ida Bauer. She was born in Vienna in 1882 to Philip and Käthe Gerber Bauer. Philip Bauer was a prosperous textile manufacturer who owned and managed textile factories in northeastern Bohemia.[8] According to Freud, he was the dominating figure in the family circle. Bauer suffered from tuberculosis and afflictions associated with advanced stages of syphilis.

Käthe Bauer was described by Freud from characterizations given him by Ida and Philip as "an uncultivated woman and above all a foolish one." Freud deduced that she was suffering from a severe form of "housewife's psychosis," being "occupied all day long in cleaning the house with its furniture and utensils and in keeping them clean to such an extent as to make it almost impossible to use or enjoy them."[9] Freud suggested that Käthe Bauer probably had contracted venereal disease from her husband because she suffered from a vaginal discharge and intestinal pain.[10]

Ida and her mother had been on unfriendly terms for many years at the time of the analysis. Ida was much closer to Philip Bauer's elder sister whom, as Freud noted, she took as a model by falling ill. This sister suffered from what Freud described as "a severe form of psychoneurosis without any characteristically hysterical symptoms. After a life which had been weighed down by an unhappy marriage," she literally starved herself to death, and died of anorexia a year or so before Ida's analysis began.[11]

The Bauer family circle was completed by a son, Otto, who was fourteen months older than Ida. As an adult, Otto manifested certain obsessional characteristics never considered serious enough to warrant analysis. Like his sister, Otto became famous, although not as a neurotic. Otto Bauer had a prestigious and influential political career as leader and chief theoretician of the Austrian Socialist Party between 1918 and 1934.[12]

This very brief review of the Bauer family's state of mental and physical health suggests that nervous illness was the special prerogative of the Bauer women. Both Bauer's sister and his wife suffered extreme forms of nervous afflictions, and his sister died of hers. This was not a state peculiar to this one family. Frau K, who plays so central a role in this case, also had a history of neurosis and had lived many years as "an invalid," obliged to spend months in a sanatorium for nervous disorders because she had been unable to walk." In late nineteenth- and early twentieth-century Europe and the United States, hysteria, as well as other forms of nervous illness, was common to women of the bourgeoisie – their language of femininity.[13]

Philip Bauer first brought Ida to Freud when she was sixteen. Her chronic nervous cough, which she had endured since she was twelve, had worsened alarmingly. She was depressed and complained of constant fatigue and lack of concentration. Freud proposed treatment at that time, but her attacks subsided and her father decided against it. Soon, she was again coughing in the characteristic manner. When, two years later, she threatened her parents with suicide, Philip Bauer firmly decided that she must undergo treatment with Freud, despite her reluctance.

During the course of the analysis, Freud discovered additional hysterical manifestations: a vaginal discharge, a limp, and a phobia which prevented Ida from walking past "any man whom she saw in eager or affectionate conversation with a lady."[14] These were Ida Bauer's symptoms, her metaphors, which Freud sought to decipher during and after the brief analysis.

Freud was inclined to believe Ida's account of Herr K's proposal to her two summers earlier. He suspected a connection between this particular "circumstance of her life" and her most recent hysterical symptoms. In the very first few sessions, Freud recognized that this was true, but only the tip of the iceberg.

The Bauers had first become friends with the K's years earlier when Philip Bauer's tubercular attacks had forced the family to move to the southern provinces where the air was fresher. Both the K's and the Bauers were unhappy as married couples. Käthe Bauer, perhaps because of her obsessions, perhaps because of her estrangement, kept away from Philip Bauer's sickroom, and Frau K nursed him during his long illness. Ida formed an intimate friendship with Frau K. She also became friends with Herr K, who often took her on walks and gave her small presents.

Sometime during the course of the first years of their friendship, Frau K and Philip Bauer began a love affair, which continued while Ida was in analysis with Freud. During these same

years, Herr K's feelings for Ida became clearly erotic. By the time
Ida was fourteen, Herr K could no longer control his passion, and
he precipitated the first of the two seduction attempts around
which Freud centered the analysis.

On the pretext of inviting Ida to join him and Frau K in viewing
a local church festival, Herr K persuaded Ida to meet him at his
place of business. When Ida arrived, however, she found Herr K
alone, for he had previously dismissed the clerks and had
persuaded Frau K to remain at home. As the procession
approached, he asked Ida to wait at the door while he closed the
outside shutters. When he returned, he "suddenly clasped the girl
to him and pressed a kiss upon her lips. . . ." At that moment Ida
experienced "a violent feeling of disgust, tore herself free from the
man, and hurried past him . . . to the street door."[15] Ida did not
mention this scene to anyone until she recounted it to Freud, four
years later. For some time afterwards, she avoided being alone
with Herr K, and she begged out of the invitation she had
previously accepted to accompany the K's on vacation. Herr K
made no further attempt at seduction until the "scene" by the
lake two years later. After this, Ida broke off relations with Herr K
entirely. However, she often met him in the street, "and he always
used to turn round and look after her; and once when he had met
her out by herself he had followed her for a long way. . . ."[16]

Shortly after the "scene" by the lake, Ida became obsessed by
her father's affair with Frau K and demanded that he break off
relations with the K's. She was enraged that her father denied her
account of the "scene." Underlying her rage was the suspicion
that her father and Herr K had formed an unspoken agreement in
which she had "been handed over to Herr K as the price of his
tolerating the relations between her father and his wife."[17] For all
intents and purposes, an exchange of women had taken place. One
can imagine the ways in which pressure was brought to bear on
Ida to keep Herr K appeased — but also remain respectable. As
Steven Marcus suggests:[18]

> If we try to put ourselves in the place of this girl between her sixteenth
> and eighteenth years, we can at once recognize that her situation was a
> desperate one. The three adults to whom she was closest, whom she loved
> the most in the world, were apparently conspiring separately, in tandem,
> or in concert — to deny her the reality of her experience. They were
> conspiring upon matters that might easily unhinge the mind of a young
> person; for the three adults were not betraying Dora's love and trust alone,
> they were betraying the structure of the actual world.

As most who have reviewed the case have pointed out, Freud agreed with Ida Bauer's perception of the actual world. He found her reproaches of her father "justified." In acknowledging reality as she perceived it, Freud undeniably touched her, and made her hopeful. He was not only the first member of Ida's class to do so, but the first father figure to do so. No doubt this legitimized Ida's complaint in her own eyes. Certainly something more than Philip Bauer's authority compelled her to appear at Freud's home each day for three months at the appointed hour. Something more induced her to comply with Freud's method, to free-associate, to speak of her sexuality.[19]

There is no way of knowing exactly when Ida Bauer first perceived, however dimly, that Freud, while affirming the structure of the actual world, was painstakingly and brilliantly constructing an analysis that would deny the structure of her psychic world. No doubt she never understood the nature of Freud's betrayal, although she understood and lived the consequences.[20] Yet, by the end of the second month of their meetings, as she brought Freud her first dream — a phantasy of betrayal and a wish for a savior — Ida Bauer was already coming to suspect that Freud would not save her, as indeed he would not.

At the most obvious and general level, Ida Bauer's hysteria signified *refusal*, "negative sexuality," as Marcus calls it.[21] Freud recognized this, but never deciphered the meaning of the refusal. While Freud's analysis is complex, his main proposition is a simple one. Freud claimed that Ida Bauer was aroused by Herr K's pursuit of her, but was unwilling to acknowledge her desire consciously. Her unwillingness, he argued, had many accidental and even healthy motives — for example, "good sense," "respectability," — but, also, importantly, a "neurotic element, namely, the tendency to a repudiation of sexuality which was already present in her. . . ."[22] Her hysterical symptoms were compromise formations that represented both her desire to yield to Herr K and a composite force rebelling against that desire. Freud further contended that underlying the present desire for Herr K was an earlier incestuous childhood wish to be seduced by her father — a wish that she summoned up to protect her from the more recent pressing threat.

I wish to suggest a very different interpretation, however. While reviewing the main evidence for Freud's proposition, I propose to demonstrate that the analysis is not only forced and ultimately unconvincing, but that it also begs the question. Ida Bauer's hysteria — her repudiation of sexuality — is not explained by Freud, but, rather, explained away, for in the course of the analysis, Freud abandons his initial concern − the elucidation of hysteria as a *compromise formation* − in order to develop an argument that is fundamentally an ideological construct, a construct that defends patriarchal phantasies of femininity and female sexuality.

By engaging in a critical dialogue with Freud's case history, I hope to offer the beginnings of a more cogent explanation for Ida Bauer's *refusal*. Proceeding from a general theoretical to a historically specific level of analysis, I will argue that at the deepest level of meaning, Ida Bauer's hysteria was exactly what it appeared to be − a repudiation of the meaning of heterosexuality. Drawing upon psychoanalytic insight, I will contend that the elementary structures within which female heterosexuality and patriarchal femininity are negotiated pose barriers to their development. These barriers can be schematically viewed as twofold. First, because sexuality is not given but *created* through activity, and because it is created in relation to a woman and the female body, its transfer to a male "object" is problematic. Second, because the essential social relations between men and women are structured in terms of dominance and submission, sexual union is understood accurately as a power relation. In sexual phantasy, this conception takes the form of what psychoanalysis terms "primal scene" phantasies. These phantasies are sadomasochistic in content and have rigidly defined masculine and feminine positions. They are, perhaps, the most profound ideology precisely because they are eroticized. These phantasies take shape at the oedipal "moment" and are intimately bound up with the process by which the child confronts and comes to terms with the patriarchal meanings of sexual difference.

Drawing upon historical evidence, and upon Ida Bauer's personal history as Freud revealed it, I will then explore the specific ways in which these contradictions were posed to Ida Bauer. I will argue that Ida Bauer's hysteria represented a non-resolution of these contradictions and that her hysteria appears for this reason to be a compromise formation, for on the one hand, as Freud of course agues, Ida's hysteria revealed attempts to comply with the patriarchal laws of her culture and to appropriate patriarchal femininity and sexuality. This is most clearly revealed in her relationship to Herr K and in her hysterical identifications with servant women. On the other hand, however, her hysteria represented a revolt against this attempt to comply, and it is precisely the forcefulness of this revolt that reveals the brittle and really superficial nature of her compliance. It is this rebellion, unconscious and therefore ineffectual, that must be understood.

I will also contend that Ida Bauer's hysteria, in so far as it expressed a wish, sought to preserve preoedipal love for the mother/woman, and retain access to the maternal/female body. This wish underlay Ida Bauer's identifications with masculinity and her primary focus on oral sexuality. In so far as her hysteria was denial, it was a repudiation not only of the feminine position in the "primal scene," and the subordination it implied, but a continual, unsuccessful attempt to repudiate the "scene" itself and the sadistic meaning of the phallus. It was an attempt to deny patriarchal sexuality, and it was a protest against postoedipal femininity.

CONTRADICTIONS

In 1897, three years before Ida Bauer's analysis, Freud wrote to Wilhelm Fliess:[23]

> I have found, in my own case too, falling in love with the mother and jealousy of the father, and I now regard it as a universal event of early childhood. . . . The Greek legend seizes on a compulsion which everyone recognizes because he feels its existence within himself. Each member of the audience was once . . . just such an Oedipus, and each one recoils in horror from the dream-fulfillment here transplanted into reality, with the whole quota of repression which separates his infantile state from his present one.

Freud had discovered the Oedipus complex, the crucible in which a disparate, infantile sexuality is organized as masculine and feminine, and out of which a gendered personality emerges. For the boy, the incestuous desire for the mother is shattered by the recognition of the Father's Law, which prohibits incest, and the Father's punishment for transgressing the Law: castration. At this moment of the discovery of the Father-as-castrator, a childhood theory about the origins of sexual difference is transposed to another register to become the primal phantasy of castration. It is a stark crystallization of the dominant social meaning of sexual difference in patriarchal culture. And, while we do not wish to reduce this phantasy in any simple way to material reality, neither can we sever it from a historically developed ensemble of social relations that ultimately, and in a variety of ways, presents masculinity as an infinitely more desirable alternative than femininity.

Freud's original concept of the Oedipus complex, and subsequent reformulations, were developed on the model of the little boy. The theoretical problems of the feminine Oedipus complex was not considered until over a quarter of a century after "Fragment of an Analysis" was written. When Freud finally did consider the issue, he found himself confronting a provocative problem.[24]

> Until about this time in Freud's work, the Oedipus complex, the shibboleth on which psychoanalysis stood or fell, had also by and large been the main starting-point of actual analysis. Without detracting from the significance of the Oedipus complex, Freud now established the importance of a new realm — the preoedipal phase, in particular for girls. Hitherto he had assumed a symmetry in the Oedipal moment: boys loved their mothers and consequently wished to get rid of their unfair rivals in love, their fathers; girls desired their fathers, hence directed their jealousy against their mothers. But very early on Freud realised there was no parity here.[25]

The asymmetry refers to the fact that both sexes enter the Oedipus complex incestuously desiring the mother. For, while Freudian theory posits a preoedipal child with a polymorphously perverse sexuality, directing passive and active desires toward both parents, the tendency is for the mother to assume primary importance because of the intensity and importance of this relationship. Indeed, it is within the context of this relationship that human sexuality emerges, initially through activity focused on life preservation itself. It is also within this intersubjectivity that the child forms its first self-image, though not yet a gendered image, and that desire is born.[26] The legacy of the preoedipal period is a tendency for sexual phantasy to be charted across the terrain of the woman's body, and for the desire of women and men alike to echo a primal childhood wish to decipher and satisfy the mother's desire.

The question of the construction of the feminine Oedipus complex provoked considerable debate among psychoanalysts. Some chose to close Pandora's box and return to the pre-Freudian view that an innate heterosexuality inevitably pushes the girl toward the father.[27] Those theorists who confront the contradiction and seek more complex solutions fall, somewhat schematically, into two divisions. The more orthodox follow the lines of Freud's own analysis which stressed the role of the castration complex.[28] Whereas in boys the phantasy of castration destroys the Oedipus complex, in girls it makes the formation of a "positive" complex possible. The girl cannot tolerate the "fact" of her castration, which she discovers and slowly comes to accept during the phallic phase. She blames her mother for her condition

and depreciates her for being castrated as well. No longer able to
believe in the phallic power of her clitoris, she renounces
masturbation and, repressing her active desires, turns her passive
desires toward her father.[29]

> the girl's libido slips into a new position along the line . . . of the equation
> "penis-child." She gives up her wish for a penis and puts in place of it a
> wish for a child: and with *that purposes in view* she takes her father as a
> love object. Her mother becomes an object of jealousy. The girls has
> turned into a little woman.

The feminine position, according to Freud, is only really
established if the wish for a penis is replaced by the wish for a
baby. However, Freud suggested that the wish for a phallus
persists in the unconscious in spite of attempts to renunciate it. He
even contended that penis envy was very possibly impervious to
analysis.[30]

The other line of explanation, formulated mainly by object-
relations theorists, finds the motivation for the girl's turn to the
father primarily in the preoedipal mother-child relationship.[31]
Here, the phantasy of castration is evoked by an all-powerful
mother, and penis envy and the transition to the father as love-
object are viewed as being motivated primarily by the girl's wish to
free herself from an omnipotent mother. Both sexes fear and
suffer a narcissistic wound at the hands of the mother; the boy,
however, overcomes this wound through the recognition of the
masculinity his phallus represents. The girl, thus, seeks the phallus
as a way of individuating from the mother. As Nancy Chodorow
explains:[32]

> The penis, or phallus, is a symbol of power or omnipotence whether you
> have one as a sexual organ (as a male) or as a sexual object (as her mother
> "possesses" her father's). A girl wants it for the powers which it
> symbolizes and the freedom it promises from her previous sense of
> dependence, and not because it is inherently and obviously better to be
> masculine: "Basically, penis envy is the symbolic expression of another
> desire. Women do not wish to become men, but want to detach themselves
> from the mother and become complete, autonomous *women*." A girl's
> wish to liberate herself from her mother engenders penis envy.

The notion of an omnipotent mother seeking to prevent her
child's individuation has a material basis. The changing meaning
and structure of the family, and the role of the mother within it,
as they have developed in Western capitalist societies over the last
two centuries, have resulted in exaggerated centripetal tendencies
in the mother-child relationship. There appears, thus, to be a

certain plausibility to the suggestion that the girl view the Father as a potential liberator.

Ultimately, however, this explanation makes sense only if we abstract away from patriarchal social relations when constructing the analysis; and this is precisely what object relations theory does. In object relations theory the triadic structure (father/ mother/child) is replaced by the dyadic structure (mother/child) as the elementary relational structure within which gender identity and sexuality are formed. Because of this replacement, patriarchal social relations necessarily lie *outside* the basic unit of analysis and, therefore, play no determining part in the process of forming gender identity and sexuality. They are brought in only after the fact — after these formations have already been theoretically accounted for. Because the content and structure of actual social relations between women and men, and the symbolic representations of these relations, are *left out* of the analytical framework, because the fundamental dilemmas of feminine gender identity and heterosexuality have been defined solely in terms of the girl's preoedipal (read prepatriarchal) relationship to the mother, the scenario in which the Father appears as liberator seems to make sense.

The obvious problem with this, however, is that even if we accept the reasonable proposition that the girl seeks to escape the centripetal and confining nature of her relationship to her mother through the socially acceptable and even socially required route of the turn to the Father, the Father and the phallus are *not* empty vessels that she can fill with whatever content she pleases — that is, with liberation. They are imbued with social meanings that are, above all, *patriarchal* and that, therefore, militate against liberation by confronting the girl with new and seemingly more permanent forms of imprisonment and dependency. It is precisely these meanings that each girl must come to terms with at the oedipal "moment," and it is these that any adequate theory of the formation of gender identity and sexuality in a patriarchal culture *must* have at the center of its theoretical framework.

Although different in crucial ways these two tendencies in psychoanalytic theory also share certain common understandings vis-à-vis this particular issue. Both acknowledge that the transition is never really perfectly achieved. Because the feminine Oedipus complex is a secondary formation, women retain more of their original bisexuality. The desire for the mother cannot be totally renounced. Both theories also, however, ultimately stress an ambivalent attitude toward the mother, the legacy of which is a *crippling* ambivalence toward women and toward the self. This is in contrast to a relatively unambivalent coveting of the phallus, either as a means of escape, or because the phallus is all there is in a patriarchal culture.

If this latter formulation is essentially complete, the barriers to the successful construction of a feminine Oedipus complex are considerably less formidable than they at first appear. The primary barrier, incestuous desire for the mother, is sufficiently overwhelmed by hostility toward her on the one hand, and by the desire for the phallus on the other.

I suggest, however, that this formulation leaves out a crucial element that makes this process far more contradictory. Neither theory seriously considers the possibility of an essential ambivalence toward the phallus itself. However, a close analysis of the phantasies that are integrally intertwined with the Oedipus complex reveals that such ambivalence *must* be the case. Psychoanalytic formulations present the phallus alternatively as signifier of desire, as symbolizing protection, invulnerability, potency, or, freedom from an all-engulfing preoedipal mother. The phantasies of castration and of the Father-as-castrator force us to posit other meanings: violence, destruction, sadism. The primal phantasy of castration depends, on the one hand, upon the equation of femininity, masochism, and annihilation, and on the other, upon the sadistic meaning of the phallus/Father.

These meanings are also clearly expressed in a second phantasy that takes form during the oedipal period and expresses the essential content of patriarchal sexual phantasy. In his analytic work Freud repeatedly discovered a phantasy in the unconscious of his analysands which he termed the "primal scene." The phantasy was the same for men and women; in it, heterosexual union, violence, and degradation were intertwined. J. Laplanche and J.B. Pontalis define Freud's notion of the "primal scene" as the "scene of sexual intercourse between the parents which the child observes or infers on the basis of certain indications or phantasies. It is generally interpreted by the child as an act of violence on the part of the father."[34] Freud first used the term in his analysis of the Wolf Man, suggesting that sex between the parents is understood by the child as "an aggression by the father in a sado-masochistic relationship. . . ."[35] In another work he noted: "Among the store of phantasies of all neurotics, and probably of all human beings, this scene is seldom absent."[36]

Freud posited the centrality of the "primal scene" in unconscious mental life as a result of clinical evidence. Another way of pursuing this phantasy is through the study of pornography. What pornography reveals, today, as in the nineteenth century, is that this "scene" is a dominant theme in sexual phantasy. Marcus documents this in his classic study of sexuality and pornography in nineteenth-century England, *The Other Victorians*.[37] After a discussion of a representative nineteenth-century pornographic novel, Marcus offers the following summary.[38]

> The chief sexual fantasies represented in *The Lustful Turk* can be rather simply outlined. They have largely to do with the sexuality of domination, with that conception of male sexuality in which the aggressive and sadistic components almost exclusively prevail. Each of the separate stories are in this sense identical with the others. Each begins with a virgin, reluctant, proud, chaste, a young women in whom Nature has not yet been awakened. She then undergoes a series of violent experiences, which ritually include beating, flogging, and defloration in the form of rape. By means of these sufferings, her pride is subdued, her chastity broken, and in their place Nature — responsiveness — is substituted. This conception of male sexuality is what I have earlier called the historically older or more traditional form, the form of aggressive domination. It is also the form in which male sexuality is represented in the overwhelming majority of pornographic works written during the nineteenth and twentieth centuries.

Let us consider the phantasy in more detail. First, the sex act, Marcus suggests, is conventionally represented as a "rape-murder-sacrifice," and typically involves the defloration of a young virgin. For example:[39]

> I quickly felt his finger again introducing the head of that terrible engine I had before felt, and which now felt like a pillar of ivory entering me. . . . My petitions, supplications, and tears were of no use. I was on the altar, and, butcher-like, he was determined to complete the sacrifice; indeed, my cries seemed only to excite him to the finishing of my ruin, and sucking my lips and breasts with fury, he unrelentingly rooted up all obstacles my virginity offered, tearing and cutting me to pieces, until the complete junction of our bodies announced that the whole of his terrible shaft was buried within me. I could bear the dreadful torment no longer, but uttering a piercing cry sunk insensible in the arms of my cruel ravisher.

Stylistically outdated, the passage seems to us more a caricature than a representation of an erotic phantasy. Yet, as Marcus points out, the theme is a central one to nineteenth-century pornographic literature.

There is a second part to this phantasy, however, which is both critical and problematic: the response of the young woman. Here is a typical example:[40]

Never, oh never shall I forget the delicious transports that followed the stiff insertion; and then, ah me!, by what thrilling degrees did he, by his luxurious movements, fiery kisses, and strange touches of his hand to the most crimson parts of my body, reduce me to a voluptuous state of insensibility. I blush to say so powerfully did his ravishing instrument stir up nature within me, that by mere instinct I returned him kiss for kiss, responsively meeting his fierce thrusts, until the fury of the pleasure and ravishment became so overpowering that, unable to support the excitement I so luxuriously felt, I fainted in his arms with pleasure. . . .

Here we have the phantasy in its pristine form: the sex act is a sadomasochistic act that is enjoyed by both sexes. Clearly, there is an odd contradiction between the two parts of this phantasy. On the one hand the phantasy involves, even depends upon, the complete objectification and degradation of the woman, of course, against her will. On the other, it demands her erotic fulfillment.

Linking these two parts is the phallus, referred to in this particular novel as "Nature's grand masterpiece," upon which, Marcus informs us, "pages of description and praise are spent."[41] In fact, sexual union, as it is described in the above passages, and as it appears in Marcus's study, is above all a celebration of an ever-potent phallus. It is the "pillar of ivory," the "terrible engine," "the ravishing instrument" that in ripping the woman apart inspires her admiration and awe. Its potency, affirmed through violence, seduces her and gives her pleasure.

Psychoanalytic theory argues that the phantasy of the "primal scene" is in fact a *mis*interpretation on the child's part, due to the influence of a specific libidinal phase – the anal-sadistic stage.[42] In contrast, I believe it is an accurate perception of the dominant patriarchal sexual phantasy. The phantasy, quite simply, expresses erotically the essential meaning of sexual difference in patriarchal culture.

Although the content may vary, the form of "primal scene" phantasies remains constant. The "scene" is one of dominance and submission, and this is the essential erotic component. Further, gender defines the positions in the "scene." For, in its archetypal formulation, the phantasy is heterosexual; it is a "scene" between a man and a woman. Even when those acting out the phantasy are of the same sex, this is its essence. The "scene" depicts the submission and degradation of whoever is in the feminine position. That is to say, ultimately and always, a woman is being degraded. The phantasy may be mild in content, or it may reach to the extreme other end of the continuum to express a sadomasochistic desire that seeks ultimate satisfaction in the total annihilation of the woman — the feminine.

If we view the Oedipus complex from this vantage point, we can see that the complex confronts the child not only with the sexual prohibitions of her or his culture, but also with the interconnected meanings of masculinity, femininity, and heterosexuality.
Precisely at the "moment" that the girl confronts the demand that she turn from mother to father, the connections between activity, possession of the phallus, sadism, and masculinity, on the one hand, and passivity, castration, masochism, and femininity, on the other, come into sharp focus. After this "moment," sexual phantasy can never again exist ignorant of the implications of gender.

These are the contradictions in barest outline. They are the product of social relations that determine sexuality will be created in relation to a woman, and that sexual phantasy will be molded by and interbound with the social meaning of sexual difference. To understand the ways in which these contradictions are posed to different races and classes of women in different periods, and the ways in which they are worked out, demands more specific levels of analysis. These are, ultimately, historical questions. In the remainder of this essay, I want to explore the way in which the dilemma was framed for Ida Bauer, and the way she sought resolution.

DORA'S HYSTERIA

Unfortunately, Freud gives relatively little information about Ida Bauer's early childhood. We know that Ida's first clearly recognizable symptom — nervous asthma — began when she was eight and was accompanied by a character change. Prior to this time, she was a "wild-creature," "but after the asthma she became quiet and well behaved" and she began to fall behind her brother in her studies. Freud guessed that Ida had been masturbating until shortly before the nervous asthma appeared.

Freud offers only fragmentary information as to the particular influences that resulted in the repression of Ida's masturbatory phantasies and the birth of her hysteria. He suggests, however, that Ida, whose bedroom was close to her parents' at this time, "had overheard her father in his wife's room at night and had heard him . . . breathing hard during coitus."[43]

> I maintained years ago that the dyspnoea and palpitations that occur in hysteria and anxiety-neurosis are only detached fragments of the act of

copulation; and in many cases, as in Dora's, I have been able to trace back the symptom of dyspnoea or nervous asthma to the same exciting cause — to the patient's having overheard sexual intercourse taking place between adults. The sympathetic excitement which may be supposed to have occurred in Dora on such an occasion may very easily have made the child's sexuality veer round and have replaced her inclination to masturbation by an inclination to morbid anxiety.[44]

Yet if this was the precipitating event, it is not clear from Freud's account why Ida would replace "her inclination to masturbation by an inclination to morbid anxiety."

Both changes in character of this kind observed in Ida and the end of masturbation are associated with the final stages of the Oedipus complex in girls. However, although clinical evidence supports the theory that girls cling to the preoedipal period much longer than do boys, eight seems a bit too long. Clearly, Ida Bauer had confronted and repressed the oedipal dilemma prior to the appearance of her hysteria. Her hysteria signaled a breakthrough of the repressed oedipal constellation.

The early appearance of Ida's hysterical symptoms is somewhat unusual. The long latency period that separates the oedipal period and puberty can offer a temporary respite from oedipal conflicts. Thus, hysteria and other forms of unconscious conflict often first appear at puberty when resolution becomes mandatory.

In this regard, Anna, the sister of the famous patient who Freud named the Wolf-Man, comes to mind. Like Ida Bauer, Anna was a spirited, intellectually curious child who during her childhood "behaved like a naughty boy."[45] In her family "it had been said that Anna should not have been born a girl but a boy."[46] Unlike Ida, however, whose hysterical attack of nervous asthma at eight signaled the inhibition of her precociousness, Anna was able to "resolve" her confrontation with the sexual phantasies of her culture in a different way.[47]

> As a child she was boyish and unmanageable, but she then entered upon a brilliant intellectual development and distinguished herself by her acute and realistic powers of mind; she inclined in her studies to the natural sciences, but also produced imaginative writings of which her father had a high opinion.

It would seem that a family myth in which Anna was given permission to "be" the son, perhaps because she was the firstborn, allowed her to escape an ultimate confrontation with femininity until many years later. She could not, however, escape forever. In his memoirs her brother explained, in his characteristically unpsychoanalytic manner:[48]

> As she was growing up, Anna's feminine traits began to appear. Apparently she could not cope with them and they turned into pathological inferiority complexes. She was enchanted with the classical ideal of beauty with which she contrasted herself. She imagined that she had no feminine charm, which was not at all true. . . .

Anna was not able to resolve the contradiction. In her early twenties, she committed suicide by poisoning herself with mercury, which she kept in the laboratory she had set up at her home for her experiments in natural science.[49]

In this particular case, a family phantasy of Anna allowed her to momentarily resolve her confrontation with the social meaning of the difference between the sexes, and with the sexual phantasies of her culture seemingly as a boy would − by repressing her preoedipal desires and love for the mother and by sublimating her sexuality through intellectual pursuits. In essence she and her family pretended she was a boy, although everyone knew she was a girl. For Anna, however, this only postponed the inevitable. At some point culture, as well as her family, demanded that she take her place as a woman. Her inferiority complex, her protestations that she was not beautiful enough to be a woman, suggest, however, that Anna did not and could not see herself as a woman.

The situation was different for Ida Bauer. Her family's myths did not offer her the option of postponing ultimate confrontation with the contradiction that structures postoedipal femininity by imagining that she was not, in fact, a girl. At eight, Ida Bauer was trapped in her oedipal struggle and would remain so for life.

We are now confronted with the problem of how Ida Bauer learned the meaning of heterosexuality. The most important source of information clearly was Käthe Bauer. If name and property were traced through patrilineal descent in Victorian Europe, phantasy was in large part matrilineal.

Quite a few times during the course of the analysis Freud noted that Ida Bauer equated heterosexuality with contamination and self-destruction. Ida knew that her father was syphilitic and, more importantly, she knew how he had become so. She understood that "her father . . . had fallen ill through leading a loose life, and she assumed that he had handed on his bad health to her by heredity."[50] At the point in the analysis when this accusation began to surface, "for several days on end she identified herself with her mother by means of slight symptoms and peculiarities of manner."[51] Ida remembered a visit she had made to Franzensbad with her mother who was suffering from abdominal pains and from a discharge. Ida, no doubt correctly, blamed her father for passing on his venereal disease to her mother. One important meaning of Ida's own vaginal discharge, which she periodically fretted over, was an identification with her mother.

Käthe Bauer was clearly obsessed with a fear of contamination. "No one could enter the Bauer apartment without taking off his shoes; on Fridays and other occasions of "thorough" cleaning, the apartment frequently had to be avoided altogether."[52] Rooms such as the salon, where Philip Bauer kept his cigars, were kept locked at all times to insure against contamination. To enter the room Käthe Bauer's permission was necessary, as she had the only key.

It seems clear that Käthe Bauer's obsessional cleaning represented her wish to rid herself of contamination. In this regard, her demands that shoes be left outside the house and that cigars be locked in the study are fascinating. Perhaps in this way she sought control over the destructive phallus. We do not know when these symptoms began; however, the phantasy of heterosexuality as destructive to the woman no doubt began as early for Käthe Bauer as it did for her daughter. She appeared to have been able to sustain a sexual relationship with Philip Bauer for only a few years; by the time he contracted tuberculosis – when Ida was six – they were already estranged. Käthe Bauer's phantasy, of course, became reality, a fact that was not lost on Ida.[53]

At one point in the case history Freud, in passing, makes the very same connection. Toward the end of the case, returning momentarily to Ida's response to Herr K's kiss, Freud noted that[54]

> Ida thought her father suffered from venereal disease – for had he not handed it on to her and her mother? She might therefore have imagined to herself that all men suffered from venereal disease. . . . To suffer from venereal disease . . . meant for her to be afflicted with a disgusting discharge. So may we not have here a further motive for the disgust she felt at the moment of the embrace?

Ida Bauer's fear that all men suffered from venereal disease was not a foolish one. "Sexual diseases" were of epidemic proportions during the late nineteenth and early twentieth centuries, and middle-class women frequently were infected by their husbands. Unfortunately, statistics on the frequency of venereal diseases during this period are unreliable and fragmentary. In the early 1900s, Christabel Pankhurst suggested in a pamphlet reprinted from *The Suffragette* that from 75 to 80 per cent of British men were infected with gonorrhea, and a considerable percentage were infected with syphilis.[55] The estimate is no doubt exaggerated for polemical purposes. Abraham Flexner's study of prostitution in Europe at the turn of the century found venereal disease to be most prevalent in the large European cities of Paris, Vienna, and Berlin, where prostitution was under government regulation. Although he cites no statistics for Vienna, he quotes a study which calculated that of the clerks and merchants in Berlin between 18 and 28 years of age, 45 per cent had had syphilis, and 120 per cent had had gonorrhea. Another study estimated that in Germany, one man in every five contracted syphilis and that gonorrhea averaged more than one attack per man.[56] Clearly, one important source of the equation of heterosexuality and contamination for bourgeois women in Victorian Europe was the fact of venereal disease.

Ida Bauer's responses to the two seduction scenes that are the focus of the case, and the hysterical symptoms that were their aftermath, illuminate both her attempted disavowal of and her preoccupation with the sadistic meaning of the phallus and the "primal scene." In the first seduction scene, which took place at Herr K's place of business when Ida was fourteen, Herr K's kiss aroused in Ida "a violent feeling of disgust." From this response Freud concluded:[57]

> In this scene . . . the behaviour of this child of fourteen was already entirely and completely hysterical. I should without question consider a person hysterical in whom an occasion for sexual excitement elicited feelings that were preponderantly or exclusively unpleasurable; and I should do so whether or no the person were capable of producing symptoms.

Freud indeed argues here that Ida Bauer was hysterical because she was disgusted by Herr K's kiss when, in Freud's opinion, she should have felt aroused. Even Freud was somewhat apprehensive about this proposition. He adds quickly: "The elucidation of the mechanism of this *reversal of affect* is one of the most important and at the same time one of the most difficult problems in the psychology of the neurosis. In my judgment, I am still some way from having achieved this end. . . ."[58]

Freud also noted that the response displayed a *displacement of sensation*. "Instead of the genital sensation which would certainly have been felt by a healthy girl in such circumstances," Freud writes, "Dora was overcome by the unpleasurable feeling which is proper to the tract of the mucous membrane at the entrance to the alimentary canal – that is by disgust." In addition, "the scene left other consequences in the shape of a sensory hallucination in which she upon occasion could still feel upon the upper part of her body the pressure of Herr K's embrace," and a phobia which prevented her from walking past any man and woman engaged in "eager or affectionate conversation."[59] Freud, quite correctly, deduced that[60]

> during the man's passionate embrace she felt not merely his kiss upon her lips but also the presence of his erect member against her body. This perception was revolting to her; it was dismissed from her memory, repressed, and replaced by the innocent sensation of pressure upon her thorax. . . . Once more, therefore, we find a displacement from the lower part of the body to the upper.

Ida's phobia was also derived from her "remembrance" of Herr K's erection. She did not like walking past any man she thought might be in a state of sexual arousal.[61]

Freud's brilliant analysis of Ida Bauer's hysterical symptoms clearly reveals that they were attempts to repudiate the memory of Herr K's erection, or, the memory of the phallus. The fact that the sensations are displaced upward to Ida's throat, which is also the focus of her other symptoms, is significant, as we shall see.

Ida Bauer's response to Herr K's sexual overtures while she and her father vacationed with the K's at the resort lake two years later was equally unambivalent. Ida slapped his face and fled. She also attempted to defend herself from Herr K while she stayed at the K's vacation house by obtaining a key to her room from Frau K; and she took the first opportunity to leave the K's by accompanying her father when he left for home three days later. This last "scene" effectively ended her relationship with Herr and Frau K, and intensified her hysteria to such a degree as to precipitate her analysis with Freud.

In the face of such consistent behavior, why should we follow Freud in his assertion that Ida Bauer's attitude toward Herr K was not what it appeared to be? That her symptoms revealed *reversal of affect*? Why should we be convinced that her behavior and her desire were at odds?

Freud persistently attempted to demonstrate to Ida that she was in fact in love with Herr K. Freud noted that Ida's coughing attacks lasted from three to six weeks, and that this was precisely the length of time Herr K's frequent business trips out of town lasted. Freud claimed that if Ida's attacks coincided with Herr K's absences, then the hidden meaning of the attacks would be a longing for Herr K. Ida allegedly imitated Frau K, who was ill when Herr K was at home, and well when he was away. Ida, Freud argued, gave her illnesses the opposite meaning. Freud was not able to establish a clear correlation between Ida's attacks and Herr

K's absences; however, he felt the correlation to be close enough to support his interpretation.[62]

Freud viewed Ida's affection for Herr K's children as a "cloak for something else that Ida was anxious to hide from herself and from other people" . . ., namely, . . . "that she had all these years been in love with Herr K."[63] While Ida for the most part did not accept this idea, she did tell Freud that other people had told her that she was "simply wild about the man!" And finally, under the influence of Freud's persistent prodding, Ida "admitted that she might have been in love with Herr K . . . but declared that since the scene by the lake it had all been over."[64]

It would be foolish to deny that Ida Bauer formed an attachment to Herr K or that she was unaware of Herr K's growing erotic feelings for her. While it seems very doubtful that "it was possible for Herr K to send [Ida] flowers every day for a whole year while he was in the neighborhood, to take every opportunity of giving her valuable presents, and to spend all his spare time in her company, without her parents noticing anything in his behavior characteristic of lovemaking," it seems all but impossible that Ida herself did not notice.[65]

It would be equally foolish, however, to overlook the utilitarian characteristics of this attachment. Ida Bauer's primary task as an adolescent woman was to resolve her sexuality, once and for all, in favor of heterosexuality. Given her hysteria and the *refusal* that lay at its core, her choice of Herr K was truly ingenious. It allowed her to comply with the demands her family and culture placed upon her while at the same time it allowed her to revolt against those demands — and to do so in the name of social propriety and social justice.[66] She could comply with her father's wishes and wear the cloak of femininity by receiving the romantic attentions of Herr K, while knowing full well that this was a doomed affair, for any respectable consummation demanded that Herr K divorce his wife and marry Ida, and this was highly unlikely, if not impossible, given the strictures of respectable fin de siècle Vienna.[67] In this light, Herr K's attempts at seduction, which could not have been completely unexpected by Ida, seemed to be ample justification for her rejection of him, as indeed they were. However, this obscured the formidable injustice of patriarchal relations in Victorian Europe, as well as the almost tragic dimensions of her defiance.

Ida Bauer's choice was ingenious in that it served another double function as well; and this function was probably her strongest unconscious motivation. Ida's flirtation with heterosexual romance, that is, plummeted her into an erotic triangle with Frau K while at the same time masking the fact that Frau K was her primary "object" of desire.[68] Freud, in fact, implicitly recognised this, despite his own formidable resistance. In a series of footnotes, Freud undid his entire analysis of Dora by suggesting that behind the "almost limitless series of displacements" that structured Ida Bauer's symptoms and dreams, "it was possible to divine the operation of a single simple factor" – Ida's "deep-rooted homosexual love for Frau K."[69] He recognized that up until the "scene" by the lake, "the young woman and the scarcely grown girl had lived for years on a footing of closest intimacy. When [Ida] stayed with the K's she used to share a bedroom with Frau K, and the husband used to be quartered elsewhere." It was with Frau K, Freud surmised, that Ida had read Mantegazza's *Physiology of Love*. Frau K had also discussed with Ida the "intimate" problems of her married life, and Ida had often praised Frau K's "adorable white body" when she spoke of her to Freud in "accents more appropriate to a lover than to a defeated rival." She also told Freud with pleasure of a time when "evidently through the agency of Frau K she had been given a present of jewelry [by her father] which was exactly like some that she had seen in Frau K's possession and had wished for aloud at the time."[70]

It seems quite clear that the intimate sexual discussions, which occupied so much of Ida and Frau K's time alone together, had erotic meaning to them both. While the discussions were unquestionably of heterosexual phantasies, these phantasies mediated the sexual relationship between the two women. In essence, the man, be he Philip Bauer or Herr K, who always stood between the two women, in phantasy and in reality, was necessary though superfluous: necessary because he masked the homosexual desires that found some degree of satisfaction in this roundabout way. Necessary also because desire, viewed backwards through the prism of the Oedipus complex, is always a triangular affair.

Philip Bauer and Herr K were crucial to the possibility of the sexual relationship between the two women. Ida was, however, always the weak link in the incestuous triangles that the K's and the Bauers formed. When Herr K demanded that Ida's romantic fantasies succumb to his sexual desire, she blew the whistle, so to speak, on everyone's phantasy – including her own. Frau K responded by siding with her husband, revealing to him that Ida read Mantegazza and spoke of "forbidden topics." Freud suggested that beneath Ida's accusation of betrayal by her father lay a deeper sense of having been betrayed by Frau K, unconscious because her love was unconscious. And this betrayal echoed an earlier, primal betrayal.[71]

> Frau K had not loved her for her own sake but on account of her father. Frau K had sacrificed her without a moment's hesitation so that her relations with her father might not be disturbed. This mortification touched her, perhaps, more nearly and had a greater pathogenic effect than the other one, which she tried to use as a screen for it, — the fact that she had been sacrificed by her father. Did not the obstinacy with which she retained the particular amnesia concerning the sources of her forbidden knowledge point directly to the great emotional importance for her of the accusation against her upon that score, and consequently to her betrayal by her friend?

In revealing Ida's "preoccupation" with sex to Herr K, Frau K not only betrayed Ida, but denied the sexual phantasy they had shared together. For it was not Ida alone who was preoccupied with sexual matters and who read Mantegazza, but Ida and Frau K together. Frau K did indeed sacrifice their erotic relationship in order to protect herself and to preserve her relationship with Philip Bauer. Frau K's actions reiterated with devastating clarity the sexual law of Ida Bauer's culture. Ida's father stood between her and Frau K as the symbolic Father stands between all women.

Yet, in a sense, Ida Bauer was an outlaw. As Freud noted, Frau K was the one person whom Ida spared, while she pursued the others with an almost malignant vindictiveness. In sparing Frau K, Ida spared herself. In this way she denied both her love for Frau K as well as its futility.

DREAMS AND THE DILEMMA

Much of Freud's analysis centered around the interpretation of two dreams that Ida Bauer brought him during the course of the analysis. Both dreams related directly to the "scene" by the lake. In both cases, Freud's interpretation of the latent dream thoughts supported his thesis that Ida Bauer was summoning up her oedipal love for her father to protect her from her love for Herr K and her desire to surrender to him. A reconsideration of this latent content, even as Freud influenced it, reveals other possibilities. It is not difficult to find in Ida Bauer's two dreams the crystallization of her oedipal struggle: disavowal of the "primal scene" and the breakthrough of repressed lesbian desire.

The first of these two dreams was a recurrent one that Ida remembered first having dreamt three nights in succession after the "scene" by the lake. Ida recounted the dream to Freud as follows:[72]

> A house was on fire. My father was standing beside my bed and woke me up. I dressed myself quickly. Mother wanted to stop and save her jewel-case; but father said: "I refuse to let myself and my children be burnt for the sake of your jewel-case." We hurried downstairs, and as soon as I was outside I woke up.

Freud interpreted the dream as a resolution and, more importantly, as a wish. Ida had responded to Herr K's proposal on their walk by slapping him in the face and fleeing. Apparently, Herr K did not take Ida's rejection well. Ida recounted to Freud that later that day she awoke from a nap in her bedroom to find Herr K standing beside her. She asked him "sharply" what he wanted, and he replied that he "was not going to be prevented from coming into his bedroom when he wanted. . . ."[73] Ida obtained a key to the bedroom from Frau K, in order to lock herself in while dressing. When she wanted to lock herself in to take her afternoon rest, she found that the key had been taken. Naturally she suspected Herr K. The dream occurred for the first time that night. Freud correctly deduced that in so far as the dream represented a resolution, Ida was in that way saying to herself, "I shall have no rest . . . until I am out of this house."[74]

There were, however, deeper meanings to the dream which Freud interpreted through two lines of association. One led back to Ida's childhood memory of her father waking her and Otto up from sleep to take them to the bathroom. This association led Freud to the discovery of Ida's childhood habit of bed-wetting and his conjecture that it was associated with masturbation. A second line of association led to a dispute between Ida's parents that had occurred when she was fifteen in which her mother rejected a bracelet Philip Bauer had bought for her; she was angry because she had requested that he buy her a particular pair of pearl drop earrings, and he had refused. In association with this memory, Ida also remembered that a short time before Herr K had made her a present of an expensive jewel-case. The German word for jewel-case, *schmuckkästchen*, is also a slang expression for the female genitals. Thus Freud deduced that in Ida's dream jewel-case represented her vagina, her virginity, and sexual intercourse. Using these associations, he made the following analysis of the main dream wish:[75]

> The meaning of the dream is now becoming even clearer. You said to yourself: "This man is persecuting me; he wants to force his way into my

room. My 'jewel-case' is in danger, and if anything happens it will be father's fault." For that reason in the dream you chose a situation which expresses the opposite — a danger from which your father is saving you. In this part of the dream everything is turned into its opposite; you will soon discover why. As you say, the mystery turns upon your mother. You ask how she comes into the dream? She is, as you know your former rival in your father's affections. In the incident of the bracelet you would have been glad to accept what your mother had rejected. Now let us just put "give" instead of "accept" and "withhold" instead of "reject." Then it means that you were ready to give your father what your mother withheld from him. . . . Now bring your mind back to the jewel-case which Herr K gave you. You have there the starting-point for a parallel line of thoughts, in which Herr K is to be put in place of your father just as he was in the manner of standing beside your bed. He gave you a jewel-case; so you are ready to give Herr K what his wife withholds from him. That is the thought which has made it necessary for every one of its elements to be turned into its opposite.

And what is the upshot of this analysis? Freud concluded to Ida:[76]

The dream confirms once more what I had already told you before you dreamed it — that you are summoning up your old love for your father in order to protect yourself against your love for Herr K. But what do all these efforts show? Not only that you are afraid of Herr K, but that you are still more afraid of the temptation you feel to yield to him. In short these efforts prove once more how deeply you loved him.

Freud's analysis of the hidden dream wish did not strike a responsive chord in Ida Bauer; Freud conceded that Ida "would not follow me in this part of the interpretation."[77] He held to it none the less.

One can never, of course, disprove a dream interpretation, especially three-quarters of a century after the fact. However, I also find that I cannot follow Freud. The main problem lies with the role of the mother in the dream. The key part of the dream is presented as a contradiction. *"Mother wanted to stop and save her jewel-case, but father said: 'I refuse to let myself and my children be burnt for the sake of your jewel-case'."*[78] Freud suggested that in one important sense Frau K is really the mother in the dream, and on one level, the suggestion makes sense. No doubt Ida wished that her father would end his barter with Herr K by saying similar words to Frau K. But the fact that the mother is trying to save her jewel-case in the dream needs further explanation. If we consider this phrase in light of the suggestion that for Käthe Bauer, as for Ida, heterosexuality equalled contamination and destruction, the dream takes on another meaning. The mother's attempt to save her "jewel-case" can have no other meaning – given this shared phantasy – than an attempt to escape heterosexuality and annihilation. Beneath Ida's wish that her father save her jewel-case lies the recognition that he, in fact, demands its destruction, as he demands the destruction of her mother's. The association leading back to Ida's bed-wetting is relevant. It is possible that the memory of Philip Bauer waking Ida to take her to the bathroom may have hidden another memory of her being awakened by her parents' "lovemaking." Freud does argue that this was the trauma that initiated Ida's hysteria. Certainly Ida Bauer understood only too well the meaning such sexual encounters had for Käthe Bauer, and it was a meaning she appropriated as her own. This is underscored by the association to the argument between Käthe and Philip Bauer over his gift of jewelry. In so far as this scene was a metaphor for sex, as Freud argues, the most significant aspect of the scene is Käthe Bauer's rejection of her husband's "gift."

The association leading back to Ida's bedwetting and masturbation is also important because it refers to the last period in which Ida expressed sexuality in an active, conscious way. In the dream, Ida's father is presented as saving her from fire, from sexuality, as he did when he awoke her and her brother as children. But, in fact, her father, in so far as he represented the symbolic Father, forced Ida to relinquish her preoedipal sexuality and to renounce its object. At the deepest level of meaning in the dream, Ida's father is represented as the enforcer of the (hetero)sexual laws and phantasies of Ida Bauer's culture.

A few sessions before Ida terminated the analysis she brought Freud her second dream.[79]

I was walking about in a town which I did not know. I saw streets and squares which were strange to me. Then I came into a house where I lived, went to my room, and found a letter from Mother lying there. She wrote saying that as I had left home without my parents' knowledge she had not wished to write to me to say that Father was ill. "Now he is dead, and if you like? you can come." I then went to the station and asked about a hundred times: "Where is the station?" I always got the answer: "Five minutes." I then saw a thick wood before me which I went into, and there I asked a man whom I met. He said to me: "Two and a half hours more." He offered to accompany me. But I refused and went alone. I saw the station in front of me and could not reach it. At the same time I had the usual feeling of anxiety that one has in dreams when one cannot move forward. Then I was at home. I must have been travelling in the meantime, but I know nothing about that. I walked into the porter's lodge, and inquired for our flat. The maidservant opened the door to me and replied that Mother and the others were already at the cemetery. I saw myself particularly distinctly going up the stairs. After she answered I went to my room, but not the last sadly, and began reading a big book that lay on my writing-table.

Among the most important associations Ida made are these:

1. Wandering in a strange town related to a memory of a brief visit to Dresden. "On that occasion she had been a stranger and had wandered about, not failing, of course, to visit the famous picture gallery. [A] cousin of hers . . . had wanted to act as a guide and take her round the gallery. *But she declined and went alone*, and stopped in front of the pictures that appealed to her. She remained *two hours* in front of the Sistine Madonna, rapt in silent admiration. When I asked her what had pleased her so much about the picture she could find no clear answer to make. At last she said, 'The Madonna.' "[80]

2. The evening before the dream occurred, the Bauers had entertained. Ida's father had asked her to fetch him brandy which he needed to sleep. During the gathering a guest had toasted her father and "had expressed the hope that he might continue to enjoy the best health for many years to come. At this a strange quiver had passed over her father's face, and she had understood what thoughts he was having to keep down. Poor sick man! Who could tell what span of life was still to be his?"[81]

3. The letter in the dream refers both to Ida's own suicide note and to the letter she had received from Frau K inviting her to the resort lake. In that letter Frau K had placed a question mark in the middle of a sentence after the phrase "if you would like to come" just as it appeared in the dream.

4. The thick wood in the dream was like the wood by the shore of the lake where Herr K made his proposal. Ida had also seen the very same wood the day before in a picture at the Secessionist exhibition. In the background of the picture, however, there had been nymphs.

Freud suggested that two phantasies structured the dream. The first was a phantasy of revenge against Ida's father, represented by his death in the dream. Freud argued that the associations relating to the thick wood in the dream suggested a second phantasy of defloration — "the phantasy of a man seeking to force an entrance into the female genitals."[82] In German the same word "nymphae" represents both "nymphs," which were in the background of one of the paintings at the Secessionist exhibition, and "Nymphae," the technical term for the labia minora. Thus at the core of this dream is the "primal scene" — but a particular version appropriate to Ida Bauer's circumstances. Here the scene is a phantasy of defloration.

Freud concluded that Ida could only have gotten the technical term "Nymphae" from reading anatomical textbooks or from an encyclopedia — the big book she goes to her room in order to read in the dream. Freud connected the two phantasies — revenge and defloration — this way:[83]

> Parents are very much in the way while reading of this kind is going on. But this uncomfortable situation had been radically improved, thanks to the dream's power of fulfilling wishes. Dora's father was dead, and the others had already gone to the cemetery. She might calmly read whatever she chose. Did not this mean that one of her motives for revenge was a revolt against her parents' [father's] constraint? If her father was dead she could read or love as she pleased.

Ida did not wish just to read about the "primal scene," however; she also wished to experience it. Freud suggested that an important key to the meaning of the dream is the association to the Sistine Madonna. The Madonna, Freud argued, was obviously Ida herself. The identification revealed Ida's concern with her virginity; it also, however, represented her wish for a child. Ida had won Herr K's affection by the motherliness she had shown toward his children and "she had had a child though she was still a girl."[84] This last reference is to Ida's false appendicitis attack, which occurred shortly after her aunt's death and nine months after the "scene" by the lake, and left Ida with a limp that periodically returned. Freud interpreted the attack as a phantasy of childbirth. Ida, he argued, regretted not having surrendered to Herr K at the lake and in her unconscious phantasy life acted as though she had. The limp symbolized her "false-step." Once again Freud concluded to Ida: "So you see that your love for Herr K did not come to an end with the scene, but that (as I maintained) it has persisted down to the present day — though it is true that you are unconscious of it."[85]

Writing of hysteria thirty years later, Freud made a very different argument.[86]

> . . . it is not hard to show that another regression to an earlier level occurs in hysteria. . . . The sexuality of female children is dominated and directed by a masculine organ (the clitoris) and often behaves like the sexuality of boys. This masculine sexuality has to be got rid of by a last wave of development at puberty, and the vagina . . . has to be raised into the

dominant erotogenic zone. Now it is very common in hysterical neurosis for this repressed masculine sexuality to be reactivated and then for the defensive struggle on the part of the ego-syntonic instincts to be directed against it.

I do not want to discuss Freud's notion that the clitoris is a "masculine" organ, and that the sexuality attached to it is "masculine." Freud was, of course, well aware that we cannot really talk of masculinity and femininity as we know it as adults until after the Oedipus complex. What Freud calls "masculine sexuality" is really preoedipal sexuality in which the "primal scene" and the meaning of the difference between the sexes are not yet fully comprehended, and in which the mother or mother surrogate is the primary object of desire. During the later stages of this period, during the phallic phase, both girls and boys direct a genital sexuality with passive and active aims toward their mother:[87]

> In regard to the passive impulses of the phallic phase, it is noteworthy that girls regularly accuse their mothers of seducing them. This is because they necessarily received their first, or at any rate their strongest, genital sensations when they were being cleaned and having their toilet attended by their mother.

The little girl wants not only to be seduced by the mother, but also to seduce her in turn:[88]

> ... intense *active* wishful impulses directed towards the mother also arise during the phallic phase. The sexual activity of this period culminates in clitoridal masturbation. This is probably accompanied by ideas of the mother, but whether the child attaches a sexual aim to the idea, and what the aim is, I have not been able to discover from my observations. It is only when all her interests have received fresh impetus through the arrival of a baby brother or sister that we can clearly recognize such an aim. The little girl wants to believe that she has given her mother the new baby, just as the boy wants to.

By Freud's own admission, the deepest level of meaning of hysterical symptoms is not a thwarted desire for the father, but a breakthrough of the prohibited desire for the mother. If we consider the dream from this point of view, it is immediately obvious that the dream is a crystallization of Ida Bauer's oedipal struggle. On one level, the dream is a clear symbolization and rejection of the "primal scene" and the feminine position Ida must assume in it. It is clear, however, that she does not assume this position in the dream. As Freud pointed out, "what was most evident was that in the first part of the dream she was identifying herself with a young man. This young man was wandering about in a strange place, he was striving to reach a goal . . . it would have been appropriate for the goal to have been the possession of a woman."[89] Freud argued that in this part of the dream Ida is identifying with a young suitor of hers who had sent her a picture of the town in which he had accepted a job as engineer. The picture forms the imagery of the strange town in which Ida is wandering in the beginning of the dream. In so far as the underlying phantasy is one of defloration, Freud is suggesting that, to the extent that Ida takes a place in the "scene," she takes the place of the man.

The letter from Ida's mother telling her "now he [Ida's father] is dead, and if you like? you can come," was directly associated with Frau K's letter inviting Ida to vacation with her and Herr K in the Alps. Certainly the obvious underlying thought was that if her father disappeared she would have Frau K to herself. In so far as Frau K's betrayal of Ida, which was precipitated by Herr K's proposal, replayed an earlier oedipal scenario, Ida's wish that her father die was not only a phantasy of revenge, as Freud suggested, but also a wish to create another sort of reality. This is one of the meanings of the Sistine Madonna in Ida's dream. For the image of the Madonna and Child is a preoedipal phantasy that suggests oral sexuality. This image, as well as the location of Ida Bauer's hysterical symptoms – chronic cough, gastric paints, mild anorexia – indicate that the conflict, which was framed in terms of genital sexuality, was transposed to and played out on the oral terrain. Ida's phantasy of Frau K and her father's mode of lovemaking, which customarily took the form of fellatio, also suggests this.[90] This transposition was an attempt to deny the phallus and the Father by constructing a mythical world where the mother/child dyad could exist undisturbed by the implications of sexual difference.

The phantasy of the Madonna denies the phallus in another way as well. Freud pointed out that the phantasy is one of a *virgin* mother. We could put the point another way, however, and call it a phantasy of the *immaculate conception*; that is, a conception in which the phallus and the "primal scene" play no role.[91] Is this not the solution to Ida Bauer's dilemma? The Madonna found her way into Ida Bauer's dream precisely because she represented the negation of the "primal scene" – the negation of masculinity and femininity.

Ida's second dream reveals that her attempts to escape the implications of femininity oscillated between attempted retreats to oral sexuality and hysterical identifications with masculinity (identification with her own suitor). Neither provided the possibility of a real resolution, however. These efforts to escape were contrasted with efforts to comply — that is, with hysterical identifications with femininity. These are revealed not only in Ida's identification with her mother, but also in her false appendicitis attack.

The attack occurred shortly after the death of Ida's favorite aunt, and nine months after Herr K's proposal at the lake.[92] Freud interpreted the attack as representing Ida's wish that she had surrendered to Herr K, and that she were having his child. Freud interpreted the limp, which periodically appeared after the attack, as a metaphor for the impropriety of her desire. Her desire to yield to Herr K demanded that she make a "false-step." The fact that Ida's hysterical attack occurred nine months after Herr K's proposal does indeed indicate that one crucial meaning of the attack was a phantasy of childbirth. The question is whether this phantasy necessarily implies that Ida Bauer had in fact regretted her response to Herr K's proposal.

At the beginning of a session that Freud planned to devote to the interpretation of Ida's second dream, she announced that she was terminating the analysis. She had made the decision two weeks earlier, but had said nothing to Freud. Freud suggested that "that sounds just like a maidservant or governess — a fortnight's warning." The suggestion proved illuminating. Ida remembered that during her stay at the lake, a governess in service with the K's gave notice to Herr K. The governess told Ida that Herr K had "made advances to her at a time when his wife was away for several weeks; he had made violent love to her and had implored her to yield to his entreaties, saying that he got nothing from his wife. . . ."[93] Herr K had used the very same words when he propositioned Ida. The governess had had an affair with Herr K who quickly tired of her. She told her parents, who at first demanded that she return home. When she waited a while before giving notice, hoping that Herr K's attitude toward her would change, her parents disowned her.

Freud concluded, correctly I think, that much of Ida's conduct after the "scene" by the lake, and an important element in her phantasies, represented an identification with this particular servant as well as with servant women in general. Ida told her parents about Herr K's proposal just as the servant had written to her parents; and Ida waited two weeks before telling them, just as the governess had waited before giving Herr K notice. In the dream, the letter inviting Ida home was the counterpart to the letter to the governess from her parents forbidding her to come home. Ida's false appendicitis attack nine months after the "scene" by the lake was also an identification with this female servant. The identification suggests that in Ida's unconscious, servitude and femininity formed a symbolic equation.

This symbolism was not idiosyncratic and had a material basis in historical circumstances. Freud recognized in a letter of Wilhelm Fliess in 1897 that his female analysands often identified in this way:[94]

> An immense load of guilt, with self-reproaches (for theft, abortions, etc.) is made possible for the woman by identification with these people of low morals, who are so often remembered by her as worthless women connected sexually with her father or brother. And, as a result of the sublimation of these girls in phantasies, most improbable charges against other people are made in these phantasies. Fear of prostitution (i.e., of becoming a prostitute), (fear of being in the street alone), fear of a man hidden under the bed, etc., also point in the direction of servant-girls. There is a tragic justice in the fact that the action of the head of the family in stooping to a servant girl is atoned for by his daughter's self-abasement.

The passage reveals, as does Ida Bauer's identification, that femininity was linked with service specifically with regard to sexuality. That is, what lies at the heart of these identifications is a particular phantasy of heterosexuality as service due men, and one explicitly based on submission and degradation.

Leonore Davidoff has suggested that the striking tendency in Victorian bourgeois ideology to an exaggerated dual vision of women had a material basis not only in the larger class structure, but also in the division of labor within the Victorian bourgeois family itself. During the latter half of the nineteenth century, domestic service became an almost exclusively female profession. Increasingly, domestic servants, who were predominantly young and unmarried, took over tasks involving manual labor and the routine aspects of childcare from bourgeois wives:[95]

> It was the nurse or maid who fed, nappied, washed, dressed, potted, put to bed, and directly disciplined the infant and small child. Within the nursery domain she had total power over her charges; yet middle-class children learned very quickly that she was their inferior and that they were both . . . subject to higher authority. It was very often these girls and women who first awakened sexual as well as other feelings in the child.

Davidoff is fundamentally concerned with the impact this actual split had on bourgeois male sexuality and psychology. This included not only the tendency to create the polar oppositions of desexualized Madonna and erotic Magdalen, but also to search for a degraded erotic object; that is, phantasy of sexuality as debasement.

If we consider what implications such splitting might have for bourgeois women, we can perceive at once the paradox. Bourgeois women enjoyed the same prerogatives of command and dominance that being members of the ruling class afforded their husbands, fathers, and brothers. They found self-affirmation in the deference showed them by servants who[96]

> stood when spoken to and kept their eyes cast down, they moved out of a room backwards, curtsied to their betters, and were generally expected to efface themselves; doing their work and moving about the house so as not to be visible or audible to their employers. In an extreme case they were made to turn their faces to the wall when the employer passed by.

But gender and class, femininity and service, were at the same time conflated – in so far as the question posed was sexuality. Bourgeois sexual phantasy did not distinguish between classes of women. In this historical circumstance, class and gender intertwined to magnify dramatically the content of the "primal scene."[97]

Freud argued that, in her identification with the K's governess, Ida Bauer revealed her desire to submit to Herr K. Yet the logic of Ida's personal history suggests that Ida's identification stemmed not from desire, but from the unconscious belief that femininity, bondage, and debasement were synonymous. In her hysterical identification with the K's governess, Ida Bauer acted out the drama of femininity. She impersonated the young servant woman whom she imagined had been seduced by her desire for Herr K, and in exchange for satisfaction, had suffered a woman's fate. If her identification symbolized a wish, perhaps she wished she could reconstitute her desire as patriarchy demanded, so that she might reclaim sexuality. But Ida Bauer's frigidity marked the depth of her protest.

In Freud's analysis, the reason for Ida Bauer's protest is repressed. However, in his choice of a pseudonym for Ida Bauer, Freud revealed his own unconscious understanding of one contradiction that aided in the birth of her hysteria. In "The Psychopathology of Everyday Life," Freud disclosed that when he searched for a name for Ida Bauer, "Dora was the only name to occur."[98] Dora was the name of a servant in the Freud family who had been his sister's nursemaid. She had been forced to give up her own name, Rosa, as it was also his sister's name. Through his choice, or lack of choice, Freud revealed his recognition that in his mind, as in Ida Bauer's, servitude was a metaphor for femininity. At the very same moment, however, Freud also confessed his wish that like Rosa, the servant woman who gave up even her name, Ida Bauer make her peace with servitude. To escape a feminine fate is the prerogative of the son, and not the daughter.

FREUD'S DORA

Assessing the reasons for Ida Bauer's abrupt termination of the analysis, Freud concluded: "I did not succeed in mastering the transference in good time."[99] As some reviewers of the case have pointed out, however, Freud's countertransference was the crucial determinant. Writing "Dora" was Freud's defense against facing what was "largely a negative countertransference – an unanalyzed part of himself."[100]

Freud arrived at his hypothesis of Ida's secret erotic love for Herr K very early in the case and, as we have seen, her pursued it with a vengeance. Each of Ida's rejections of this analysis was met by Freud with feigned disregard and even more elaborate displays of his intellectual prowess.

At the beginning of the case, Freud assumed that he was replacing Ida's father in her imagination:[101]

> But when the first dream came, in which she gave herself the warning that she had better leave my treatment just as she had formerly left Herr K's house, I ought to have listened to the warning myself. "Now," I ought to have said to her, "it is from Herr K that you have made a transference onto me. Have you noticed anything that leads you to suspect me of evil intentions similar . . . to Herr K's?"

It would indeed appear that by the time of the first dream Ida was identifying Freud with Herr K. But what is even more evident as the case progresses is that Freud was identifying himself with Herr K as well, and he was doing so with a passion. Although Freud's early high opinion of Ida's father changed considerably as the case unfolded, Herr K was spared all criticism. Freud did not find it unusual that Herr K had, somewhat deviously, set the scene for the seduction of his close friend's fourteen-year-old daughter. He found Ida at fault for not responding. After all, as Freud pointed out, Herr K "was still quite young and of prepossessing appearance."[102] Herr K's total denial of the "scene" by the lake, his speaking of Ida to her father "with disparagement," his "reflection that no girl who read such books and was interested in such things could have title to a man's respect," were not seen by Freud as indications that something was terribly wrong with Herr K. In fact, Freud took Herr K's side and considered Ida maladjusted because she did not keep the whole matter to herself:[103]

> I looked upon her having told her parents of the episode as an action which she had taken when she was already under the influence of a morbid craving for revenge. A normal girl, I am inclined to think, will deal with a situation of this kind by herself.

Freud did not find Herr K's seduction and abandonment of the family governess shortly before he propositioned Ida of any concern. Nor did the fact that Herr K used the very same line on Ida as he had on the governess rouse Freud's suspicions. Freud could not understand Ida's "having been so deeply injured by Herr K's proposal . . . as I was beginning to realize that Herr K himself had not regarded the proposal . . . as a mere frivolous attempt at seduction."[104]

Ida's termination of the analysis was a serious blow to Freud. In the postscript to the case, he reproaches Ida in a tone that reveals his narcissism. "Her breaking off so unexpectedly, just when my hopes of a successful termination of the treatment were at their highest, and her thus bringing my hopes to nothing — this was an unmistakable act of vengeance on her part." Freud then ponders whether "I might perhaps have kept the girl under my treatment if I myself had acted a part, if I had exaggerated the importance of her staying on, and had shown a warm personal interest in her." His identification with Herr K is revealed in his very next thought: "Nor do I know whether Herr K would have done any better if it had been revealed to him that the slap Dora gave him by no means signified a final 'No'."[105]

If this were Freud's story, we would have to go beyond feminist polemics and search for the sources of the negative countertransference — the unanalyzed part of Freud — that brought the analysis to an abrupt end. The search would lead to the conjecture that Freud's identification with Herr K was really only secondary; that it was a defense against a more fundamental identification with Ida Bauer's hysteria. The search would lead to the many relationships with men in which Freud acted out his own passive desires — his femininity: Maynert, Charcot, Breuer, and Wilhelm Fliess. It would lead in short to Freud's hysteria.[106]

But here, we are only concerned with the implications this negative countertransference held for Ida Bauer. When, fifteen months after the termination of the analysis, Ida returned to Freud, "to finish her story and ask for help once more," Freud declined her request. "One glance at her face . . . was enough to tell me that she was not in earnest over her request."[107]

Freud had finished writing "Fragment of an Analysis" over a year before Ida Bauer's return.

Each time I reread Freud's study, I am struck, as others have been, by one statement Freud makes in the postscript. After tying up every loose end in the analysis, after skillfully introjecting the same meaning into Ida Bauer's every symptom, every action, every unconscious and conscious thought, Freud acknowledges, "I do not know what kind of help she wanted from me. . . ."[108] Because of the meaning Freud gave to Ida Bauer's desire, she remained a mystery to him.

Writing of hysteria in our own time, a disciple of Freud's voices a similar sentiment. "Hysteria," he writes, "still poses similar difficulties to those of the past, though they are perhaps more sophisticated."[109]

> Hysteria still provides the analyst with the illusion of power which the patient takes away after having tempted him to believe he possessed it. Hysteria's subtle intrigue obliges one to overcome a prejudice, to solve a mystery, but, in the end, this is perhaps the mystery of femininity.

But is the mystery really so insoluble, or is it perhaps that its solution would demand the shattering of a precious phantasy?

Precious to some, painful to others.

NOTES

I would like to thank Robert Brenner, Shirl Buss, Lynn Fonfa, Stella Menatos, and Victor Wolfenstein for their critical comments on earlier versions of this essay. In particular, I am indebted to Dawn Baker and Temma Kaplan for countless fascinating and fruitful discussions about "Dora" and about psychoanalysis in general. Of course, the errors are mine alone.

[1] Adrienne Rich, "Sibling Mysteries," *Chrysalis* 1 (1977): 117-18.

[2] The phantasy that determined Freud's choice of the name, Dora, is explained below.

[3] Sigmund Freud, "Fragment of an Analysis of a Case of Hysteria," in *The Standard Edition of the Complete Psychological Works of Sigmund Freud*, ed. James Strachey, 24 vols. (London: Hogarth Press and the Institute of Psycho-Analysis, 1973), 7: 3-112.

[4] Sigmund Freud, *Dora: An Analysis of a Case of Hysteria*, ed. Philip Rieff (New York: Collier Books, 1971).

[5] See, for example: E.H. Erikson, "Reality and Actuality," *Journal of the American Psychoanalytic Association* 10 (1962): 451-74; M.M. Gill and H.L. Muslin,

"Transference in the Dora Case," *Journal of the American Psychoanalytic Association* 26 (1978): 311-32; Robert Langs, "The Misalliance Dimension in Freud's Case Histories: I. The Case of Dora," *International Journal of Psychoanalytic Psychotherapy*, 5 (1976): 301-17; Karl Lewin, "Dora Revisited," *Psychoanalytic Review* 60 (Winter 1973-74): 519-32. Samuel Slipp, "Interpersonal Factors in Hysteria: Freud's Seduction Theory and the Case of Dora," *Journal of the American Academy of Psychoanalysis* 5 (1977): 359-76, offers a stimulating interpretation of the case based on a modified version of Freud's seduction theory. An interesting summary of contemporary Psychoanalytic views on hysteria is reported by J. Laplanche, "Panel on 'Hysteria Today,' " *International Journal of Psycho-Analysis* 55 (1974): 459-69.

[6] Steven Marcus began the feminist critique of this case history with his perceptive article, "Freud and Dora: Story, History, Case History," in *Representations* (New York: Random House, 1976). This essay has influenced my reading of the case considerably. Recent feminist rereadings of the case include Hélène Cixous, *Portrait de Dora* (Paris: Editions des Femmes, 1976); Hannah S. Decker, "Freud and Dora: Constraints on Medical Progress," *Journal of Social History* 4 (Spring 1981); 445-64; Temma Kaplan, "Female Nature and Nurturance: Freud and the Dora Case," (unpublished ms, 1979); and Jacqueline Rose, " 'Dora' − Fragment of an Analysis," *m/f* 2 (1978): 5-21.

[7] Juliet Mitchell, *Psychoanalysis and Feminism* (New York: Pantheon, 1974). Mitchell's important contribution to feminist theory was her insight that classical psychoanalysis, which has as one object of study the formation of gender identity and sexuality in patriarchal culture, is a useful tool for feminism. The critical task is to separate those aspects of the theory that are ideological from those that are insightful and useful − if incomplete.

[8] Arnold A. Rogow, "A Further Footnote to Freud's "Fragment of an Analysis of a Case of Hysteria,' " *Journal of the American Psychoanalytic Association* 26 (1978): 342.

[9] Freud, "Fragment of an Analysis," p. 20.

[10] These symptoms are associated with advanced stages of untreated gonorrhea in women. Most likely, Philip Bauer had contracted gonorrhea, as well as syphilis.

[11] Freud, "Fragment of an Analysis," p. 19.

[12] Rogow, "A Further Footnote."

[13] Henri F. Ellenberger, *The Discovery of the Unconscious* (New York: Basic Books, 1970) and Ilza Veith, *Hysteria: The History of a Disease* (Chicago: University of Chicago Press, 1965) both argue that hysteria increased significantly in the mid- to late nineteenth century and afflicted predominantly upper-class women. It is not clear at present to what extent working-class women suffered from hysteria during this period. They were not, however, immune. The Salpêtrière, where Charcot and Janet studied hysteria, was a mental hospital for the poor. Carroll Smith-Rosenberg notes that in the United States in the late nineteenth century, physicians connected with almshouses and urban hospitals reported hysteria to be common among immigrant and tenement-house women. Carroll Smith-Rosenberg, "The Hysterical Woman: Sex and Role Conflict in 19th Century America," *Social Research* 39 (Winter 1972): 659.

[14] Freud, "Fragment of an Analysis," p. 29.

[15] Ibid., p. 28.

[16] Ibid., p. 34.

[17] Ibid.

[18] Marcus, "Freud and Dora," p. 256.

[19] Gill and Muslin, "Transference in the Dora Case." The authors present an interesting discussion of the transference/countertransference relationship. Following Freud, they argue that Ida Bauer's abrupt termination of the treatment signaled her total identification of Freud with Herr K and her fear of surrendering to the temptation to give in to Freud sexually. They further argue that Freud's countertransference was

highly eroticized as well.

[20] Ida Bauer remained a chronic hysteric. For a discussion of her life after leaving the analysis, see Felix Deutsch, "A Footnote to Freud's Fragment of an Analysis of a Case of Hysteria," *Psychoanalytic Quarterly* 26 (1957): 159-67.

[21] Marcus, "Freud and Dora," p. 309.

[22] Freud, "Fragment of an Analysis," p. 88.

[23] Freud, Letter to Wilhelm Fliess, *Complete Psychological Works*, no. 71, I: 265.

[24] Freud's main essays on female sexuality and femininity are: "Some Psychical Consequences of the Anatomical Distinction Between the Sexes," "Female Sexuality," and "Femininity," all in *Complete Psychological Works*, vols. 19 and 21.

[25] Juliet Mitchell, "On Freud and the Distinction Between the Sexes," in *Women and Analysis*, ed. Jean Strouse (New York: Dell Publishing Co., 1974), p. 46.

[26] See Jean Laplanche's masterful work, *Life and Death in Psychoanalysis*, trans. Jeffrey Mehlman (Baltimore: Johns Hopkins University Press, 1976).

[27] See, for example, Karen Horney, *Feminine Psychology*, edited with Introduction by Harold Kelman (New York: W.W. Norton, 1967); and Ernest Jones, *Papers on Psychoanalysis* (Baltimore: Williams and Wilkins Co., 1950).

[28] This line of argument is presented by Mitchell, *Psychoanalysis and Feminism*, and by Gayle Rubin, "The Traffic in Women: Notes on the 'Political Economy' of Sex," in *Toward an Anthropology of Women*, ed. Rayna R. Reiter (New York: Monthly Review Press, 1975).

[29] Freud, "Anatomical Distinction Between the Sexes," *Complete Psychological Works*, 19: 256.

[30] Freud, "Analysis Terminable and Interminable," *Complete Psychological Works*, 23: 250-1.

[31] This line of argument has found favor with North American psychoanalytically oriented feminist theorists. It is cogently presented by Nancy Chodorow, *The Reproduction of Mothering: Psychoanalysis and the Sociology of Gender* (Berkeley: University of California Press, 1978), and by Dorothy Dinnerstein, *The Mermaid and the Minotaur: Sexual Arrangements and Human Malaise* (New York: Harper Colophon Books, 1977). Also, Jane Flax, "The Conflict Between Nurturance and Autonomy in Mother-Daughter Relationships and Within Feminism," *Feminist Studies* 4, no. 2 (June 1978): 171-89. The argument is made in popular form by Nancy Friday, *My Mother/ My Self* (New York: Delacorte Press, 1977).

For prominent examples of object relations theory, see Melanie Klein, *Contributions to Psycho-Analysis, 1921-1945* (London: Hogarth Press, 1948); W.R.D. Fairbairn, *An Object-Relations Theory of the Personality* (New York: Basic Books, 1952); Margaret Mahler, *On Human Symbiosis and the Vicissitudes of Individuation, vol. 1: Infantile Psychosis* (New York: International Universities Press, 1968); D.W. Winnicott, *Playing and Reality* (New York: Basic Books, 1971); and Michael Balint, ed., *Primary Love and Psycho-Analytic Technique* (New York: Liveright Publishing, 1965).

[32] Chodorow, *Mothering*, p. 123. Chodorow is citing Janine Chasseguet-Smirgel, "Feminine Guilt and the Oedipus Complex," 1964, in *Female Sexuality*, ed. J. Chasseguet-Smirgel (Ann Arbor: University of Michigan Press, 1970), p. 118.

[33] This "slippage" leads these theories, and the feminists who use them, to focus primarily on mother-daughter and mother-son ambivalence. At the same time, this focus results in a tendency to explain crucial aspects of the social whole as being fundamentally determined by the dynamics of this *single* relationship. Thus Chodorow and Dinnerstein locate the origins and reproduction of misogyny in the mother-child relationship.

[34] J. Laplanche and J.B. Pontalis, *The Language of Psychoanalysis*, trans. Donald Nicholson-Smith (New York: W.W. Norton and Co., 1973), p. 335.

[35] Ibid. See Freud, "History of an Infantile Neurosis," *Complete Psychological Works*, 17: 3-123.

[36] Laplanche and Pontalis, *Language of Psychoanalysis*, p. 335.

[37] Steven Marcus, *The Other Victorians* (New York: Basic Books Inc., 1964).

[38] Ibid., pp. 211-12.

[39] Ibid., p. 198.

[40] Ibid., p. 206.

[41] Ibid., p. 199.

[42] Laplanche and Pontalis, *Language of Psychoanalysis*, p. 421.

[43] Freud, "Fragment of an Analysis," p. 79.

[44] Ibid., p. 80.

[45] Muriel Gardiner, ed., *The Wolf Man* (New York: Basic Books, 1971).

[46] Ibid., p. 24.

[47] Freud, "Infantile Neurosis," 17: 21.

[48] Gardiner, ed., *Wolf Man*, p. 24.

[49] Ibid., p. 23.

[50] Freud, "Fragment of an Analysis," p. 25.

[51] Ibid.

[52] Rogow, "A Further Footnote," p. 343.

[53] Käthe Bauer's phantasy also affected Otto Bauer's sexuality. His low libidinal drives would seem to have been, in part, a response to his mother's abhorrence of sex (see Rogow, "A Further Footnote").

[54] Freud was not content to leave it at that, however, and went on to argue that ultimately Ida's disgust was related to her own leukorrhea which he linked to her childhood masturbation (Freud, "Fragment of an Analysis," p. 84).

[55] J.A. Banks and Olive Banks, *Feminism and Family Planning in Victorian England* (Liverpool: Liverpool University Press, 1964), p. 112.

[56] Abraham Flexner, *Prostitution in Europe* (New York: The Century Co., 1914), p. 367.

[57] Freud, "Fragment of an Analysis," p. 28.

[58] Ibid.

[59] Ibid., p. 29.

[60] Ibid., p. 30.

[61] Many analysts who have commented on this part of Freud's analysis have argued that Freud's main deficiency was his inability to place Ida Bauer developmentally. Marcus notes that "at one moment in the passage [Freud] calls her a 'girl,' at another a 'child' – but in point of fact he treats her throughout as if this fourteen-, sixteen-, and eighteen-year-old adolescent had the capacities for sexual response of a grown woman." (Marcus, "Freud and Dora," p. 286). Another reviewer has suggested that Freud's libidinous countertransference prevented him from recognizing the absurdity of his expectations that Ida, at fourteen, respond sexually to Herr K as would a "mature woman" (Gill and Muslin, "Transference in the Dora Case," p. 324).

Although objections along this line have validity, particularly with regard to this scene, they prove problematic in light of Ida Bauer's prior and subsequent development. At what age, we may ask, should Ida the "girl" have become Ida the "mature woman," sexually speaking? If Ida Bauer had been repulsed at Herr K's embrace when twenty-one, would she then, by this theory have been hysterical? If Ida's symptoms were the result of her inability to deal with the unspoken pressure that her father exerted to make her submit to Herr K, her hysteria might have begun when she first understood the nature of the barter. It would have abated once she had asserted her will in the matter. But, in fact, Ida's symptoms began when she was eight and continued to plague her throughout her life. The point is that we must interpret the meaning of Ida

Bauer's response to this particular scene within the context of her entire history of hysteria.

[62] Freud, "Fragment of an Analysis," p. 39.

[63] Ibid., p. 37.

[64] Ibid.

[65] Ibid., p. 35.

[66] Recent feminist discussions of hysteria stress its element of compliance. See, for example, Hannah S. Decker, "Freud and Dora," pp. 453-54. Hysteria as simply compliance is argued by Luce Irigaray, *Speculum. De l'autre femme* (Paris: Editions de Minuit, Collection Critique, 1974). For an excellent critique of Irigaray's position, see Monique Plaza, " 'Phallomorphic' Power and the Psychology of 'Woman,' " *Feminist Issues* 1 (Summer 1980).

[67] See Marcus, "Freud and Dora," pp. 305-7.

[68] Jacqueline Rose points out that "in his analysis of the hysterical symptom-aphonia or loss of voice, Freud is forced towards the beginnings of a concept of component sexuality (a sexuality multiple and fragmented and not bound to the genital function), since the symptom is clearly not only a response to the absence of Herr K (impossibility of communication desired), but also a *fantasied identification with a scene of imagined sexual satisfaction between Dora's father and Frau K*" (my italics). Rose, "Dora," p. 11.

[69] Ibid., footnote, p. 105. On page 120, in a final footnote to the case, Freud writes: "The longer the interval of time that separates me from the end of the analysis, the more probable it seems to me that the fault in my technique lay in this omission: I failed to discover in time and to inform the patient that her homosexual . . . love for Frau K was the strongest unconscious current in her mental life. . . ."

[70] Ibid., p. 61.

[71] Ibid., p. 62. This betrayal by Frau K duplicated at least one prior betrayal by a woman. Ida had been on intimate terms with her governess who "used to read every book on sexual life and similar subjects, and talked to the girl about them," while demanding secrecy from Ida about these goings-on. When Ida discovered that the governess was secretly in love with her father and, she supposed, indifferent to her, Ida had her fired. Freud noted that Ida's own behavior toward Frau and Herr K's two children owed something to an identification with this governess. She was the first of two servant women with whom Ida would make such an identification (Freud, "Fragment of an Analysis," pp. 36, 60).

[72] Ibid., p. 64.

[73] Freud, "Fragment of an Analysis," p. 66.

[74] Ibid., p. 67.

[75] Ibid., pp. 69-70.

[76] Ibid.

[77] Ibid.

[78] Ibid., p. 64.

[79] Ibid., p. 94.

[80] Ibid., p. 96.

[81] Ibid., p. 97.

[82] Ibid., p. 100.

[83] Ibid.

[84] Ibid., p. 104.

[85] Ibid.

[86] Freud, "The Disposition to Obsessional Neurosis," *Complete Psychological Works*, 12: 325-26.

[87] Freud, "Female Sexuality," 21: 238.

[88] Ibid., p. 239.

[89] Freud, "Fragment of an Analysis," p. 96.

[90] Freud noted that Philip Bauer was impotent and that fellatio was the primary form their lovemaking took (Freud, "Fragment of an Analysis," p. 47).

[91] Juliet Mitchell, reviewing Karl Abraham's work on femininity, makes a passing reference to phantasies of immaculate conception as representing an unconscious attempt to deny the importance of the phallus. Such disavowal reveals, of course, a protest against the social meaning of sexual difference (Mitchell, *Psychoanalysis and Feminism*, p. 124).

[92] Unfortunately, our ability to interpret the attack at all its levels of meaning is hindered by the fact that Freud was unable to unearth the line of association that must have existed linking Ida's attack and her aunt's death. This aunt, who Freud informs us in the beginning of the case had been the model upon which Ida patterned her hysteria, is conspicuous by her absence in Ida's unconscious. Yet, she must have had important meaning to Ida if Ida copied her unconscious metaphors so closely. Freud noted that part of the material for Ida's second dream was derived directly from Ida's memory of her aunt's death; yet, the meaning of this memory is not evident (Freud, "Fragment of an Analysis," p. 126).

[93] Ibid., p. 105.

[94] Sigmund Freud, Letter to Wilhelm Fliess, 1897, no. 61, *Complete Psychological Works*, 1: 248.

[95] Leonore Davidoff, "Class and Gender in Victorian England: The Diaries of Arthur J. Munby and Hannah Cullwick," this volume.

[96] Ibid., p. 97.

[97] Recently, the stereotype of the sexually frigid bourgeois woman has been challenged by F. Barry Smith, "Sexuality in Britain, 1880-1900: Some Suggested Revisions," in *The Widening Sphere: Changing Roles of Victorian Women*, ed. Martha Vicinus (Bloomington, Indiana: University of Indiana Press, 1977); and Carl Degler, "What Ought to Be and What Was: Women's Sexuality in the Nineteenth Century," *American Historical Review* 79 (December 1974): 1469-90. Such critical questionings of traditional stereotypes are crucial. However, it will be essential, I think, to bring to the historical evidence some theory of the genesis and nature of human sexuality in general, and of female sexuality in particular. If we discover that hysteria did indeed occur among this class of women often enough to warrant considering it a historically significant phenomenon, then, we will have to explore the conjecture that the historical circumstances in which Victorian bourgeois women found themselves tended to exacerbate problems inherent in the development of female sexuality. Hysteria would represent an extreme response.

[98] Freud, "The Psychopathology of Everyday Life," *Complete Psychological Works*, 6: 241.

[99] Freud, "Fragment of an Analysis," p. 118. See, for example, Gill and Muslin, "Transference in the Dora Case"; and Marcus, "Freud and Dora."

[100] Marcus, "Freud and Dora," p. 309.

[101] Freud, Fragment of an Analysis," p. 118.

[102] Ibid., footnote, p. 29.

[103] Ibid., p. 95.

[104] Ibid., p. 115.

[105] Ibid., p. 109.

[106] See Rene Major, "Revolution of Hysteria," *International Journal of Psycho-Analysis* 55 (1974). Also, Henry Ellenberger, *The Discovery of the Unconscious* (New York: Basic Books, 1970).

[107] Freud, "Fragment of an Analysis," p. 120.

[108] Ibid., p. 122.
[109] Major, "Revolution of Hysteria," p. 391.

3 Servants, Sexual Relations and the Risks of Illegitimacy in London, 1801-1900

JOHN R. GILLIS

For Victorians, illegitimacy was a moral litmus test. Although less obviously censorious, historians have used the incidence of bastardy in a similar manner, as one of the few available means for exploring the otherwise obscure relationship between the sexes in past generations. Illegitimacy statistics provide the principal evidence for Edward Shorter's well-known thesis concerning female emancipation in the nineteenth century. His critics, including Joan Scott and Louise Tilly, use virtually the same evidence to come to the opposite conclusion that women, while acting in new ways dictated by their new industrial and urban circumstances, continued to be motivated by traditional values.[1]

What follows will not settle this dispute. On the contrary, the evidence presented here suggests that the above participants are wrong in assuming that there is a single general cause of illegitimacy. Concepts of "modernization," "urbanization," and "industrialization" will scarcely suffice as explanations for a phenomenon which has always been, and remains, immensely complex and diverse. In nineteenth-century Britain, bastardy varied enormously by region, culture, and by class; its character and implications differed according to the specific circumstances and values of the women and men involved. The experience of the pregnant Banffshire dairy maid differed strikingly from that of the unwed mother in a Lancashire cotton town. The events which added a London servant's child to the Registrar General's annual bastardy count had yet another configuration.[2] In each case factors peculiar to the backgrounds, work, and class positions of the women and men shaped the outcome of sexual relations. The study of London servants suggests the limits of generalization. But at the same time, it provides a mode of analysis that, when applied to other groups of women, could ultimately provide a fuller understanding not only of the causes of historical illegitimacy but also of relations between the sexes, as these have been transformed in capitalist industrial societies.

Understanding illegitimacy among servants requires careful attention to their work, leisure, income, and especially their social relations with their employers. Service differed from other female employments not only because of its live-in character, but also because the servant was involved in the elaboration of the employer's life-style—a role that required not only discipline and specific skills but also unique character traits and demeanor. Among higher servants in particular, the work demanded a conformity to upper-class standards of respectability, rules of behavior which, even when not wholly internalized, had important effects on servants' social relations in and outside the household. Examination of these factors, together with the unique conditions of London life, casts new light on servants' sexual relations and their peculiar vulnerability to illegitimacy.

Country girls, humble in station, innocent in the ways of the world and seduced by predatory city men, socially their superior— these are the images of fallen servants that embellished charity appeals and provided material for didactic novels throughout the nineteenth century. The plot is familiar enough, owing much to the eighteenth-century literary theme of seduction and betrayal and to the realities of master-servant relations of earlier periods.[3] By the nineteenth century, however, literary convention no longer comprehends the full reality of unwed motherhood, which by then included many mature women in respectable domestic employment; women experienced in the ways of the city, conscious of its risks as well as its opportunities. Equally, the description of the seducer must be revised in light of the fact that sexual relations leading to illegitimacy were now rarely between servant and master but between persons similar in background and social standing.

Victorians found it difficult to understand how respectable servants could find themselves in such a predicament. Dinah Mulock Craik was puzzled by what she and her friends observed:

Another factor, stranger still to account for is, that women who thus fall are by no means the worst of their station. I have heard it affirmed by more than one lady, and by one in particular whose experience is as large as her benevolence, that many of them are the very best—refined, intelligent, truthful, and affectionate. . . . Some of my most promising village girls have been the first to come to harm; and some of the best and most faithful servants I have ever had have been girls who have fallen into shame, and who, had I not gone to

the rescue, and put them on the way to do well, would invariably have become lost women.[4]

The first systematic study of illegitimacy in Britain, published
by Dr. William Acton in 1857, confirmed the worst fears of Victorians. Utilizing records of births in the workhouses of London's
St. Marylebone, St. Pancras, and St. George's (Southwark) parishes,
Acton found domestic servants constituted the majority of unwed
mothers in all three, despite significant differences in the social and
employment structures of their respective locations. Servants averaged 57.2 percent of all the single women confined there, a proportion considerably higher than that of servants in the parishes' population of unwed, fertile women.[5] An 1883 survey of ten thousand
unwed mothers in Scotland found forty-seven percent to be servants. High percentages of servants were most common in commercial, residential cities such as London, where Queen Charlotte's
Hospital, one of the major maternity charities, reported that 71.3
percent of the single women in its wards were servants. When
another general survey was made in 1911, it was found that 46
percent of the illegitimate children in Britain were born to women
who had been in service.[6]

Unlike France, where registration of bastards was required, the
legal record is of only minimal assistance in providing a more precise profile of servants' backgrounds and ranks. Bastardy orders,
workhouse records, and settlement examinations tell us more about
the males than the females, but not enough about either to provide
a really satisfactory account of urban illegitimacy.[7] The problem
in part is one of faulty registration of births, in error as much as
30 percent in London before 1874. But even if the past were
accessible to direct sociological investigation, reconstruction of
maternities legally defined as illegitimate, especially those involving
married women, would be a formidable, if not impossible, task.[8]

Fortunately, the newly opened records of the London Foundling
Hospital provide a remarkably abundant source for the study of
urban illegitimacy during the nineteenth century. The information
contained in approximately five thousand successful petitions for
admission of infants corroborates the findings of Acton and others
that London illegitimacy was primarily, if not exclusively, a problem involving domestic servants. In the twelve hundred cases on
which this study is based, servants of all types accounted for 65.6
percent of the women successfully applying to the Foundling Hospital. The servants' proportion varied somewhat over time, but
never did the next largest category of women—those employed
in the clothing trades—ever come close to their percentage. The

admission requirements of the Hospital, limiting applicants to single women and emphasizing demonstrated need and good character, undoubtedly inflated the servants' proportion to some extent.[9]

Table 1   Occupations of Unwed Mothers Whose Children Were Admitted to the London Foundling Hospital, 1801-1900

		Professions and Teaching	Retail and Distribution	Personal Service	Clothing Trades	Other Manufactures	Listed as Helping at Home	Not Employed or Unemployed	Not Stated
1801-1810	n=119	0	0	69.2	10.0	4.2	3.3	10.8	2.5
1811-1820	n=118	1.7	0.8	64.7	7.6	5.0	3.4	16.0	0.8
1821-1830	n=124	2.5	1.7	68.3	10.8	0.8	4.2	10.8	0.8
1831-1840	n=117	0	0.8	59.2	20.0	1.7	2.5	15.0	0.8
1841-1850	n=115	0.8	0.8	65.0	13.3	1.7	5.0	13.3	0
1851-1860	n=120	0.8	0.8	65.0	7.5	1.7	11.7	12.5	0
1861-1870	n=117	1.7	2.5	64.5	10.7	3.3	5.8	11.6	0
1871-1880	n=119	1.7	1.7	69.7	6.7	4.2	3.4	12.6	0
1881-1890	n=120		4.2	70.0	10.0	1.7	5.0	9.2	0
1891-1900	n=120	0.8	5.0	60.5	7.6	5.0	6.7	12.6	1.7
Average for Century	n=1189	1.0	1.8	65.6	10.4	2.9	5.1	12.5	0.7

As an occupational title, domestic service can obscure almost as much as it reveals. The lowly kitchen "skivvy" had scarcely anything in common with the dignified lady's maid, except perhaps a common mistress or master. The higher ranks of female servants (cooks, housekeepers, nurses, lady's maids, and governesses) were considered, and considered themselves, to be significantly superior both socially and culturally to the lower ranks of general servants: kitchen- and housemaids, parlor-, laundry-, and scullery- maids. It comes as something of a surprise, therefore, that the petitioners to the Foundling Hospital should have included so many of the better type of London servant, as measured not only by rank, but also by age, social background, and literacy level. Table 2 shows that higher servants, including cooks, lady's maids, governesses, and others who served in capacities "above stairs" tended to be proportionally more numerous among the Foundling Hospital applicants than among the London servant population at large. The ages of the applicants also indicates that servant petitioners were an exceptionally experienced group. The group's superior literacy is another indication that a surprisingly large number were a cut above the ordinary working woman.[10]

Table 2   Social Characteristics of Domestic Servants Whose Children Were Admitted To the London Foundling Hospital, 1801-1900

	In Higher Ranks of Service	Literate	Average Age	London Origins	Social Class by Father's Occupation*				
					I	II	III	IV	V
1801-1810	13.3	84.0	insufficient information			15	31	31	23
1811-1820	20.0	79.3	23.61	"	7	7	46	13	27
1821-1830	37.0	78.5	23.83	"		17	42	33	8
1831-1840	42.0	92.1	24.39	"		11	45	44	
1841-1850	30.3	87.7	22.79	"		16	36	37	11
1851-1860	53.8	89.2	22.66	41.9		9	43	43	5
1861-1870	44.2	94.8	22.86	39.1		16	32	32	20
1871-1880	49.4	92.9	21.63	44.4		15	38	38	9
1881-1890	31.3	93.4	21.59	44.3		6	63	24	7
1891-1900	35.3	100.0	21.67	40.4		9	30	43	18
Average for Century	35.7	89.19	22.78	42.01	0.7	12.1	40.6	33.8	12.3

*See Appendix A for classification categories used here and Table 4.

The social background of these women corresponds to what one would expect of a group containing so many ranking domestic servants. Overwhelmingly, they were from either the ranks of the lower-middle class or the upper levels of the working classes. The single largest group were daughters of artisans and other skilled laborers; shopkeepers, small farmers, and similar small property owners also saw their daughters enter service. We cannot determine geographical origins before 1850, but it is likely that rural women were even more predominant then than they were after mid-century. However, whether rural or urban in origin, these women remained consistently superior in status and training to servants as a group and the London female population at large. It is reasonable to assume that the Foundling Hospital rules of admission favored higher servants over lower servants to some extent. Nevertheless, it is clear that illegitimacy among ranking servants was by no means exceptional; and it provides an opportunity to inves-

tigate how domestic service, together with the economic and social
system of which it was a part, affected sexual relations.

Domestic service was by far the largest employer of women in the
metropolis. Unlike England's northern industrial centers, factory
work was exceptional. Young women bent on London employment
had really only one major alternative to service; namely, the highly
unstable, casualized occupation of the numerous clothing trades.
Abundant opportunities as shop assistants, secretaries, or minor
clerks did not open up until the very end of the century and traditional types of nonmanual work, mainly teaching, accounted for
only about 5 percent of the total volume of London employment
for women. With few exceptions, women's work beyond service
was poorly paid, subject to seasonal unemployment and, in the
absence of trade union organization, vulnerable to the worst type
of exploitative practices. Access to the clothing trades was highly
dependent on personal contacts within intricate channels of sub-
contracting that constituted its basic structure.[11] To many women,
particularly those from outside the metropolis, domestic service
was not only more accessible, but considerably more attractive.
There was no worry about finding a place to live or eat; the wages
of service kept pace with the rise in the cost of living; and there
was, of course, the promise of greater job security for those willing
to put up with the loss of freedoms service inevitably involved.[12]
Service in nineteenth-century London incorporated an immense
variety of situations and conditions, bisected by a reasonably clear
division between the higher and lower ranks of the occupation.
Housekeepers, cooks, nurses, lady's maids, and (depending on the
household) governesses, were separated from general servants, kitchen maids, housemaids, parlormaids, and maids of the scullery
and laundry by certain clearly defined social boundaries, derived
in part form the differences in function but also from the higher
social origins and pretensions of the women occupying the higher
ranks. The position of governess required a certain level of education and social respectability, however much this might clash with
the essential servility of the position.[13] Women recruited as cooks
or lady's maids were less likely to feel the ambiguity of their situation; but they too were recruited in part for the graces and steady
habits that employers could expect to find in girls from the lower-
middle or upper-working classes. They might start with the less
promising girls at the level of house- or kitchenmaids, but by their
twenties they were likely to be promoted. In London this subtle
distinction was paralleled to a large degree by the division between
the rural-born and native-born. The higher ranks were more likely

to be of rural origin, not only because gentry households brought their help with them from the country, but also because the resident middle-classes preferred well-bred country girls for their reputation for reliability.[14]

The lower ranks were more likely to be born in London. Daughters of working-class families, they might start in the kitchen or laundries of the wealthy West End, but rarely stayed very long. They were found in great numbers in the working-class districts of the East End or, after 1860, in the expanding suburbs north and south of the Thames, to which the lower-middle class and better off laboring men were migrating. These were primarily single-servant households, the lowest paid and probably hardest worked situations in London. Yet the young London girls who occupied these places did not usually intend to make a career of service. Most left it when in their late teens or early twenties, either to seek other employment or to marry.[15]

There were women, London-born and of working-class backgrounds, who moved up the ranks, becoming nurses or cooks in the West End households where such employment was most available, but they were probably the exception. In any case, advancement in wage and rank usually involved change of place, even location. Promotion within a household was rare and when women advanced to higher ranks, usually in their early twenties, they often went from a small household, employing one or perhaps two girls, to one of the larger establishments with its full complement of male as well as female staff, including butler, footman, cook, parlormaid, and housemaid. In London, these larger establishments, which in 1891 employed almost 30 percent of the city's female domestics, were located primarily in the West End. It was there that women bent on making a "career" of service were most heavily concentrated.

Table 3 Ages, and Remuneration of Female Indoor Servants in 1891[16]

Age	London		England and Wales excluding London	
	% of Servants	Average Wage	% of Servants	Average Wage
		£/s		£/s
under 15	4.1	£ 7 2s	8.4	£ 6 7s
15-20	27.9	£11 9s	33.4	£11 2s
20-25	26.5	£17 –	24.3	£16 1s
25-35	23.3	£21 6s	17.8	£20 2s
35-45	9.1	£27 6s	7.0	£23 5s
45+	9.1	£26 8s	9.1	£25 1s

The structure of domestic service in the metropolis was different from that of England and Wales as a whole. London servants were not only older, but higher ranking. While the city had only a slightly higher proportion of servants over thirty-five years of age and noticeably fewer in the ranks under age twenty, its peculiarity lay in the disproportionate number of cooks, nurses, lady's maids and others in their early twenties to early thirties, women at the peak of the wage and position scale. After age thirty-five, a woman's wages did not increase with her experience; and the position of "old maids," in the double sense of that term, was an unenviable one. If the proportion of older women among the London servant population is any indication, however, it would appear that most managed to escape this fate. They may have married somewhat later than the London population at large, but most had departed service by their early thirties.

In this almost exclusively celibate occupation, marriage marked a definitive end to a female servant's career. Occasionally a woman would return to service upon the death of a husband; but for the most part it was premarital employment, an opportunity to accumulate savings and domestic skills, though among servants in general, and the higher ranks especially, there was precious little else that was directly transferable as earning power or seniority in any other respectable trade. Particularly among the higher levels, the woman who entered service did so with the ultimate objective of marriage clearly in mind. Wages of London's higher servants were sufficient so that, with equal portions of luck and thrift, modest amounts could be accumulated. In the later nineteenth century, a woman beginning at age fifteen, with seven pounds, two shillings per annum could expect to be earning at least nineteen pounds, eighteen shillings by her mid-twenties, assuming she proved capable, acquired the necessary character references, and moved up through the ranks with sufficient alacrity.[17] To wages must be added free room and board, gifts from employers and trades people, and the considerable value of "perks," leftovers and castoffs, to which the higher servants normally had claim. According to contemporary estimates, the total value made service the best paid of all women's employment during the nineteenth century and explains why this occupation, despite its obvious drawbacks, remained popular almost to 1900.[18]

Living in the place of employment, wearing uniform dress, hair plainly cut and forbidden cosmetics or jewelry, servants were the least subject to the temptations of consumption. Therefore savings in the range of five to twenty pounds were not uncommon. One Foundling Hospital applicant had even managed to accumulate almost fifty pounds in gifts and wages, an amount equal at the time to more than a year's income of a skilled worker.[19] "There can be little doubt that from a monetary point of view the advantages of a servant's life are great," wrote an observer, "and it is not uncommon to find girls who dislike its restraints and suffer much from homesickness, willing to endure it for a long time in order to be able to send home the help which its remuneration enables them to spare."[20]

A servant's hours were not necessarily longer than those of women otherwise employed, but her time was rarely her own, always at the command of the mistress or, as in large establishments, the authority of ranking servants. Higher servants might enjoy somewhat more leisure, but this too was hedged by many limitations. Part of Sunday was usually free, and there might be another half day during the week; but it was not until the very end of the century that longer holidays were usual. Then, too, the servant was subject to a great deal of involuntary mobility. The wealthy household would be in London for "The Season" from February through August, then back to the country or off to the Continent for the rest of the year. Acquaintances outside a large household were difficult to make and even harder to maintain.

In lesser places there was less traveling and, as a consequence, stronger bonds with the neighborhood. Almost certainly the lower servant had greater contact with people outside the household. Elizabeth Thomas, a maid-of-all-work to an Upper Thames Street timber merchant, met Thomas Pullen, a weekly jobbing carpenter, because, as her employer testified, "they necessarily mixed their employment." Mary George, servant to a Lambeth baker, was much in the company of Horace Coville, his journeyman, before Coville made love to her.[21]

By contrast, the larger places tended to restrict a woman's acquaintances to male servants, members and guests of the master's family, and those tradesmen who were permitted to call at the house for business reasons. Life in London's larger households was more interior, and subject to greater scrutiny and censure. Friendship with any man aroused suspicion. Eliza Howard lost her place as cook in Islington because Frederick Repnell came once too often to her kitchen; and a Regents Park linen draper felt justified in sacking both his porter and cook for what he regarded as undue "familiarity of conduct."[22] "No Followers" was the iron rule in many places. One housekeeper in a place near St. James insisted that nursemaids were "not supposed to visit the Park, as they generally do, without someone to attend them—on account of Red Coats and Music which are tempting things to in-

experienced girls. . . ." As an example of what was commonly
called "scarlet fever," there was poor Mary Rose, seduced by a
musician in the Horse Guards band.[23]

Violation of house rules frequently meant dismissal without a
character reference; and prudent servants learned to avoid all situations, however innocent, that might appear suspicious to employers or arouse the latent jealousy of fellow servants. Bored, restless
women were forced to resort to back alley rendezvous; secretive,
closet courtships were the inevitable result of employer vigilance.
No less constricting were the restraints that servants, particularly
the higher ranks, imposed on themselves to protect their jobs,
reputations, and self-respect.[24]

Domestic service is sometimes called an anomaly in the developing industrial capitalist society of the nineteenth century. Eric
Richards has described it as an aspect of female underemployment,
a temporary phase that would disappear with the passage of time.
Certainly service bore but slight resemblance to industrial occupations. It involved no production for a market; the work was neither
centralized nor mechanized; and wages constituted only a part of
the reward. On the other hand, the conditions of work bore close
resemblance to those of industrial captialism. Both the means of
production and the control of the labor process were in the hands
of the employer. One can even speak of the proletarization of service, a gradual shift from eighteenth-century conditions, when the
servants, male and female, had a greater degree of control over their
work time, the labor process, and even the means of production.
Servants had previously tended to be more like intermediaries between their masters and the larger world. In the eighteenth century,
they had access to a much wider range of additional sources of income, both through the recognized custom of "vails" (tips) and by
quasi-legal appropriation of goods in dealings with tradesmen and
the like.[25]

Complaints about the liberties and acquisitiveness of servants
were heard with increasing frequency during the late eighteenth
century, and the whittling away of their intermediate position was
well-advanced by the beginning of the next century. The femini-
zation of service was one way masters sought greater control, but
both male and female servants were by 1850 closely supervised.
Wages were regularized and many forms of appropriation defined
as felonious. Vails, a symbol of servants' earlier right to additional
sources of income, were suppressed. Certain perquisites remained,
particularly to the butler, cook, and those servants most likely to
have dealings with tradesmen; but employers had gained tighter

control over both the means of production and the labor process itself.[26] The locked pantry and minute-by-minute daily schedule had become standard in most larger households.

The new labor discipline was accomplished by direct supervision, either by the employer or by superior servants. It was also further-ed by the reorganization of the work process itself, a division of labor that created a more sharply defined hierarchy within the household. This effectively separated the lower-ranking servants from the superior employees. Kitchen maids, housemaids, and unskilled general servants were restricted to the manual elementary processes of food production, cleaning, and laundering. Their work required little training, and their roles were easily interchangeable. Among what were called general servants there was considerable turnover; both because they were so easily replaced and because their work, being unskilled, could be applied just about anywhere, not just in large but in small households, in hotels as well as private homes, and, of course, in marriage itself. The lower-ranking female servants were not only likely to change places more frequently, but to marry early. They were attractive brides to men of the unskilled working class, where the tendency toward early marriage was strongest. It was from this group that most lower servants came; and it was to that class that they would return.[27]

The situation of higher-ranking servants was distinctly different. Their role was not in basic material production as such, but in the elaboration of the social and cultural symbols appropriate to the social status of their employers. Lady's maids, cooks, and governesses were regarded as specialists, whose skills in hairdressing, *haute cuisine*, and elementary French were rewarded with higher wages and superior status. They were recruited from the lower-middle or upper-working classes, and were expected to be more refined in speech and manners. Their training accustomed them to command the less-polished lower servants, whom they were taught to regard as their inferiors.[28]

As the new urban upper classes expanded and codified the standards and rituals appropriate to acceptance in their ranks, the demand for higher servants increased. High demand in the mid-nineteenth century did not mean, however, that these higher ranks were any more independent than the inferior general servants. Their relationship to masters or mistresses may have been more intimate and their tenure more secure, but they were cut off from alternative employments in ways general servants were not. Because their skills were appropriate to a certain kind of household, their employment opportunities were more limited. Although better paid, they were subject to stringent discipline because their work was so much more personal and visible to their employers. The protection of being distinctly "below stairs" was not available to them. They were more a part of the middle- or upper-class world, yet unable to transform that experience into any real material asset. Fancy cooking or the arts of dress and speech had little application outside the upper-class household; such skills did not lead to other employments and had little usefulness in working-class life generally. It was not their skills that made these women attractive as brides; rather it was the status and savings that they accumulated. Therefore the higher ranks tended to stay in service longer and marry later, if they married at all.

Thus, everything about the upper servants' position in Victorian society, including their sexual relations, must be seen in light of these specialized roles in the upper-class household, especially their peculiar position in the elaboration of a distinctive class culture that, while not their own, had a powerful effect on their behavior and, to a lesser extent, their values.

It would appear (according to Table 2) that the vulnerability of upper servants was greatest in the period 1850-1880, at precisely the historical moment when the elaboration of the servant-keeping middle class was at its peak. The number of upper servants was expanding at this time, but not sufficiently to explain the increased vulnerability of that group. The reasons lie instead in both the conditions of employment and the aspirations which women brought to careers in service. Chief among the latter was the hope for respectable marriage, and for this reason careful selection of husbands was perhaps more important to servants than to any other group of women apart from the daughters of the propertied classes. Because, as wives, they would become almost wholly dependent on their mates' earning power, it is not at all surprising that servants were attracted to men in steady employment: either skilled workers among the laboring classes or clerks, shopkeepers, and small farmers among the nonmanual strata. Although detailed examination of the marriage patterns of individual occupational groups remains to be done, general marriage data would seem to indicate that the class of women who appear so frequently in the Foundling Hospital records could normally expect to occupy a kind of marital middle ground between the lower-middle class and upper-working class. There appears to have been considerable marital interchange between the children of these two groups both nationally and within London itself.[29] On occasion, higher servants might even wed members of the lesser professions, notably teachers. However, they rarely aspired to husbands much higher than this on the social scale, and only at the risk of the kind of scorn heaped on Ann Marsden when she announced herself engaged to a Scottish gentleman. Mrs. Hewetson, a distant relation, saw it her duty to protect Ann against what she called the "foolish vanity of becoming a Lady," and effectively terminated the relationship.[30]

On the other hand, higher servants rarely sought mates much below the skilled working class, and almost never wittingly among the casually or menially employed. They were traditionally wary of men such as soldiers and sailors. One servant refused to marry a seafarer even after she became pregnant: "He would have married her after seduction, but she had no opinion of him after having seduced her and besides he had no way of getting his livelihood."[31] Susanah Carter's master warned her against Joseph Weaver, a former silk dresser, now a seaman, because of his "not being of any trade."[32] Soldiers were similarly avoided.

Conversely, there was a strong tendency for men of both lower-middle class and skilled working-class background to seek brides among upper servants. Similarity of background, certified character and steadiness of habit were qualities that the respectable artisan, shopkeeper, or minor clerk would look for. Scarcely less important was the nest egg that many servants were presumed to have, an amount considered sufficient to launch a journeyman tailor or butcher's apprentice in his own business.[33] In London, marriage meant the establishment of a new household; and when Henry Cockcraft borrowed eight pounds from his fiancée it was to set up their future home.[34] Quarrels over money were common. It was John Wave's eagerness to have Betsy Andrew's inheritance of one hundred and fifty pounds to set himself up in the carpentry business that caused a rift between them. Betsy refused him and was abandoned.[35]

The stakes were rarely so high, however, and most couples were satisfied if they had a little left over after anticipated expenses. The old cliché "two can live cheaper than one" applied. In 1850 the estimated cost of living of one adult was seven shillings per week, but a couple could live for eleven shillings. However, once the first child arrived, often less than nine months after the marriage, the costs became considerably more taxing. Maternity costs, the expense of baby linen, additional food and space, all these raised the couple's costs 42 percent according to one estimate.[36] Most of the working classes and even a portion of the lower-middle strata could expect to fall below the poverty line until the time their children were old enough to earn for themselves.[37] Avoidance of this fate was to some degree a matter of luck, although the right choice of partner was viewed as a guarantee against future destitution.

Romantic attraction played its part, but by necessity courtship was a serious, intricate matter of mutual assessment, with a strong element of shrewd bargaining on both sides. It would appear that women and men were deliberately cautious in arriving at any final decision. Their relatively high age is one measure of this prudent character; another is the extended, ritually protracted nature of their courtships, in which long acquaintance was followed by formal (sometimes written) betrothal pledges, and only then the final preparations for marriage.[38] Jane Watson was a housemaid in West End service when she met a Hoxton watchmaker, Alexander Hay. For seven months they met regularly on Sundays after church. It appeared a good match. He was one of the minority of working men who could afford an engagement ring, and, furthermore, he took care to put his promises in writing:

> Dear Jane Watson
> I solemnly promise to marry you
> my dear girl.
> 18 December 1840   Yours affec.
>   Alex Hay

Jane began to accumulate household items. She resisted intercourse at first, but once the banns were promised she gave in on two occassions. Then things began to turn sour. Jane was pregnant and Alex was experiencing difficulties of his own. Obviously distressed, he wrote to her that he was going to America: "Although I have basely seduced you under a solemn promise of marriage yet circumstances which I cannot explain to you will not permit me to redeem my promise. I write then to end all suspeance [sic] on your part and I pray God to support you in the trouble in which you are involved by my shameful rascallity."[39]

Such extreme formality was not exceptional and was a reflection of the cautious, eminently practical cast of mind that typified not only the nineteenth-century lower-middle class but the higher grades of working men and women as well. The language is that of contract. Promises are given and redeemed in a market of social exchange that is subject to its own tight rules. Solemn bethrothal was apparently viewed, as it had been for centuries, as a significant commitment which permitted considerable intimacy.[40] Women like Jane Watson resisted intercourse until they were sure of the man's intentions. The cook at one Hyde Park establishment knew that the lady's maid had slept there with her lover seven or eight times over a three-month period, but "did not think [it] was wrong as she expected they would have been married."[41]

According to the women's own testimony, the incidence of intercourse after bethrothal was probably less frequent than this example would suggest. Servants reported an average of only four instances of intercourse prior to pregnancy, a relatively low frequency and one not likely to produce very many pregnancies.[42] There appears to have been a good deal of self-restraint on the part of both men and women. A Finsbury Park grocery clerk wrote to his fiancée: "I am grieved at the thought of loosing [sic] self-control, but as to the consequences in the future I am thoroughly satisfied. I think that there is no cause to trouble about that."[43] Conditions of employment, especially the lack of time and privacy also inhibited sexual intimacy.

The question of how these women viewed sexual intercourse is not easy to determine. However, there is very little evidence of obsessive prudery or intense anxiety, at least during the first decades of the century. Fertility was still regarded as an asset and there is little evidence that before the 1860s many servants attempted to terminate pregnancy by abortion.[44] Several used their sexual attractiveness to encourage and, when necessary, retain the affections of a potential husband. In the case of Emma Stoke, relations began with a sexual assault by a fellow servant. She slept with him again, however, "this in the hope that he would marry her." Similarly, Priscilla Perk, a Marylebone general servant, continued to encourage Charles Banks: "Fearing I should be in the family way, I kept up the acquaintance but there was no repetition of the criminality. . . ."[45] Steady and deliberate by nature and training, most servants approached pregnancy, even when unwanted, with surprising composure.

Chagrin was more frequent than remorse; only a few were paralyzed by self-recrimination; even then, there were only one or two instances of attempted suicides. Many continued to count on the marriage promise. If servants rarely invoked public pressure to redeem a man's vow, this had less to do with ingrained guilt-ridden passivity than the fact that it was to the servant's advantage to keep the pregnancy from the employer and fellow servants for as long as possible. Betrothed couples arranged for the woman to stay in service up to the last possible moment, thereby allowing the master to absorb the costs of room and board. The wedding date would be arranged at the convenience of both partners, often, in London at least, at holiday times like Christmas and Whitsun, when couple, family, and friends would have adequate time for celebration.[46]

Sexual relations were not planned with a wedding date in mind and therefore brides were prepared to arrive at the altar at various stages of pregnancy.[47] Conception did not stampede couples into sudden marriages. Instead, they appear to have kept their own time and counsel, waiting for the right moment from the financial point of view, even if this should occur after the birth of the child. Under these conditions, even the best intentions could go awry. Herbert Walker, a traveling photographer, found himself unable to marry Bessie Clark when she became pregnant in 1894. His business had been depressed by a long stretch of rainy weather and he had no money. He wrote to her father: "I assure you my intentions are honorable and we wish to be married as soon as possible. . . . I am always travelling and what has been the principal thing, I have had scarcely any money having had such severe weather." Mr. Clark, a carpenter in Tunbridge Wells, who had eight children in addition to Bessie, was impatient, however, and threatened to summon Walker to the bench once the baby was born. An infant ultimately arrived and Herbert, disowned by his own father, pleaded for time: "I don't see that a few months difference in the time we are married can matter much, as that cannot alter the birth of our dear little girl." Despite his letters, the summons was served, Walker fled, and the child was given up to the Foundling Hospital.[48]

Most of the couples behaved initially as if pregnancy were a prelude to eventual marriage. Where courtship had been prolonged and marriage possible, as it was in most of the cases involving higher servants, many men continued to support the women up to birth and even afterwards. The stereotype of the cruel seducer applies mainly to those cases where interclass liaisons' were involved. As for the majority of the servants, their relations up to abandonment are scarcely distinguishable from those of similar background who successfully completed courtship and marriage. Only the outcome was different.

Why then was a group as sober and experienced as the higher domestic servants so peculiarly vulnerable to illegitimacy? The answer lies in their efforts to combine customs of courtship and marriage appropriate to women of their class backgrounds with the standards of conduct expected of them by their employers. The contradictions were inherent in servants' conditions of employment, especially the restrictions on their social and economic autonomy. Away from home and subject to strict supervision, it was rare for them to meet men in the traditional settings of courtship, namely dances, hiring fairs, and festivals or at home and among friends. Foundling Hospital mothers were more likely to have met the man on their own, either at their place of work (fellow servants, jobbing tradesmen, local shopkeepers) or, by chance, on the street and while traveling. First meetings were almost never arranged and subsequent relations were rarely attended by the publicity associated with traditional courtship.[49] Conditions of employment dictated a peculiarly private kind of liaison. Couples met "by appointment" on days off; and then, unobtrusively, out of the way of employers and fellow servants. Courtship was necessarily furtive and clandestine, particularly where the "No Followers" rule applied. Coffee houses, stables, and railway carriages provided a minimum of privacy. One couple's intimacy was regulated by the metropolitan railway schedule, their lovemaking confined to the few minutes when the train stopped at a dark siding.[50] Similarly, the necessity of secret betrothals restricted the kind of public interest and pressure to which courting couples were normally subjected.

Servants had the opportunity to meet a wide range of men, but almost always under restrictive circumstances. Furthermore, while most of the partnerships were between equals, a distinct minority were disparate in one way or another. Servants were often enough thrown into proximity with men clearly socially superior to themselves. At the same time, they found themselves associating with men who were their inferiors. In both cases, such relationships made for instability and faulted courtships.

The class distribution of males was clearly dissimilar to that of the women (see Table 2). At the upper end of the scale, males were five times more frequent than females, though it is important to note that, contrary to literary convention, the disparate liaison between servant girl and gentleman was a statistical rarity. Far more significant is the fact that the greatest number of female servants were from Class III, while their partners were concentrated among groups of semi-skilled workers, shop assistants, and lower servants, all of whom belong to groups a step below them. Liaisons with male servants were particularly frequent, though not always by choice and certainly not to the women's advantage. An unusually large number of the relationships with such men began with some kind of forced seduction. Because a portion of men in service were married (although often keeping it secret) there was an additional hazard. But even among that majority of servant liaisons in which there was no impediment to marriage, there were other inherent dangers. Service was not a man's career in the usual sense. Except for a few butlers and senior coachmen, most male servants were young and highly transient. Better wage and position required frequent change of place and John Brooks, a hotel servant, owned up that "his wandering mode of life would not allow him to marry. . . ."[51]

Table 4   Social Characteristics of the Partners of Domestic Servants Applying to the Foundling Hospital, 1801-1900 (With Comparison to Total Male Population in 1861 and 1891)*

	Male's Social Class (by percentages)					Social Characteristics of Male London Population Over 10 Years of Age. Calculated by Stedman Jones, p. 387.						
	I	II	III	IV	V							
1801-1810 n=82	5	1	32	55	7							
1811-1820 n=80	6	10	35	45	4							
1821-1830 n=85	9	7	41	41	2							
1831-1840 n=75	3	16	38	43			I	II	III	IV	V	Others
1841-1850 n=73	5	15	23	52	5	1861 Census	7.2	16.3	31.7	11.3	20.1	13.4
1851-1860 n=82	9	13	30	45	3	1891 Census	6.5	19.1	25.0	12.7	21.6	15.1
1861-1870 n=80	4	24	34	31	7							
1871-1880 n=78		13	46	33	8							
1881-1890 n=90		13	42	38	7							
1891-1900 n=71		17	38	39	6							
1801-1900 n=796	4.1	12.9	35.9	42.2	4.9							

*See Appendix A for definition of categories used here.

Another problem lay in the fact that male servants were not well-matched socially with their female counterparts. On the whole, they tended to be recruited from a slightly lower social station and lacked the chances for social mobility possessed by other males. A few remained in service their entire lives; others, also a minority, accumulated sufficient capital to start their own small drink or service enterprises. But a greater part appear to have dropped into the world of casual labor once they had lost the youthful appearance that was a prime requirement of male service. Like their female counterparts, their prior role in social production for a particular class provided them with few transferable skills and thus only slim prospects as breadwinners and husbands.[52]

Because female servants outnumbered male in London five to one in 1891, this type of liaison was highly unfavorable to women. When the partners were both in service, it was not uncommon for the women to be older and of more elevated backgrounds than the men. Although this disparity was perhaps not out of the ordinary in earlier centuries, the pattern in the nineteenth century was for women to marry men older than themselves.[53]   Men sought brides slightly younger and socially inferior to themselves, a condition that, together with London's extremely unfavorable sex ratio, worked to the disadvantage of servants generally, but especially those of higher age and rank. When such women took up with men below them in age or status, they not only violated the custom of their peers but risked parental disapproval. One family sent its daughter to the London Female Penitentiary to get her away from a farm laborer; and Caroline Lane's father refused to press her seducer, a mere laborer, because, as he put it, "there was no good to be got out of him."[54]

If female servants were likely to be thrown together with men inferior to them, they were also unusually accessible to men of clearly superior age and rank. Although exploitation of servant girls by their masters appears to have been far from common, nevertheless, the lecherous employer or rakish lodger did present a danger.[55] Cautious and realistic, servants would rarely overreach themselves by falling for an older gentleman. When these women became involved with middle-class men it was usually with the young and the unsettled, men still struggling for status: commercial travelers, clerks, students, apprentices to the lesser professions; the sort of bachelors who inhabited the hotel and lodging house world of the metropolis, lonely men, who had little access to women of their own age and background, and who were naturally attracted to those women who served in these establishments. Some were notorious seducers, con men or rapists, but the majority to whom these women gave any encouragement appear to have been more self-deceived than deceiving, men who sought a steady, promising relationship as a counterweight to the transience imposed by their work or education. The previously mentioned Herbert Walker, a traveling photographer, was not free to marry because of his job. Charles Hamilton, an engineer's secretary, encountered a different kind of impediment when he announced his intention to marry Esther Long, a laborer's daughter. Hamilton recognized he was superior by birth, but told her that "he didn't want a fine lady for a wife as he could not afford it." Unfortunately, his father thought differently and packed him off to America before the marriage could take place.[56]

In all, disparate relationships accounted for less than one-quarter of the relationships involving female servants. The greater part of servant illegitimacy was generated by couples apparently well-matched and genuinely betrothed. The percentage of relationships involving promise of marriage remained relatively constant throughout the century, averaging 55 percent. By contemporary standards, these were couples with superior marital prospects. If their expectations differed not at all from those who successfully married, then the causes of separation lie not in their sexual behavior, which appears indistinguishable from that of others of similar background, but rather in the contradictions between the marked immobility of women in service and the contrasting rapidity of movement of the men to which such women most frequently found themselves attached. Movement of job and place was particularly accentuated among the kind of men who made up more than one-third of the partners, namely, the aristocrats of labor, the skilled workers. Quite apart from seasonal and trade cycles of employment, the careers of skilled men were accompanied by a high degree of movement from job to job, area to area. This was particularly true of artisans in their twenties, journeymen and even young masters, who gained their greatest bargaining power by changing jobs frequently. These were men who began their extended training in their teens at wages lower than those obtained by semi-skilled and even common laborers of a similar age. However, while the earnings of other working men had peaked by the time they were in their late teens or very early twenties, the maximum earnings of the skilled man were still ahead of him. This was one of the reasons why the aristocracy of labor tended to delay marriage longer than other working men.[57] Movement became even more rapid as marriage approached and men looking for maximum wages often went on the road. One witness explained the separation of Mary Wright and Joseph Reynolds by the fact that, as he was a journeyman baker, young men "in that trade are so frequently shifting about."[58] In the first half of the century, when so many of the skilled trades were facing devastating competition from industry organized on a factory basis, artisans were often compelled to move just to survive. After 1860, it was more common to find men like Charles Howard, a housepainter, shifting about, as he put it, to "get better money."[59] Either way, the results were much the same.

In London in particular there was a strong correlation between skill and geographical mobility. Unskilled, casual laborers were tied to locales such as the dockland of the East End, where they depended on local employers or, in the absence of work, the credit of the corner shopkeeper. This type of economy produced a high degree of endogamy and a pattern of relatively early marriage. Skilled workers ranged further afield and were more likely to be found in the West End and those suburban areas where their work was to be found. There, where the majority of female servants were also concentrated, the age of marriage was higher and partners were less likely to be from the same parish or even the same district.[60]

The type of skilled worker with whom the servant was most likely to become involved was the type connected with the building trades: carpenters, masons and bricklayers, men mainly on temporary assignment, working on houses in the more affluent neighborhoods. In a similar situation were gardeners and landscape workers. A large number of relationships began soon after the men arrived on the job and only began to suffer difficulties when work was completed and the man moved on, either to another part of London or beyond the city. Charles Brown's movements as a house painter never brought him back to his fiancée. The same happened when Walter Howard, a jobbing gardener, courted Sarah Stoner when he was working during the summer of 1866 at her Kensington place. He wrote in December complaining that winter weather had put him out of work. With no money and dependent on his brother, it was impossible for him to marry.[61]

Another kind of contact, though less frequent among servants, was with men employed in the skilled trades of tailoring, shoemaking, and furniture finishing, all of which normally serviced fashionable households. These men were more likely to be resident in the servant-keeping districts of London, but they too were subject to the vagaries of season and trade cycle that caused the perpetual motion of London's most skilled workmen. Couples caught up in cycles of economic depression present particularly poignant cases. When Ann Westmoreland met William Richey he was a promising young tailor's journeyman in the Barbican district. They lived as husband and wife for a time in 1809 before he was called for the Hereford militia. Their problem was complicated still further when Richey's mother fell ill. He might have supported both had not trade collapsed in 1810 and he wrote to Ann: "For I am very Short at Present and any Business is Extremly [sic] Dead. So that is all against mee [sic] for my Mother has been verry [sic] ill, and almost lost her eye Sight. . . ."[62]

Ironically, workers who had lost their independent standing as artisans and were employed in the sweated, mass production work concentrated in London's East End seem to have been better situated as suitors. Sweated East End tailors do not appear in the Foundling Hospital record as frequently as do employees of the better Oxford Street establishments, probably because they were more likely to seek brides from their own locales. The structural underemployment and periodic destitution of slop work may have wrought their own particular kind of marital havoc, but it was in the proletarian East End that young marriages were most frequent and illegitimacy rates the lowest.[63]   Poverty, caused by low wages and casualized employment, was not a direct cause of illegitimacy. More significant than actual wages were those conditions of employment which, by encouraging male mobility, posed a hazard to stable relationships. The very characteristics that made the skilled worker respectable in his own eyes and in the estimation of society; namely, ambition, mobility, and the willingness to postpone immediate gratification for future reward, were accompanied by the necessity of delaying marriage to the point that illegitimate birth was sometimes the regretable result.

Much the same set of causes operated in the case of the other group of men with whom servants were most likely to become involved, namely clerks, shopkeepers, and other men of the lower-middle class. Here again a certain degree of geographical mobility was prerequisite to success, encouraging delay of marriage in order to complete an apprenticeship or accumulate enough money to begin a small business. In order to finish his engraver's apprenticeship, twenty-two year-old John Bucking put off marriage until it was too late to patch things up with his fiancée.[64] Few men of his status would accept the idea of a wife working and it was therefore imperative that he reach his full potential as a breadwinner before marriage. Similarly, the junior clerk or assistant butcher was faced with an intolerable dilemma should his fiancée become pregnant. To marry prematurely meant possible forfeit of that which these men prided themselves on being able to bring to a marriage: secure livelihood and a measure of status associated with the attainment of superior position. Anything less was shameful and irresponsible, as bad, if not worse, as outright abandonment. For them, the choice was not between good and evil, but between alternatives equally disastrous socially and economically.

That great expectations and superior prospects could have led to the gates of the Foundling Hospital seemed inconceivable to contemporaries. They preferred to believe sexual promiscuity and loose morality was the major cause. However, the incidence of intercourse reported by the mothers is not at all suggestive of erotic abandon.[65] Even had servants wished more frequent sexual relations, their conditions of employment would not have made it possible. Nevertheless, these same conditions, and especially the severe moral regime to which servants were subjected, were also major factors contributing to illegitimacy because extreme emphasis on propriety often prevented couples from realizing their original intentions. Employers tended to be concerned mainly with the appearances of morality, and, as such, did not bother to inquire into the context of sexual relations once a pregnancy was revealed.

Their reflex was likely to be punitive, resulting in dismissal or, what was often worse from the point of view of servants' marriage prospects, a form of social quarantine, preventing the girl from seeing the man involved. Knowing this, Charlotte Richards revealed her pregnancy to no one because she feared losing her place. But she was no better off than Elizabeth Rayum, whose mistress forbade her lover to visit once the pregnancy was known. Both women lost contact with their lovers.[66]

The real feelings of the couple scarcely mattered to the busy master confronted with the unpleasant news of a pregnant kitchen-maid. Yet, paternalism was not always reflected in punitive actions. Sometimes pity, coupled with financial aid, was offered to the woman. A helping hand was rarely extended to her partner, however. Men were expected to be responsible and self-sufficient; charity, especially if it lifted the man's burden, was regarded as inappropriate. Therefore, the men were the first to be turned away by employers. Robert Grimby, a twenty-two-year-old gardener, was in tears when he was told he must leave the household; and when Herbert Strong, a grocer's foreman, refused to marry Harriet Meadows on the spot, he was ruined by their mutual employer, who withdrew his letters of recommendation.[67] Although a number of women were kept on until soon before the birth and their confinements paid for or a ticket of admission to a charity hospital provided, the man, if he were a fellow employee, was invariably sent off without a recommendation, thereby condemned to a very uncertain future. In the name of female virtue, masters felt no reluctance to sacrifice the public reputation of the men involved. Even John Kingman, a groom of six years good standing, was packed off with a "certificate of reserved character," making it virtually impossible for him to get another place and support his fiancée.[68] The women were sometimes accomplices in this defamation, but most were aware of the fact that moral condemnation, when pushed too far, was disastrous. For this reason, they struggled to keep matters quiet, especially from gossiping fellow servants.

Once any kind of separation was imposed, contact was very difficult to reestablish. In other circumstances, in which the courtship was public and personal expectations were reinforced by those of family, friends and community, the chances of eventual marriage were far better. Sometimes employers would confront the man, demand that he marry or, at the very least, support the child. Toward the end of the century, when a larger proportion of servants were London-born, the girl's parents were more actively involved, alternately threatening and cajoling the prospective husbands. However, this kind of pressure could backfire, for instead

of reinforcing the man's sense of honor it could just as easily call
it into question, with adverse results. Harry Crown, a coachman,
admitted to getting Annie Balham "in trouble" and was willing to
work out a settlement with her parents. But when Mr. Balham
threatened him with a summons his pride erupted and he wrote to
the father: "Fellows of my breed won't stand that kind of pressure and you seldom find them a coward."[69] George Singly and
Emily Marshall's master offered to buy the marriage license and
set them up, but he absconded.[70] A builder, Joseph Radnor, had
moved on to another job and had begun to court another girl when
he was told of Mary Brady's trouble. He told Mary that he would
not have abandoned her "if he had known my condition," but now
the publicity of the situation had become intolerable and "he could
not face her and those around him that were acquainted of the way
she was in."[71] James Willard, a coppersmith, became so angered
at his fiancée's mother that he declared he would not come to her
house in the future.[72] The fear of public exposure that would result from a court appearance concerning a bastardy order was Herbert Walker's greatest anxiety: "Of course, it matters little to you
as you were not born and brought up in the place," he wrote to his
Bessie, "but to me it means complete disgrace and I'm unable to
help myself."[73] Even more dramatic was the response of William
Muller, a married cabinetmaker, who was willing to support Emma
Rowley, but could not risk marriage to her because unable to afford
divorce, he could then be charged with bigamy. He posted his last
letter to her from Victoria Station: "Had you not persisted in that
[the marriage demand], I would have remained here and seen you
through your trouble. . . . I have had quite enough of you to drive
a man to do something worse that [sic] I do."[74] Shame, transformed into resentment, caused William to leave town.

   A surprisingly large number of men supported the women through
their confinements. It was more common for the expectant mother
to stay in service as long as possible, then to exist on her savings,
thereby using up the capital basis of possible marriage. We have already noted that the moment the woman left service for home or
lodgings her main source of earnings was behind her. Needlework
or other home employment might cover some expenses, but these
were difficult to obtain on short notice. Jane Raines, a servant with
six years' experience and a savings of five pounds, found herself,
unable to get work, destitute after three months in lodgings.[75] Maternity cost, even without complications, was rarely less than one
guinea, a reason why ever-larger numbers of women were resorting
to public or private charitable institutions as the century progressed.[76]
The financial advantages of the workhouse or charity ward were off-

set, however, by the loss of status and freedom attendant on entering them. Begging a charity ticket to Queen Charlotte's was perhaps a little less humiliating than workhouse confinement; but in both cases women were virtually imprisoned during the birth and recovery, a period often stretching to two weeks. It was Queen Charlotte's Hospital policy to isolate unwed mothers, permitting them no visitors for ten days.[77] The more self-respecting the man, the more likely he was to be repelled by the humiliating conditions of charity. However well-meaning, hospital and workhouse personnel provoked reactions of shame and fear among both men and women, thus making separation more likely.

Even after the birth there was still the chance of marriage. Wedding could not legally legitimize the child, but it could prevent abandonment of the child.[78] Once again, however, servants were at a disadvantage in maintaining a relationship after birth. A woman in another occupation could continue to work, supporting herself and her child until a convenient time for marriage. But servants had not the accumulated skills or prior experience in the broader labor market; and many were forced to rely on family and friends, or, when this failed, to accept the most restricted form of service, namely, wet-nursing. Among the unwed mothers applying to the Foundling Hospital, servants were the most likely to become wet nurses. Until the 1880s, this occupied an average of 12 percent of the women leaving their children. It paid well above the wages available to the ordinary domestic, but it virtually prohibited further contact with the father and thus diminished the chances of marriage.[79]

Needlework, washing, and casual prostitution also supported unwed mothers, but with equally sad results.[80] When health failed, savings were exhausted, and the last piece of respectable clothing was pawned, the workhouse became almost inevitable. Only a few women resorted to the courts for child support. The New Poor Law of 1834 had made bastardy orders difficult to obtain and even when successful legal action was brought the amount of support was discouragingly small.[81] Most women were simply put off by the court costs and the attendant publicity, but there was an additional reason why even those women who bore the shame and expense so rarely got a favorable judgment. Women who had been correct and discreet in their relations with the man had no proper witnesses to call. As one court officer explained:

The more respectable the women, the less likely she is to be able to produce the corroborative evidence in a material point which is essential in obtaining an order, and for the simple reason that in all probability she had more carefully concealed her condition with the attendant circumstances, from the knowledge of everyone who would be likely to be of assistance to her at the hearing of the summons.[82]

The contradictions inherent in the status of respectable domestic servant were manifest at every point from the beginning of court-ship, through pregnancy, to abandonment. Of course, many other women of lesser stations, lodging out and casually employed, also found themselves pregnant outside marriage. However, London evidence suggests that the poor and transient were more likely to find some kind of support, if not in legal marriage or in some form of common-law arrangement, then among friends and relations. This is not the place to inquire into these differences; that must await the kind of investigation of specific economic and social circumstances that has been applied here only to servants as a group. The problems of women employed in the better places and most intimately involved in the elaboration of the life-styles of their employers had their own unique and desperate dimensions. They were the women who were supposed to represent, even in-ternalize, the stern moral values of the upper classes. Although it is doubtful that servants adopted upper-class attitudes with the same alacrity that they appropriated the masters' external symbols of wealth and status, it is nevertheless clear that years in service did raise a woman's expectations and inculcate a prim, superficially correct form of behavior. London's servants, par-ticularly at the higher levels, appear to have been reasonably chaste and, when given their choice of men, quite discerning, if not a little snobbish. However, no amount of caution could compensate for the peculiar contradictions inherent in the servant's conditions of employment and residence. Regretably, these turned pride into shame and transformed private virtue into public disgrace.

APPENDIX A

I have adopted the classification used by G. Stedman Jones in his *Outcast London: A Study in the Relationship between Classes in Victorian Society* (Oxford: Oxford University Press, 1971), pp. 350-57. The following is his brief description of the five classes:

Class I — large employers, merchants, bankers, higher officials in shipping and insurance, property owners, and the liberal professions: civil service, church, law, medicine, army, navy, science, fine arts, architecture, etc.

Class II — small employers, small dealers, wholesalers, retailers, caterers, local government officials, teachers, entertainers, musicians, subordinate officers in insurance, church, clerical occupations

Class III — artisan crafts, skilled labor (mostly in construction and manufacture), lower-class traders, higher class domestic service

Class IV* — semi-skilled or intermediate workers mainly in transport, agriculture, wood, metals, textiles; soldiers and sailors; subordinate government and local government service, police

Class V — general unskilled labor, unskilled workers in land and water transport, service and manufacture, municipal labor, street traders.

*I have included the lower ranks of service in Class IV. Journeymen and apprentices also belong here, whatever their aspirations or future status might be.

NOTES

I wish to thank the members of the Rutgers Social History Group, the Davis Seminar of Princeton University, members of my graduate seminar, and the very able editors of this journal for their stimulating and critical suggestions. The present article is part of a study of conjugal relations in nineteenth-century Britain.

[1] Shorter's argument is developed in his *Making of the Modern Family* (New York: Basic Books, 1975), chap. 3. Joan W. Scott and Louise A. Tilly, "Women's Work and the Family in Nineteenth Century Europe," *Comparative Studies in Society and History* 17 (1975): 36-64; Joan Scott, Louise Tilly, and Miriam Cohen, "Women's Work and European Fertility Patterns," *Journal of Interdisciplinary History* 6, no. 3 (1976): 447-76.

[2] Among the studies which suggest enormous regional variations in the nature of illegitimacy are William Cramond, *Illegitimacy in Banffshire* (Banff, 1888); W. Rhys Jones, "A Besom Wedding in the Ceirog Valley," *Folk-Lore* 39 (1928): 148-62; Michael Flinn, ed., *Scottish Population History from the 17th Century to the 1930s* (Cambridge: Cambridge University Press, 1977), pp. 349-68. The value of local studies that pay attention to mode of production and culture is underlined by David Levine's *Family Formation in an Age of Nascent Capitalism* (New York: Academic Press, 1977). Current research on historical illegitimacy is summarized in Peter Laslett, *Family Life and Illicit Love in Earlier Generations* (Cambridge: Cambridge University Press, 1977).

[3] On illegitimacy in the eighteenth century, see Lawrence Stone, *The Family, Sex and Marriage in England, 1500-1800* (New York: Harper & Row, 1977), pp. 627-48.

[4] Quoted in Arthur Leffingwell, *Illegitimacy and the Influence of the Seasons upon Conduct* (New York: Scribner's 1892, pp. 139-40.

[5] William Acton, "Observations on Illegitimacy in London Parishes at St. Marylebone, St. Pancras and St. George's, Southwark, during the year 1857," *Journal of the Royal Statistical Society* 22 (1857): 491-502.

[6] Figures for Scotland from Leffingwell, *Illegitimacy*, p. 67; *Annual Report of Queen Charlotte's Hospital*, 1880; The 1911 survey cited in Nigel Middleton, *When Family Failed: The Treatment of Children in the Community in the First Half of the Twentieth Century* (London: Gollancz, 1971), p. 270.

[7] None of the English court or administrative records provide the kind of detail given by the French declarations of pregnancy. See Alain Molinier, "Enfants trouvés, enfants abandonnés et enfants illégitimes en Lanquedoc aux XVIIe et XVIIIe siècles," *Sur la population francaise au XVIIIe et au XIXe siècles: Hommage à Marcel Reinhard* (Paris: Société de démographie historique, 1973), pp. 445-73; Alain Lottin, "Naissances illegitimes et filles-mères à Lille au XVIIIe siècle," *Revue d'histoire moderne et contemporaine* 17 (1970): 278-322; Jacques Depauw, "Amour illégitime et société à Nantes au XVIIIe siècle," *Annales: ESC* 27 (1973): 1155-82; Cissie Fairchilds, "Female Sexual Attitudes and the Rise of Illegitimacy: A Case Study," *Journal of Interdisciplinary History* 8, no. 4 (Spring 1978): 627-67.

[8] The role of married women in illegitimacy cannot be determined with any degree of accuracy even by contemporary sociologists. On this problem, see Virginia Wimperis, *The Unmarried Mother and Her Child* (London: Gollancz, 1960), chap. 1. Ambiguities concerning what constituted legal marriage existed up to Lord Hardwicke's marriage act of 1753, and, in the popular mind, even well into the nineteenth century. See Stone, *The Family, Sex and Marriage*, pp. 30-37.

[9] This study is based on a 25 percent sample of approximately five thousand successful petitions for admission to the Foundling Hospital, 1801-1900. In assessing the typicality of the cases, it is important to note that the admission process, routinized in 1801 and only slightly modified thereafter, stipulated that only illegitimate children under one

year of age were to be accepted. Furthermore, care was taken to investigate whether the mother had been "of previous good character" and the "the Father of the child (if living) had deserted the Mother and child; and that the reception of the child will, in all probability, be a means of replacing the Mother in the course of virtue, and in the way of an honest livelihood." Emphasis on need and good character was meant to exclude women with repeated illegitimacies, women alleged to be promiscuous, and proven prostitutes. Mothers petitioning for the admission of their children initially filled out their life histories, which were then checked by the Hospital's inspectors, who made written and personal inquiries, often interviewing numerous persons as to the truth of the petitioner's deposition. Their casework, preserved in the archives of the Foundling Hospital, is remarkably thorough. Petitioners who were found to conceal evidence were normally rejected. I have used only the successful cases for the purpose of this study. It should also be noted that all names have been changed in accordance with archival regulations. Records for the period 1801-1880 are deposited at the Greater London Record Office; while the petitions for the years 1881-1900 remain with the Thomas Coram Foundation for Children. I wish to thank Mr. J. G. B. Swinley, Director and Secretary of the Coram Foundation, for his permission to use both sets of documents. Because these documents are not yet catalogued, all references to the petitions in this article refer to the year and the original petition number. Thus the 97th petition for the year 1851 is cited here as: Foundling Hospital 1851/97.

[10]When the Registrar General began reporting female literacy rates in 1841, the average for England the Wales was 51.1 percent. In 1881 it had risen to 82.3 percent, but did not reach 96.8 percent until 1900. Richard D. Altick, *The English Common Reader* (Chicago: University of Chicago Press, 1957), p. 170. I define as literate those applicants who were able to sign their petitions.

[11]Gareth Stedman Jones, *Outcast London: A Study in the Relationship between Classes in Victorian Society* (Oxford: Oxford University Press, 1971), especially chap. 6: Charles Booth, ed., *Life and Labour of the People in London*, 2nd series: *Industry*, 5 vols. (London: Macmillan & Co., 1903), 4: 208-25; and Sally Alexander, "Women's Work in Nineteenth Century London: A Study of the Years 1820-50," *The Rights and Wrongs of Women* (Harmondsworth: Penguin, 1977), pp. 59-111.

[12]Theresa M. McBride, *The Domestic Revolution: The Modernization of Household Service in England and France. 1820-1920* (London: Croom-Helm, 1976), chaps. 2 and 3; Pamela Horn, *The Rise and Fall of the Victorian Servant* (New York: St. Martin's, 1975), chaps. 2 and 3; W. T. Layton, "Changes in the Wages of Domestic Servants during Fifty Years," *Journal of the Royal Statistical Society* 71 (1908): 515-24; Sheila J. Richardson, " 'The Servant Question': A Study of the Domestic Labor Market, 1851-1911," unpublished M. Phil. thesis, University of London, 1967; Clara E. Collet, "Report on the Money Wages of Indoor Domestic Servants," *Parliamentary Papers* (1899), 44, pp. 15-30.

[13]M. Jeanne Peterson, "The Victorian Governess: Status Incongruence in Family and Society," *Victorian Studies* 14, no. 1 (September 1970): 7-26.

[14]McBride, *The Domestic Revolution*, pp. 34-47.

[15]Booth, *Life and Labour*, 2nd series, 5: 22.

[16]1891 figures cited in Richardson, "The Servant Question," p. 162.

[17]Figures are for 1894, cited in Booth, *Life and Labour*, 2nd series, 4: 224.

[18]McBride, *The Domestic Revolution*, pp. 50-69; Horn, *Rise and Fall*, pp. 184-88.

[19]McBride, *The Domestic Revolution*, pp. 84ff. Foundling Hospital 1853/19.

[20]Booth, *Life and Labour*, 2nd series, 4: 224.

[21]On holidays and mobility, see Horn, *Rise and Fall*, pp. 95-97; and Leonore Davidoff, *The Best Circles: Society, Etiquette and the Season* (London: Croom Helm, 1973), chap. 2; and Foundling Hospital 1818/3.

[22]Foundling Hospital 1865/229, 1856/216.

[23] Ibid., 1805/3.

[24] Richardson, "The Servant Question," chap. 8; Mrs. Nassau Senior, "Report on the Education of Girls in Pauper schools," Local Government Board, Third Annual Report, *Parliamentary Papers* (1874), 25, pp. 314-85.

[25] Eric Richards, "Women in the British Economy since about 1700: An Interpretation," *History* 29 (October 1974): 347-48. On the greater independence of servants in the previous century, see J. Jean Hecht, *The Domestic Servant Class in Eighteenth Century England* (London: Routledge and Paul, 1956), especially chap. 6. In addition to vails, which were suppressed from the 1760s onwards, there was board and tea money, together with the "poundage" and Christmas boxes extracted from tradesmen.

[26] Leonore Davidoff, "Mastered for Life: Servant and Wife in Victorian and Edwardian England," *Journal of Social History* 7 (1974): 406-22; Frank E. Huggett, *Life Below Stairs* (New York: Charles Scribner's Sons, 1977); Horn, *Rise and Fall*, pp. 49-91; and *Useful Toil*, ed. John Burnett (London: Allen Lane, 1974), pp. 164-67.

[27] Booth, *Life and Labour*, 2d. series, 4: 213.

[28] *Useful Toil*, pp. 150-53.

[29] There is as yet no systematic study of marriage patterns in nineteenth-century London. Some figures on interclass marriage are available in Hugh McLeod, *Class and Religion in the Late Victorian City* (London: Croom-Helm, 1974), pp. 293-98; and *48th Annual Report of the Registrar General*, 1887. On the basis of these published figures, together with unpublished data provided me by Professor David Glass, I make these very tentative statements. I hope to gather adequate data in the future.

[30] Foundling Hospital 1842/8.

[31] Ibid., 1816/6.

[32] Ibid., 1817/6.

[33] Stedman Jones, *Outcast London*, p. 29.

[34] Foundling Hospital 1870/9.

[35] Ibid., 1825/6.

[36] Alan Armstrong, *Stability and Change in an English Country Town: A Study of York, 1801-1850* (Cambridge: Cambridge University Press, 1974), p. 50; Michael Anderson, *Family Structure*, pp. 31-32.

[37] Anderson, *Family Structure*, pp. 31-32; B. Seebohn Rowntree, *Poverty: A Study of Town Life* (New York: H. Fertig, 1971), pp. 152-72.

[38] *48th Annual Report of the Registrar General*, 1887; McBride, *Domestic Revolution*, p. 91.

[39] Foundling Hospital 1842/170.

[40] A study of Ashford, Kent, for the period 1840-1870 found 38.4 percent of the brides pregnant. Carol G. Pearce, "Some Aspects of Fertility in a mid-Victorian Community," *Local Population Studies* 10 (Spring 1973), pp. 25-29.

[41] Foundling Hospital 1849/119.

[42] This calls into question Edward Shorter's main argument about the erotic revolution of the nineteenth century. On the other hand, until we know more about the traditions of courtship and marriage it would be a mistake to assume, as do Joan Scott and Louise Tilly, that this behavior is "conservative." A similar point is made by Fairchilds, "Female Sexual Attitudes," pp. 653-54.

[43] Foundling Hospital, 1889/83.

[44] John R. Gillis, "Changing Balances of Sexual Power in Nineteenth-Century England," unpublished paper given at International Conference in Women's History, November 1977, University of Maryland, College Park, Maryland.

[45] Foundling Hospital 1844/17, 1857/169.

[46] This point is elaborated in John R. Gillis, "Big Wedding/Little Wedding: Changing Forms of Marriage Ceremony in Britain, 1700-1900," unpublished paper; also Olive Anderson, "The Incidence of Civil Marriage in Victorian England and Wales," *Past and Present*, no. 69 (November 1975): 50-87.

[47] *Annual Report of Queen Charlotte's Hospital*, 1877 and 1878.

[48] Foundling Hospital 1896/11.

[49] On traditions of public courtship, see Shorter, *Making of the Modern Family*, pp. 120-48; John R. Gillis, *Youth and History: Continuity and Change in European Age Relations, 1770 to Present* (New York: Academic Press, 1974), pp. 30-31, 62-64.

[50] The woman later used the railway schedule to substantiate her story. Foundling Hospital 1877/16.

[51] Foundling Hospital 1816/3.

[52] Booth, *Life and Labour*, 2d series, 4: 227-30.

[53] In less than 10 percent of the cases was the woman socially superior to the man. Most of these were the highest ranks of female servants.

[54] Foundling Hospital 1845/82, 1841/143.

[55] Master-servant seductions may have been more prevalent in the eighteenth century when relations between employer and employee were more fluid and less routinized. See Stone, *The Family, Sex and Marriage*, pp. 642-47.

[56] Foundling Hospital 1888/109.

[57] Ibid., 1829/48.

[58] Ibid., 1882/99.

[59] Anderson, *Family Structure*, pp. 132-34.

[60] McLeod, *Class and Religion*, pp. 2-9; Stedman-Jones, *Outcast London*, part 1.

[61] Foundling Hospital 1867/220.

[62] Ibid., 1810/8.

[63] Leffingwell, *Illegitimacy*, pp. 26-33; Charles Booth, *Life and Labour*, 3d series: *Religious Influences*, 7 vols. 1: 56, 2: 97.

[64] Foundling Hospital 1870/16.

[65] At the rates of intercourse testified to by the servants, very few pregnancies would have resulted.

[66] Foundling Hospital 1831/28, 1826/7.

[67] Ibid., 1878/106, 1874/62.

[68] Ibid., 1859/184.

[69] Ibid., 1875/81.

[70] Ibid., 1880/3.

[71] Ibid., 1869/195.

[72] Ibid., 1885/62.

[73] Ibid., 1896/11.

[74] Ibid., 1900/23.

[75] Ibid., 1871/35.

[76] Maternity costs calculated from cases.

[77] Regulations of Queen Charlotte's Hospital as stated in annual reports.

[78] In Ashford, 1840-70, 3 percent of maternities occurred before marriage. See Pearce, "Some Aspects of Fertility," pp. 30-31.

[79] A poignant fictional example is provided by George Moore, *Esther Waters* (Oxford: Oxford University Press, 1974), chap. 18. The problem of nursing in London is extensively documented in "Report of the Select Committee on the Protection of Infant Life," *Parliamentary Papers* (1871), 7.

[80] The relationship between domestic service and prostitution is a complicated one. Former servants may have made up between one-third and one-half of London prostitutes during the nineteenth century, but it is not clear that women went on the streets to support illegitimate children. See Helen R. E. Ware, "The Recruitment, Regulation and Role of Prostitution in Britain from the Middle of the Nineteenth Century to the Present Day," unpublished Ph.D. dissertation, London University, 1969, pp. 122-24, 333ff, 361, 374-84, 422. Also *Downward Paths: An Inquiry into the Causes Which Contribute to the Making of the Prostitute* (London: Women's Cooperative Guild, 1916), pp. 164-69;

McBride, *Domestic Revolution*, chap. 6; Horn, *Rise and Fall*, pp. 133-38; also Judith Walkowitz, *Prostitution and Victorian Society: A Study of the Contagious Diseases Acts*, forthcoming, Cambridge University Press.

[81] U. R. Q. Henriques, "Bastardy and the New Poor Law," *Past and Present* no. 37 (July 1967): 103-29; Ivy Pinchbeck and Margaret Hewitt, *Children in English Society*, 2 vols. (London: Routledge & Kegan Paul, 1969), 2: 200-222.

[82] Foundling Hospital 1876/81.

4 Free Black Women and the Question of Matriarchy

SUZANNE LEBSOCK

In 1853, Eliza Gallie, a middle-aged, free black woman of Petersburg, Virgina, was arrested and charged with stealing cabbages from the patch of Alexander Stevens, a white man. She was tried in Mayor's Court and sentenced to thirty-nine lashes. There was nothing unusual in this; free black women were frequently accused of petty crimes, and for free blacks, as for slaves, whipping was the punishment prescribed by law. What made the case a minor spectacle was that Eliza Gallie had resources, and she fought back. She filed an appeal immediately, and two weeks later she hired three of Petersburg's most eminent attorneys and one from Richmond as well. "If the Commonwealth, God bless her, has not met her match in Miss Liza," a local newspaper commented, "it won't be for lack of lawyers." The case came up in Hustings Court in March 1854. Gallie's lawyers argued first of all that her ancestors were of white and Indian blood and that she should therefore be tried as a white person. The court was unconvinced. On the trial's second day, her counsel argued that she was innocent of the theft. The court was again unconvinced. Gallie was pronounced guilty and sentenced to "twenty lashes on her bare back at the public whipping post. . . ." At first she set another appeal in motion, but deciding that the case was hopeless, Eliza Gallie dismissed her lawyers and took her punishment.[1]

Gallie's case was in many ways an unusual one, and yet her story cuts straight to the central contradiction in our common image of the historic black woman. Eliza Gallie was, relatively speaking, a powerful woman, propertied, autonomous (divorced, actually), and assertive. But she was helpless in the end, the victim of the kind of deliberate humiliation that for most of us is past imagining. So it is with our perception of the history of black women as a group. On the one hand, we have been told that black women, in slavery and afterward, were formidable people, "matriarchs" in fact. On the other hand, we know that all along, black women were dreadfully exploited. Rarely has so much power been attributed to so vulnerable a group.

The contradiction can be ironed out, with sufficient attention to definition and evidence. All the evidence used here comes from Petersburg, Virginia, and it comes mainly from the Petersburg of Eliza Gallie's youth, when the first generation out of slavery, the women emancipated in the wake of the American Revolution, established a pattern of female responsibility radically different from that prevailing among whites. Petersburg had fewer than seven thousand residents in 1820, but for its time and region, it was a city of some consequence. Flour milling, tobacco manufacture, and the commerce generated by the farmers of Southside Virginia sustained Petersburg's growth, while the horse races and the theater gave it touches of urban glitter. Only two cities in Virginia had larger populations, and no other Virginia town had a higher proportion of free blacks among its people. Before the statute of 1806 brought manumissions to a near standstill, Petersburg's free black population grew at a prodigious pace, its size swelled by a high rate of emancipation in the town itself and by the hundreds of migrants from the countryside who came in search of kin, work, and community. By 1810, there were over one thousand free blacks in Petersburg; nearly one-third of Petersburg's free people (31.2 per cent) were black.[2]

Some definitions are called for. The term "matriarch" has been used in so many different ways that it has become almost useless as a descriptive term. But it should be understoof that the word "matriarch" would never have been applied to black women in the first place were it not for our culture's touchiness over reduced male authority within the family. It is a telling fact that "matriarchy" has most often been used as a relative term. That is, women are called matriarchs when the power they exercise relative to men of their own group is in some respect greater than that defined as appropriate by the dominant culture. Given this standard, women need not be the equals of men, much less men's superiors, in order to qualify as matriarchs. The acquisition by women of just one commonly masculine prerogative will do, and hence it becomes possible to attribute matriarchal power to some of society's most disadvantaged people. The woman who had no vote, no money, and no protection under the law was nonetheless a "matriarch," so long as she also had no husband present to compete with her for authority over her children.

Concern over the reduction of male authority has also been the touchstone of scholarship on black family life (relatively little has been written on the history of black women per se). For all the disagreements among scholars on the character of the historic black family, it has been assumed on almost all sides that female-headed families are, and were, pathological. There were two key assertions in the classic thesis advanced by E. Franklin Frazier four decades ago and revived in 1965 in the Moynihan Report. First, as a result of slavery and continued discrimination, an alarming proportion of black families were "matriarchal," that is, the husband/father was either absent or (Frazier added) he was present, but of negligible influence. Second, the woman-dominant family was unstable and disorganized, at once the symptom and cause of severe social pathology among black people.[3] The Frazier-Moynihan thesis came under heavy fire in the 1970s when scholars began to check the matriarchy image for historical accuracy. And yet the historians, too, reinforced the prevailing prejudice against female-headed households. Working for the most part with census data from the second half of the nineteenth century, several historians found that female-headed households were outnumbered by two-parent households. This, along with additional evidence of the statistical insignificance of the woman-headed household, was offered in defense of the Afro-American family: Black families were not generally matriarchal/matrifocal/female-headed (the term varies), therefore they were not disorganized, unstable, or otherwise pathological after all.[4]

This is a dangerous line of defense, and its problems are highlighted when we encounter evidence like that for early Petersburg. Here was a town in which well over half of the free black households were headed by women. Shall we therefore label it a nest of social sickness? It would make better sense to disentangle our evidence from conventional, androcentric value judgments on what is healthy and what is not.

For the time being, it would seem wise to set aside the issue of the integrity of black family life (by what standard, after all, are we to judge it?) and to concentrate instead on the impact of racial oppression on the status of women and on the distribution of power between the sexes. When we do this for Petersburg, we are confronted once again with the dual image of strength and exploitation. Women were prominent among Petersburg's free blacks. They outnumbered the men three to two, they headed more than half of the town's free black households, and they constituted a large segment of the paid labor force of free blacks.

Yet this was for the most part the product of wretched poverty and persistent discrimination. The "matriarch" and the victim, it turns out, were usually the same woman.

Still, the fact remains that among free blacks there was less inequality between the sexes than there was among whites; when black women of the present say they have always been liberated, they have a point. Among those free blacks who managed to accumulate property in early Petersburg, a high proportion — about 40 per cent — were women. And because they were more likely than their white counterparts to refrain from legal marriage, free black women were more likely to retain legal control over whatever property they did acquire. It may well have been that free black women valued their relative equality and did their best to maintain it.

How all this came to be is not entirely clear, for census data are sketchy, measures of wealth are crude, evidence on the occupational structure is thin, and vital records do not exist. It seems likely, however, that the preponderance of women in the free black population began with the cumulative decisions of emancipators: Women slaves stood the better chance. Before the Virginia legislature tied the hands of would-be emancipators in 1806, 173 slaves were manumitted in Petersburg.[5] Ninety-four of them (54.3 per cent) were female. Of the manumitted adults, meanwhile, 59.3 per cent (54 of 91) were female. Sexual intimacy, antislavery principle, and economic calculation could all have been responsible for women's easier access to emancipation.

That a number of manumissions resulted from sexual unions would seem to be a good bet for a town full of well-to-do bachelors, many of whom were a long way from home. Documentable cases, however, are few. Only one white emancipator was known to have acknowledged his kinship with his former slaves, and in only two instances is there strong circumstantial evidence of a sexual connection. In 1814, Mary Moore, a "great, large, fat, bouncing-looking" Irish woman, manumitted Sylvia Jeffers, as she was authorized to do by the will of her late brother John Jeffers. Sylvia was apparently John's daughter; in any case, in 1853 she talked the local court into escorting her across the color line, claiming descent from Indians and whites only.[6] Betsy Atkinson, too, won the special affection of her owner. A week after James Gibbon freed her, he wrote his last will. To Atkinson, he left a slave and furniture already in her possession, some livestock, and three hundred dollars.[7]

Anti-slavery principle may also have accounted for the women's edge in emancipation. Under Virginia law, the child inherited the status of the mother. To free a man, therefore, was to guarantee the freedom of but one person. The emancipation of a woman in her childbearing years might secure the freedom of generations.[8]

In the short run, meanwhile, the emancipation of a woman meant a lesser loss of income for the owner. Women suffered a distinct disadvantage in earning power, a disadvantage that began in slavery and that showed in the inability of slave women to purchase themselves. Hiring oneself out was illegal, but both women and men did it, and most of them got away with it.[9] The women who hired themselves out did not, however, command wages equivalent to those of men, or so it appears from the incidence of self-purchase. Self-purchase was uncommon in this period; from 1784 to 1820, just nine of the two hundred slaves emancipated bought themselves. Amy Jackson, who paid her master $410 in 1819, was the sole woman among them.[10]

The same disparity in earning power limited the numbers of slaves whom emancipated women managed to free in turn. Altogether, free blacks themselves were responsible for thirty-three manumissions (one-sixth of the total to 1820), and although about one-half of the black emancipators were women (7 of 15), no woman was able to liberate more than one slave. Graham Bell showed what could be done with a remunerative skill (shoemaking), hard work, and business sense. In 1792, Bell set free his wife, or possibly his daughter, and five sons. From 1801 to 1805, he emancipated his brother, two women, one of whom he had purchased "for the express purpose of manumitting or emancipating her," and a child.[11] No one else came near Bell's record, but four of the other men did manumit at least two slaves. In the years after 1820, several women would join the ranks of the multiple emancipators. Meantime, one apiece was the best they could do.[12]

Emancipation was itself a step up on the economic ladder; the woman at last owned her person and her labor. In Petersburg, she was not likely to own anything else, not in the beginning anyhow. White emancipators expected their former slaves to fend for themselves. James Campbell made it explicit in 1802 when he freed forty-two-year-old Sally, "whom I have reason to believe is an honest woman, and one that will earn by her labour a proper support for herself."[13] A few emancipators may have granted their former slaves some kind of economic assistance, but in only one deed was something promised in writing. Persons manumitted by will did not fare much better. Of the twenty-seven slaves whose freedom was directed by will, only four were staked by their masters, and three of the four were men.[14]

The emancipators no doubt believed they were giving their former slaves an even chance. Given the circumstances under which many of the women were freed, however, making a living would be an uphill struggle. Some emancipators freed the children with the mother, and while this spared the women from trying to save to buy their children (and from the pain of being unable to save enough), it did mean extra mouths to be fed. Most of these women had one child or two, but three or four or five was not unusual.[15] Age was important as well. The emancipators who stipulated the ages of the persons they freed were too few to provide a reliable sample, but the ages that were recorded suggest that relative to the men, the women were disproportionately middle-aged. A large proportion of the women set free were, or would soon be, past their best wage-earning years.

Table 1 Age at Emancipation

Age	Women	Men
18-30	9	4
31-40	1	4
41-50	8	2
51 and up	0	1

The most significant handicap, however, was the near absence of occupational options. The vast majority of free black women engaged in domestic employment of one kind or another. This was not a matter of choice, and it was more a matter of sex than of race. Nothing made the women's occupational bind plainer than the apprenticeship orders issued by the court for free black children. Among the masters who took on free black boys as apprentices were a carpenter, a cabinetmaker, a painter, a cooper, a barber, a blacksmith, a hatter, a boatman, and a baker. So limited were the girls' options that the clerk hardly ever wasted ink on specifying the trade. The few specific orders contained no surprises. In 1801, Lucy Cook was ordered bound "to learn the business of a Seamstress & Washer." On the same day Polly Flood was "bound to Abby Cook, to learn to Sew & Wash &c untill of lawful age — being now about 9 years of age." Polly was bound to a second master "to learn Household business" five years later. And Polly White, an orphan just five years old, was apprenticed "to Mrs. Brewer to learn the duties of a House Servant."[16]

There were some women who broke the mold and engaged, at

least part time, in more specialized occupations. Betty Morris and
Aggy Jackson were nurses, Judy Denby and Judy Darvels were
midwives. A few engaged in legitimate commerce. Amelia Gallé
ran a bath house, Lurany Butler operated a dray, Nelly White was
a baker, and Elizabeth Allerque and Sarah Elliott were licensed
storekeepers.[17] As with white women, just as many pursued
illegitimate commerce. At least five black women were nabbed by
the Petersburg Grand Jury for keeping a "tippling house" or for
selling liquor without a license.[18] The fact that specific
occupations can be identified for only a dozen black women is
testimony to the predominance of domestics among them. Cooks,
cleaning women, washerwomen, seamstresses, and child-nurturers
did not advertise, nor were they likely to surface in any of the
public records.[19]

If the gentlemen of the Grand Jury had been asked, they would
probably have identified prostitution as a major enterprise of free
black women. In 1804, the Grand Jury registered a grievance
against the invasion of free black "strangers," many of whom
"come only for the purpose of Prostitution. . . ."[20] There is no
telling whether or how often free black women in fact resorted to
prostitution, but the Grand Jury was right about the invasion.
Dismal as economic opportunities were in Petersburg, they were
apparently worse in the countryside, particularly for women.
Black migration from the country was thus spearheaded by
women. By 1820, the sex ratio among free blacks aged fourteen
and above was 85.0 (males per 100 females) for eastern Virginia
as a whole. In Petersburg it was 64.5.[21]

Petersburg was, relatively speaking, a land of opportunity, and
a few of the women emancipated there did register gains. Betty
Call was freed on Independence Day, 1786, and within four years
she managed to buy her grown son, London, from an Amelia
County owner. After ten years, she set him free. Betty Call never
did own any real estate, but she was taxed on a female slave
(evidently hired) for years, and when she died in 1815, the sale of
her household goods netted just over seventy dollars.[22]
Emancipated on the same day as her mother, Teresa Call saved for
nine years. In 1795, she purchased a small lot and continued to
live there for decades.[23] Dolly Clark acquired a female slave five
years after her manumission. On the other hand, women like
Nancy Hall and Sally Steward accumulated no traceable property.
Emancipated in 1799 and 1805, respectively, their continued
residence in Petersburg was confirmed by entries in various public
record books, but neither of them owned the land or slaves or
horses or carriages that would have resulted in their appearance on

the tax lists.[24]

New arrivals fared worse than the natives. Only nine free black women were among the town's taxpayers in 1810, and most of them were old-timers. All but one had lived in Petersburg as free women for at least six years. Betty and Teresa Call had both been free for twenty-four years, while Sarah Vaughan held the record for longevity on the tax lists. Vaughan owned real estate when Petersburg's first land tax book was assembled in 1788, and thirty years later she still held, and presumably rented out, her "4 small tenements."[25] On the average, the nine women had been paying taxes for almost nine years, and they held on to what they had. In the decade after 1810 three of them died, but the remaining six, all landowners, were still paying real estate taxes in 1820.

By that time they had more company. In 1820, there were thirty-eight free black women among the taxpayers. However one chooses to measure it, this was an impressive relative increase. In 1810, black women constituted but 2.2 per cent of (9 of 413) of the town's taxpayers. In 1820, their proportion was 5.5 per cent (38 of 687). The increase is not attributable to any relative growth in the free black female population. A count of the percentage of taxpayers among heads of families does help control for possible population shifts; similarly, it indicates a doubling of property holding among free black women. In 1810, 5.1 per cent (7 of 138) of the black women designated as heads of families in the census schedules were also listed in the tax books; by 1820, the proportion had risen to 10.1 per cent (17 of 168). All in all, blacks were gaining on whites, women were gaining on men, and black women were gaining on black men.[26]

At least three developments accounted for the sudden economic ascent of a portion of the free black female population. With the deaths of propertied men, a few black women claimed their inheritances. More important were the hard-won savings of the women themselves. And third, it looks very much as though the Panic of 1819 forced slaveholders to put their slaves on the market at prices more women could afford.

Among the black female taxpayers of 1810, only Molly James had acquired her property by inheritance. James was the heir to the house and lot her husband had owned at his death in 1804. By 1820, two more legacies marked the passing of the first generation of prosperous black men. Graham Bell in 1817 left to his wife, Mary, a life estate in one of his town lots, while Elizabeth Graves was daughter and one of two surviving heirs of Richmond Graves, a livery stable operator.[27] Mary Ann Vizonneau and Amelia Gallé, meanwhile, were heirs of white merchants. Vizonneau's

Scottish father, John Stewart, had threatened to disown her when she married Andre Thomas Vizonneau. But moments before his death in 1813, Stewart relented and directed that Mary Ann be given "all the money he then had in the Bank and the house & Lot he then lived on," on the condition "that her husband . . . might have no manner of Controul over, or right, to the same." This was a considerable bequest, worth over eighteen thousand dollars, and it made Mary Ann Vizonneau one of the wealthiest women in Petersburg.[28]

Amelia Gallé was also the heir of a white merchant. She had earned her inheritance. Amelia Gallé was still a slave when she first arrived in Petersburg, and she was known by a slave name, Milly Cassurier. In 1800, French merchant Jean Gallé bought her for eighty pounds, and he emancipated her four years later, after she had borne him a son. Jean Gallé died in 1819, and while in his will he termed Milly "my housekeeper," it was clear from the provisions of the will that she had been his wife in every sense but the legal one. He acknowledged her son Joseph as his natural son. He left to the two of them the greater part of his estate. And he enjoined Milly to act as mother to his "mulatto Girl slave" Catherine Gregory, charging her "to support the said Catherine and bring her up to lead a moral and religious life."[29]

Jean Gallé also left to Milly Cassurier his bathhouse, a business she had apparently been running for years. When she assumed sole management of the bathhouse in the spring of 1820, she became the first black businesswoman in Petersburg to exploit the full possibilities of newspaper advertising. At first she settled for a two-sentence announcement that the bathing season had arrived. By midsummer, however, her appeal was more effusive.

> The character of this bath, is so well known that it needs no comment. The subscriber is resolved if possible to improve it, by consulting the comfort and convenience of the visitants — and to enable her to do so more effectually, she humbly solicits a continuation of that patronage which has so liberally supported the institution till this time. Having had several years experience in this business, the subscriber believes she will generally succeed in pleasing — and therefore, with stronger confidence humbly solicits a portion of the public support. . . .

For several years thereafter, she opened the season with just a brief announcement. Two or three months later, as the heat of the Virginia summer grew tediously oppressive, she would follow with greater fanfare. "She has the pleasure of tendering to her patrons," came the notice of May 1823, "her most grateful thanks for their former encouragement, and begs a continuance of the same." August brought the harder sell.

HEALTH
Purchased Cheap!

In consequence of *Small Change* being scarce, and wishing to contribute towards the health of the ladies and gentlemen, the subscriber has the pleasure to inform her patrons and the public, that she has reduced the price of her baths to 25 CENTS for a single one. She will make no comments on the necessity of Bathing in warm weather: − suffice it to say, that with Mr. Rambaut's FAMILY MEDICINES, and some Cold or Warm BATHS, the health of her friends will keep at a proper degree of the thermometer, without the aid of Calomel or any other mineral Medicines.[30]

These advertisements were not just a means of drumming up business. They were also the means by which a free black claimed for herself the respect due a propertied widow. In her first advertisement, she signed herself "Milly Cassurier." In the second, she was "Milly Galle." She signed the third "Amelia Galle." In the fourth, she was "Amelia Galle, widow." How far others accorded her the respect she asked for is an open question. She made some progress with the census taker, who listed her as "Milly Gallie," but to the tax collector she was still Cassurier, "cold at Galle's."[31]

Amelia Gallé, Mary Ann Vizonneau, Elizabeth Graves, and Mary Bell were the only black female taxpayers of 1820 whose property was (documentably) acquired by inheritance. More significant was the economic maturation of the women themselves, and here the foremost success story belonged to Elizabeth Allerque. "Madame Betsy," she was called, "a French colored woman" who was probably a refugee from St. Dominigue. She was, in any case, well connected with Petersburg's French immigrant community, and the connections in combination with her commercial talent spelled steady financial progress. Allerque first opened a store in 1801. At some point she added a partnership with French merchant André Vizonneau (Mary Ann Vizonneau's father-in-law), who in 1809 made sure that Allerque would be paid her full share of the proceeds when the firm was dissolved by his death: "I declare that the partnership which I had entered into with Elizabeth Alergues was joint and equal both as to capital and profit. . . ." Five years later, French physician L.J. Hoisnard wrote his will, charging Allerque with the care and legal guardianship of his daughter. Moreover, "in consideration of her good attention to me during the latter part of my life," Hoisnard left to Allerque and her two

children a legacy of a thousand dollars.[32] Even without this
bequest, Elizabeth Allerque would have done well for herself. She
first invested in real estate in 1806 and improved it several times
thereafter. In 1806, too, she became a slaveholder for the first
time. Allerque was one of Petersburg's few black commercial
slaveholders; in 1806 she advertised in the Richmond and Norfolk
newspapers for the return of her runaway woman Charlotte.
Madame Betsy died in 1824, free of debt and the owner of land
and six slaves.[33]

Most free black women had neither the skills nor the
connections of an Elizabeth Allerque, but a few had enough
savings to take advantage of the Panic of 1819. While the general
economic dislocation that surrounded the Panic must have caused
great suffering among many black women, it also afforded the
betterplaced the opportunity to hire or purchase slaves for the
first time. (The tax lists, unhappily, do not indicate whether the
taxpayer owned or hired the slave.)[34] As more and more whites
scrambled to find the money to pay their debts, more and more
slaves were put up for hire or sale, and probably at bargain prices.
There is no estimating just how many slaves changed hands during
the Panic years. In 1819 and 1820 alone, however, Petersburg
owners mortgaged over 240 slaves; these slaves would be sold at
auction for whatever they would bring if the owners failed to pay
their creditors on schedule.[35]

For the master class the time was unnerving, for the slaves it
was potentially disastrous, but for the free black woman with
some savings, here was a rare opportunity, a chance to acquire a
loved one or a laborer. Three-quarters of the black women taxed
in 1820 (27 of 38) made their debuts on the tax lists in 1819 or
1820. And all but two of the newcomers were taxed on one or
more slaves.

It was in slaveholding that black women registered their greatest
gains by 1820 and in slaveholding that they came closest to
economic parity with black men. In 1820, forty-six slaves were
held by black men, forty-five by the women. Women were farther
from equality in other measures of the black sex ratio of wealth,
but they were gaining on the men. Two-fifths (13 of 32) of the
black landowners of 1820 were women, a somewhat larger
fraction than in 1810.[36] Two-fifths of the black taxpayers of 1820
were women, up from one-fourth in 1810. And two-fifths of the
tax collected from free blacks in 1820 was collected from women,
again, up from one-fourth in 1810.

Measured against comparable figures for whites, these were
stunning proportions. In 1820 women were but 12.8 per cent of

the white taxpayers (76 of 593), and they accounted for only 3.5 per cent of the tax money collected from whites.

This glaring disparity in the status of black and white women relative to men of the same race fades somewhat when sex ratios are taken into consideration. It should also be said that free black women were more likely than were white women to maintain their legal eligibility to control property. Virginia was a common-law state, and the common law made razor-sharp distinctions between single and married women. Single women and widows had the same property rights and obligations as men. But the instant a woman married, she surrendered both her rights and her obligations to her husband; if she had owned taxable property, the surrender was manifested in her summary disappearance from the tax lists.[37]

It is impossible to estimate how many of Petersburg's free black women shunned lawful matrimony, but the qualitative evidence suggests that the proportion was high, higher than among whites. The sex ratio, the law, poverty, and preference conspired to keep a great many free black women single, and to the extent that women remained single, they remained free agents in the economic realm.

The sex ratio and the law together dictated the single life for one-third of Petersburg's free black women. Because blacks were not permitted to marry whites, and slaves were not permitted to marry anyone, the pool of marriageable men was restricted to free blacks, and there were simply not enough of them to go around. A few black women did take up with whites, and more, apparently, were coupled with slaves. These matches yielded some interesting economic arrangements. Milly Cassurier, when she was still known by that name, acquired property in her own right while she was living with Jean Gallé, something she could not have done had the two of them been married.[38] When a free woman cohabited with a slave, meanwhile, here were the legal materials for a complete sex-role reversal, for the woman assumed all legal rights and responsibilities for the pair. In 1800, a slave named David White was jailed for going at large and trading as a free person. The fine for White's misdeeds fell on his wife, Polly Spruce, a free woman who had hired White for the year and who was therefore legally answerable for his behavior. Nearing her death years later, Jane Cook found it necessary to make special provision for her slave husband, Peter Matthews. Cook had purchased two small boats, "the Democrat and the experiment," as her husband's agent and with his money. These she bequeathed to Matthews, appointing a free black man to act as his agent and to stand guardian to her daughter, to whom she left her own property.[39]

The women whose mates were white or enslaved had no choice but to remain technically single, but it is by no means certain that all of them would have married had they been given the chance. When free black women entered into partnerships with men who were also black and free, legal wedlock was not the inevitable result. For one thing, marrying did cost money. Ministers were authorized to charge one dollar for their services, and the clerk's fee was a quarter. If a poor couple found that amount an obstacle, they likely found it well-nigh impossible to locate a third party willing to post the $150 bond required to obtain the license.[40]

Nonmarriage among free blacks, however, was evidently as much a matter of ethics as of expenses, for even the propertied showed no consistent tendency to make their conjugal ties legal ties. Christian Scott was hardly well-to-do, but he did own some animals and a goodly stock of household furniture; "having for some time past lived with Charlotte Cook by whom I have a son called Jesse Mitchell. . . ," Scott explained, "And being desirous from the friendship & Regard I bear to the said Charlotte Cook & affection to my said Son, to convey the property aforesaid to them," Scott deeded them the property, dividing it exactly as it would have been divided had Scott married Cook and then died intestate (without a will). James Vaughan was far wealthier than Scott. He was also in trouble. In 1806 Vaughan was tried for the murder of "his supposed wife," Milly Johnston. After his conviction, a contrite Vaughan was permitted to write a will to direct the distribution of an estate that included cash and bonds worth over two thousand dollars, a town lot, three horses, and four slaves. Vaughan gave half of his estate to Sarah Vaughan, his daughter by Polly Hull. The other half went to John Vaughan, his son by Ann Stephens. Whether James Vaughan's relationships with Johnston, Hull, and Stephens were simultaneous or sequential is both unclear and beside the point. The point is that he did not marry any of them.[41]

So much the better for the women's control over their property and wages. Polly Hull, for example, bought a town lot a few months before James Vaughan wrote his will and was taxed on it for more than a decade thereafter.[42] There were other free black women in roughly similar circumstances. Charlotte Rollins was part of an uneasy triangle that included a free black named Captain Billy Ash and a slave named Julius. Ash was tried for "shooting and wounding" Julius in 1802, and Rollins's sister and brother-in-law were examined in the case: "On their being asked if Charlotte was wife of the prisoner, it was answered, that they both, the prisoner & Julius, resorted where she was." It is unclear what became of Billy Ash, but Charlotte Rollins never married him or anyone else. In 1810, she was listed as the head of a three-person family, and in 1817, she disposed of her household furniture and kitchen utensils by deed of gift, a probable substitute for the writing of a will.[43] Nelly White, unhappily, was unable to enjoy the property she had acquired in her baking business. In 1811, White was examined on suspicion of knifing a free man named Tom, and a witness described their relationship. "Tom & the Prisoner had lived in the same House, in different apartments — and been considered as man & wife but lived badly together after wrangling." White was convicted in District Court and sent to the penitentiary. She left behind "some property & Estate," and the town sergeant was ordered to look after it while she served her sentence.[44]

A member of one of Petersburg's most prominent free black families, Molly Brander married once, but opted for cohabitation the second time around. The first time, she married Nathan James. After his death in 1804, Molly began a new family, taking James Butler "as her husband tho not lawfully married," and adopting her orphaned niece. Because she did not marry Butler, Molly James retained her rights to the house and lot she had inherited from her first husband, and when she died intestate in 1812, her mother and brothers inherited the property in turn. Before her death, however, Molly James had told her family that she wanted the lot to pass to James Butler and her adoptive daughter; the family complied in 1815 by means of a deed of gift.[45]

Just how commonly black women acquired some kind of property and retained legal control over it by not marrying the men in their lives is a mystery, for evidence surfaces only sporadically in trial reports (hence the prevalence of violent crime in the preceding paragraphs) and in a very occasional deed. Moreover, these few documents give no clues as to whether the women deliberately refused marriage for the sake of maintaining their property rights. The legacy and continued presence of slavery no doubt provided cause enough. Slave marriages were necessarily based on mutual consent; for a good many black couples, consent was sufficient in freedom as well, an attitude that the black churches would combat with mixed success in the decades that followed.[46] Still, it may have been that women so recently emancipated, and women accustomed to providing for themselves, did not give up their legal autonomy lightly.[47] Certainly free black women had unique incentive for staying single. For the woman who hoped to buy an enslaved relative, legal wedlock meant that her plan could be sabotaged at any time by her husband or by her husband's impatient creditors. The common-law disabilities of married women added an ironic twist to chattel slavery's strange fusion of persons and property: Matrimony could pose a threat to the integrity of the free black woman's family.

Whether by necessity, deliberation, or default, sufficient numbers of free black women avoided legal marriage to constitute a major departure from the white norm. The contrast with the experience of white women was sharper still in the extent to which black women shouldered the burden of supporting their families. If most of the women listed by the census taker as "heads of families" were primary breadwinners, then the magnitude of economic responsibility borne by free black women was truly staggering. In 1810, 56.3 per cent (138 of 245) of the free black households of Petersburg were headed by women. For 1820, the figure was 58.1 per cent (168 of 289). In 1820, these female-headed households sheltered over one-half (52.3 per cent) of all free black persons living in black households and an even larger proportion (57.3 per cent) of free black children under fourteen.

So uninformative are these early census returns, and so suspect the given numbers, that no satisfactory reconstruction of household composition is possible.[48] From the unembellished hashmarks that made up the 1820 schedules, the one safe conclusion is that there was no typical free black household structure. The most commonplace household type (87 of 289) was, it appears, the female-headed family containing one woman and her (?) children. Further guesswork suggests that the second most frequent arrangement was the male-headed household containing an adult couple and their children (51 of 289).[49] Thirty-seven households were composed of but one person, twenty-nine of them female, and there were apparently twenty-four childless couples. The remaining households, about one-third of the total, contained persons of ages and sexes that defy categorization. Worth noting, however, is the incidence of extended or augmented families. One-fifth of all free black households contained at least one "surplus" person over the age of twenty-five.[50]

It should be emphasized that there was no typical household structure among whites either.[51] The difference was that Petersburg's multiform white households were overwhelmingly male-headed. The proportion of white households headed by women was 15.7 per cent in 1810 and 17.0 per cent ten years after. In addition, a disproportionately small number of whites lived in these female-headed households. The census taker of 1820

found only 13.3 per cent of white children under sixteen resident
in female-headed households, while 12.8 per cent of all white
persons lived in households headed by women.[52]

Nineteenth-century census data usually raise more questions
than they answer, and this is particularly true of the early returns.
It is impossible to discern the precise family structure within
households, much less assess the meaning of familial roles played
by neighbors and nonresident kin. This last blind spot is especially
troublesome given the probability that for numerous free blacks,
spouses and close kin remained the slaves of white owners. Least
of all does the census tell us anything about love, commitment,
giving children a chance in life — those qualities that despite our
disclaimers usually lurk behind our reading of the numbers.

These problems only begin the list of the source limitations that
frustrate any attempts to recapture the experience of the mass of
free black women. We do know that there was a flourishing free
black Baptist church in Petersburg before 1820 and that in 1820 a
Sunday school run by free blacks had girls as well as boys among
its two hundred students.[53] But there are no records for the
church in this period and none at all for the Sunday school.
Newspapers reported next to no local news. The whites whose
correspondence is preserved wrote of their own kind; only rarely
did they discuss their slaves, and free blacks were never
mentioned. While the local public records are surprisingly rich,
they are decidedly slanted toward the property owners. The
majority of free black women thus appear to us only as names —
or worse, as numbers — on the census schedules.

The conclusion nevertheless stands. In a slave society of the
early nineteenth century, there developed among free blacks a
relatively high degree of equality between the sexes. There is not
much material here for romanticizing. For free black women, the
high rate of gainful employment and the high incidence of female-
headed households were symptoms of oppression. Neither was
chosen from a position of strength; both were products of a
shortage of men and of chronic economic deprivation. The high
incidence of female property holding, meanwhile, was largely the
consequence of a system that limited the achievement of black
men.

Yet there was autonomy of a kind, and the fact that its origins
lay in racial subordination should not detract from its significance.
The autonomy experienced by the free black women of Petersburg
was relative freedom from day-to-day domination by black men.
We cannot say for certain how free black people looked on this.
The fact that so many couples refrained from legal marriage,

however, at least suggests that the women valued their autonomy and that one way or another the men learned to live with it. The tragedy for the nineteenth century – or one of many tragedies – was that white people were unable to use the free black example to call their own gender arrangements into question, that no one outside the free black community took anything positive from the free black experience. Perhaps we can do better.

NOTES

The author wishes to thank the Colonial Williamsburg Foundation and the Woodrow Wilson National Fellowship Foundation Program in Women's Studies for their support of the research on which this article is based. She would also like to thank Sharon Harley for her comments on an earlier version of the article.

[1] *South-Side Democrat*, 29 November, 12 December 1853 (first quotation), 17 March, 18 March, 20 March 1854; Minutes, 15 December 1853, 16 March, 17 March 1854 (second quotation).

All references to minutes, deeds, wills, accounts, and marriages are to the records of the Petersburg Hustings Court, on microfilm in the Virginia State Library, Richmond, Va. References to land books, personal property books, and legislative petitions are to the original manuscripts in the Virginia State Library.

[2] Calculated from *Aggregate Amount of Persons Within the United States in the Year 1810* (Washington, 1811), p. 55a. According to this census, Petersburg contained 1,089 free blacks, 2,173 slaves, and 2,404 whites. The town's free black population grew to only 1,165 by 1820. In reading these figures, allowance should be made for probable undercounting.

[3] E. Franklin Frazier, *The Negro Family in the United States* (Chicago: University of Chicago Press, 1939); U.S. Department of Labor, Office of Policy Planning and Research, *The Negro Family: The Case for National Action* by Daniel P. Moynihan (Washington, D.C.: U.S. Government Printing Office, 1965.) More detailed summaries of these works may be found in the articles by Gutman, Lammermeier, and Shifflett, cited in note 4.

[4] John W. Blassingame, *Black New Orleans 1860-1880* (Chicago and London: University of Chicago Press, 1973), pp. 79-105; Frank F. Furstenberg Jr., Theodore Hershberg, and John Modell, "The Origins of the Female-Headed Black Family: The Impact of the Urban Experience," pp. 211-33; Herbert G. Gutman, "Persistent Myths About the Afro-American Family," pp. 181-210; Crandall A. Shifflett, "The Household Composition of Rural Black Families: Louisa County, Virginia, 1880," pp. 235-60, all in *Journal of Interdisciplinary History* 6 (Autumn 1975); Herbert G. Gutman, *The Black Family in Slavery and Freedom, 1750-1925* (New York: Pantheon Books, 1976), pp. 432-60; Paul J. Lammermeier, "The Urban Black Family of the Nineteenth Century: A Study of Black Family Structure in the Ohio Valley, 1850-1880," *Journal of Marriage and the Family* 35 (August 1973): 440-56; Elizabeth H. Pleck, "The Two-Parent Household: Black Family Structure in Late Nineteenth-Century Boston," *Journal of Social History* 5 (Fall 1971): 3-31. Pleck, however, does point out the value-laden nature of terms like "family disorganization," and in *Black Migration and Poverty: Boston 1865-1900* (New York: Academic Press, 1979), has reevaluated the

significance of two-parent households.

[5] This may be a slight overcount; of the two dozen slaves directed freed by will, some may have remained in slavery due to owners' indebtedness or to litigation. The law of 1806 discouraged manumission by requiring all newly freed persons to leave the state within one year of emancipation, and for a time it was extremely effective. There were no emancipations in Petersburg from 1807 to 1810. Emancipations began again in 1811, but from 1811 to 1820 were granted at less than half their pre-1807 rate, even though a new statute of 1816 made it easier for the manumitted to obtain permission to remain in Virginia.

The female advantage in emancipation seems to have been more than a reflection of the sex ratio among slaves; calculations from the Personal Property Book for 1790 show that females constituted only a 51.5 per cent majority of slave adults.

[6] Mary Cumming to Margaret Craig, December 1811, Margaret and Mary Craig Letters, Virginia Colonial Records Project, Alderman Library, University of Virginia, Charlottesville, Virginia (quotation); Wills I, 238 (1796); Deeds IV, 304 (1815); Luther P. Jackson, "Manumission in Certain Virginia Cities," *Journal of Negro History* 15 (July 1930): 310. John Jeffers's will also authorized the emancipation of Sylvia's mother.

[7] Deeds V, 324 (1818); Wills II, 163 (1819).

[8] Luther P. Jackson counted the deeds of emancipation recorded in Petersburg and Richmond from 1784 to 1806 and found more in Petersburg, even though it was the smaller city. This he attributed to the early presence in Petersburg of antislavery Methodists. See Jackson, "Manumission," pp. 281-82. By my count, six Methodists accounted for almost one-fifth of Petersburg emancipations to 1806.

[9] Six women were apprehended and jailed for hiring themselves out. The court had the choice of selling them or fining their masters; two of the six were ordered sold. Minutes, 5 April 1802, 5 September 1803, 2 January, 9 February, 4 April 1809, 6 May 1811. See William Waller Hening, *The New Virginia Justice, Comprising the Office and Authority of a Justice of the Peace in the Commonwealth of Virginia . . .* 2nd. ed. (Richmond: Johnson & Warner, 1810), p. 549.

[10] Deeds VI, 51 (1819).

[11] Deeds II, 157 (1792), III, 58 (quotation), 74 (1802), 236 (1805).

[12] Two of the women freed their sons; no relationship was stated by the others. Deeds II, 174 (1792), 581 (1799), 701 (1800), 737 (1801), Deeds III, 75 (1802), 116 (1803), Deeds V, 325 (1818).

[13] Deeds III, 78 (1802).

[14] Deeds III, 267 (1805); Wills II, 69 (1812), 114 (1815), 139 (1817), 161 (1819).

[15] At least sixteen women were manumitted with their children (this does not include those freed by husbands or other kin from whom they could expect financial assistance). Six had a single child, five had two children, and five had three or more.

[16] Minutes, 1 June 1801, 6 January 1806, 7 August 1809.

[17] Accounts I, 31, 55 (1808), 37 (1809), Accounts II, 189 (1821); Luther Porter Jackson, *Free Negro Labor and Property Holding in Virginia, 1830-1860* (New York and London: D. Appleton-Century Co., 1942), p. 221; Personal Property Books, 1801-1820.

[18] Minutes, 2 November 1790, 5 August 1799, 2 March 1812.

[19] There were probably more gainfully employed women among free blacks than among whites, but because the whites were more likely to escape (paid) domestic service, they are far more visible; specific occupations can be identified for more than 150 white women. These women, with a few exceptions, were milliners, dressmakers, midwives, teachers, and keepers of taverns, boardinghouses, and stores. Meanwhile, the only female occupations in which no free black women were found were teaching and millinery.

[20] Minutes, 4 November 1804.

[21] Calculated from the United States *Census for 1820* (Washington, D.C.: Gales and

Seaton, 1821). The imbalance may also have been due to a higher rate of male migration to the free states. It does not appear to have been due to higher mortality rates among men, because the sex ratio was higher (71.3) among free blacks aged forty-five and above.

[22] Deeds I, 270 (1786), Deeds II, 116 (1800); Personal Property Books, 1795-1804; Accounts I, 75 (1817).

[23] Deeds I, 303 (1787), Deeds II, 379 (1795); Land Books, 1795-1820.

[24] Deeds II, 205 (1792), 593 (1799), Deeds III, 237 (1805); Personal Property Books, 1797-1802; Wills II, 69 (1812); Minutes, 5 October 1812, 8 August 1815, 5 March 1816, 17 July, 16 October 1818.

Few of the persons emancipated in Petersburg can be traced. Emancipators stated last names for fewer than one-third of the slaves freed (black emancipators were more prone than whites to state surnames), and because ex-slaves hardly ever took the name of the last owner, inference is of little help.

[25] Land Book, 1820.

[26] Taxable property consisted of land (taxed according to its annual rental value), slaves over twelve years of age (taxed by the head), horses, carriages, and exports from the tobacco warehouses. My calculations include all taxes paid by living individuals, except those paid on tobacco exports, there being no comparable taxes on other businesses.

It should be emphasized that all along, white men controlled the lion's share of the taxable wealth, ranging from 85 per cent in 1790, when town matriarch Mary Marshall Bolling was in her heyday, to 94 per cent in 1820. The best way to characterize the trend for the decade after 1810 is that more white women and blacks of both sexes were acquiring small pieces of an expanding pie. The following table shows the proportion, in per cent, of the persons listed in the census schedules as head of families who also paid taxes:

	1810	1820
White men	60.1	61.8
Black men	21.5	24.8
White women	14.8	30.3
Black women	5.1	10.1

[27] Deeds III, 300 (1806), Deeds IV, 351 (1815); Wills II, 141 (1817).

[28] Legislative Petitions, 23 December 1839; Wills II, 94 (1814).

[29] Deeds III, 156 (1804); Wills II, 161 (1819). Amelia Gallé's son Joseph later on became the husband of Eliza Gallie.

[30] Petersburg, *Republican*, 18 April, 7 July 1820, 23 May, 22 August 1823.

[31] United States Manuscript Census Schedule, 1820; Personal Property Books, 1819, 1820.

[32] Accounts I, 91 (1814) (first quotation); Deeds IV, 332 (1815) (second quotation); Wills II, 40 (1809) (third quotation), 95 (1814) (fourth quotation).

[33] Accounts II, 68 (1824-1826); Deeds III, 279 (1806); Land Books, 1806-1820; Personal Property Books, 1801-1820; *Republican*, 29 October 1816.

[34] Slave sales were not usually publicly recorded, and this adds to the difficulty of determining the extent of slave ownership.

[35] The number of slaves mortgaged was calculated from the deed books. During the same two years, Petersburg newspapers advertised the sale of about eighty slaves "according to a deed of trust," in other words, for owners' indebtedness. Both figures given here are lower than the actual totals, because the advertisements and deeds of trust did not always stipulate the precise numbers of slaves involved. Anyone prone to discount the significance of the threat of forced sale would do well to sample some

deed books. In 1819 and 1820 alone, at least one-tenth of Petersburg's slaves were put up as collateral for owners' debts.

[36] In 1810, eight of twenty-three black landowners were women.

[37] By using the legal loopholes provided by the equity tradition of jurisprudence, a few married women were able to exempt their property from the control of husbands and husbands' creditors. Mary Ann Vizonneau provides one example. Her father's stipulation that her inheritance was not to be controlled by her husband set up a "separate estate," which was formalized in 1818 by a separation agreement executed by Vizonneau and her estranged husband. Deeds V, 284 (1818). In this period, however, separate estates were still very rare.

[38] In his will, Jean Gallé apprised his executors that the woman slave Faith and all but two of the beds in his house belonged to Cassurier and not to his estate. Wills II, 161 (1819).

[39] Minutes, 3 September 1800; Wills II, 192 (1822).

[40] Joseph Tate, *A Digest of the Laws of Virginia, which are of a Permanent Character and General Operation; Illustrated by Judicial Decisions: To which is Added, An Index of the Names of Cases in the Virginia Reporters* (Richmond: Shepherd and Pollard, 1823), pp. 415-18, secs. 1, 11, 13. Because the Marriage Register did not stipulate race, not even a rough estimate of black marriage rates can be made.

[41] Deeds V, 124 (1817); Minutes, 21 November 1806; Wills II, 182 (1821). Vaughan was born free and the son of the Sarah Vaughan who appeared year after year on the tax lists.

[42] Deeds III, 376 (1807); Land Books, 1809-1820.

[43] Minutes, 27 January 1802; Deeds V, 197 (1817).

[44] Minutes, 6 April 1811 (first quotation), 6 May 1812 (second quotation).

[45] Land Books, 1806-1812; Deeds IV, 330 (1815) (quotation).

[46] Records of the Gillfield Baptist Church suggest that as late as 1860, there was still ambivalence on the marriage issue. An entry of 29 January 1860, for example, reads: "It was moved & 2nd that the Past Action of the church be reconsidered of mutual consent being considered Man & Wife Carried – non considered Man & Wife But those joined together By Matrimony." Gillfield Baptist Church Record Book, Alderman Library.

[47] Two cases suggest that some free black women were aware of the law and concerned about its consequences. Two days before she married Jacob Brander, Nancy Curtis deeded her furniture and livestock to her teenaged children, a clear attempt to protect the rights of her own heirs. Lydia Thomas maintained her property rights in a slave and some furniture, despite her marriage to John Stewart, by entering into a prenuptial contract with him. This gave her a separate estate, much like that of Mary Ann Vizonneau. Deeds IV, 335 (1815), Deeds V, 288 (1818); Marriages, 1814, 1817.

[48] The 1810 census listed the names of free black heads of households, but the only further information given was the total number of free blacks (with a separate total for slaves) living in each household. The census for 1820 is somewhat more informative, supplying the number of persons of each sex in each of four age categories (under fourteen, fourteen to twenty-five, twenty-six to forty-four, and forty-five and above).

[49] The first figure is the total of all households in which one female from fourteen to twenty-five was listed along with one or more children under age fourteen, and in which one female of twenty-six or above was listed along with one or more persons under age twenty-six. The same age categories were used for the second figure.

[50] For female-headed households, surplus adult is defined as anyone over twenty-five listed in addition to the head. For male-headed households, surplus adults are those listed in addition to one man and one woman. There were twenty-one surplus women and six men in male-headed households, thirty surplus women and twenty-three men in female-headed households.

[51] Even counting resident slaves and free blacks out of the analysis, fewer than one-third of the households headed by whites can be reasonably classified as nuclear, that is, as being composed of an adult couple or an adult couple with their children with no surplus persons.

One-tenth of Petersburg's free blacks were listed as residing in households headed by whites. Three-fifths of these free blacks were males, and they outnumbered females resident in white households in every age group except the over-forty-four category.

[52] The incidence of female-headedness among poorer white households was considerably higher, as might be expected. In 1810, 27.1 per cent of the households of nontaxpaying whites were female headed. Comparison of white and black households is complicated by the fact that different age categories were used for the two groups.

[53] Luther P. Jackson, *A Short History of the Gillfield Baptist Church of Petersburg, Virginia* (Petersburg: Virginia Printing Co., 1937); *Republican*, 17 October 1820.

5   The Power of
Women's Networks

MARY P. RYAN

One of the first impulses of the feminist historians in the early
1970s who set about discovering women's past was simply to chart
the course of sexual inequality and the oppression of women. The
advances of women's scholarship since then have raised more complicated historical issues. Women's historians are now looking to
the past for evidence of women's power and autonomy rather than
their simple subordination. Within segregated female spheres and
women's networks they have discerned evidence of the ability of
women to maximize their freedom and exert considerable social
influence. This trend in women's history has given new currency
to Mary Beard's notion, first enunciated in the 1940s, that contrary
to being oppressed and victimized, women have acted throughout the
American past to shape events and to make history. This scholarly
perspective has given us a richer, multi-dimensional picture of wom-
en's history. There are, at the same time, some hazards inherent in
this emphasis on women's culture and women's power. The first
possible risk is that by exonerating the women of the past from
the charge of being eternal victims and passive objects of history,
we will also lose sight of the societal inequality which has consistently marked womanhood and been a central component of nearly
every sex/gender system. Secondly, we are in some danger of over-
simplifying the historical process. If women are a force in history,
if they make their own history, then we must also face the possibility that females have participated in creating and reproducing
the less-sanguine aspects of the gender system. We are now in a
position, after scarcely a decade of intense research, to recognize
women as full agents in history, who for all their power and freedom have not circumvented the constraints, ironies, and contradictions that confront human beings in the past and into the future.[1]
This paper explores one manifestation of this more complex historical relationship drawn from the annals of antebellum American

reform movements. The American Female Moral Reform Society seems to represent women entering history in a powerful, militant, some have said feminist posture. More than 400 chapters of the national moral reform association grew up throughout New England and the Middle-Atlantic States in the 1830s and 40s. Their goal was to reform standards of sexual morality and regulate sexual behavior in their communities. They assailed the double standard, forcefully pursued and exposed licentious men, and extended their protection to seduced women and reformed prostitutes. In Female Moral Reform, Carroll Smith-Rosenberg has found expressions of women's discontent with their assigned sphere, contempt for tyrannical males and militant defense of members of their own sex. More recently, Barbara Berg has relied heavily on the records of the American Female Moral Reform Society to argue that the origins of American feminism lay not in the abolitionist movement but in the women's benevolent organizations that flourished in the nineteenth-century city and often dated from an earlier period.[2] At the same time any casual reader of the Society's periodical, *The Advocate of Moral Reform*, will also notice a contrary tendency. The *Advocate* reveled in portraying the innate purity, domestic virtue, and maternal priorities of the female sex. In fact they were among the earliest and most enthusiastic exponents of these features of the nineteenth-century stereotype of "true womanhood." Female Moral Reform, in other words, presents two apparently contradictory uses of woman's power: to attack the double standard, on the one hand, and to celebrate a domestic feminine stereotype, on the other. Thus the case of Female Moral Reform offers an excellent opportunity to examine the relationship between women's power and the history of the sex/gender system. It may illuminate the nature, sources, and ambiguous historical impact of women's efforts to exert influence on society at large.

This historical objective is best achieved by minute analysis at the level of local reform organization. This narrow but sensitive compass can locate the specific origins of the female moral reformers' power. The focus of this inquiry is a chapter of the American Female Moral Reform Society founded in Utica, New York in 1837. The Utica Society was also served by rural tributaries, including chapters in such satellite farming and factory villages as Whitesboro, Clinton, New York Mills, and Westmoreland. In the 1830s and 40s, Utica and these surrounding towns of Oneida County were alive with moral reform, and consequently prolific of documents for historians of women.

Female moral reform grew up in the interstices of the expanding agricultural market economy which centered in the village of Utica.

As late as 1800, Utica was merely a river crossing and trading post situated in the midst of a few pioneer homesteads. The commercial preeminence of the town was established in the 1820s when it became a port along the Erie Canal, bustling with trade and exploding with a population of eight thousand. By the mid 1830s, the canal boom had subsided and the population stabilized at around twelve thousand people. The majority of the employed males of the newly incorporated city made their livelihoods as small merchants or manufacturers—shopkeepers and artisans who served the nearby commercial farmers. Utica also boasted a number of banks and insurance companies; many stockholders in the nearby railroads and textile factories; and a bevy of ambitious entrepreneurs, large and small, who proudly announced themselves as capitalists. Just on the outskirts of the town stood the industrial village of New York Mills, one of the nation's largest textile producers outside of New England. Yet neither large-scale manufacturing nor wage labor dominated local economic activity. Rather the small independent producer, whether a farmer or artisan, characterized the regional economy and made Utica a bustling, open marketplace.[3]

At this precise historical moment—while still a small, youthful, preindustrial, but flourishing, market economy—Utica earned its place of moderate renown in American social history. The plethora of religious revivals and reform activity which Whitney Cross portrayed in his classic study, *The Burned-Over District*, originated in and around Oneida County. The region had been overrun with evangelism since the first settlers arrived from New England in the late eighteenth century. The inaugural Christian benevolent association, a missionary society, was founded in Utica in 1806, and the long, lively, revival cycle ensued soon thereafter: beginning in 1814, peaking in 1826, and dissipating late in the 1830s. It was in the 1830s and 40s that the "Burned-Over District" spawned the species of reform organization to which female moral reform properly belongs. The city directory for 1832 listed no less than forty-one voluntary associations. These groups performed a multitude of community functions; care of the poor, instruction of children, self-improvement of young men, and simple conviviality for their members.[4]

The first associations, founded at the turn of the century, generally united men or women of elite status in order to perform community services, such as providing relief for the poor in a condescending fashion. The voluntary associations of the 1830s were set up for a different purpose—to reform individuals and institutions—and exhibited a new mode of organizing. Most were congregations of peers: members of similar age groups, occupations,

and ethnic backgrounds. Most rejected a rigid governing hierarchy
and condescending manners. The Washingtonian Temperance
Union was the most extreme expression of this leveling tendency,
enthusiastically welcoming even acknowledged inebriates into its
fraternal embrace. All these associations occupied a distinctive
space in the social order of the community, somewhere along a
muted boundary between private and public life. The "association" or "society" as it was alternately called, was clearly not an
enclosed private space. Yet it was not exactly public, at least not
in the way Utica's New England founders used the term: to desig-
nate the formal institutions of town and church where male heads
of households met to exercise official authority. Rather, the association relied on informal but expansive social ties, a voluntary network of like-minded individuals, as its organizational machinery
and political leverage. Combined, these associations actually functioned as a major structure of social organization for Utica in the
1830s and 40s. Whatever the community need—be it police or fire
protection, a new industry, poor relief, education, an orphanage—
some association rose to meet it.

    Social organizations of this nature are particularly receptive to
female participation. Sex, first of all, was a legitimate common
characteristic around which to form an association of peers. Furthermore, the blurred distinction between private and public space
which characterized the association effectively removed a barricade
which so often consigned females to domestic confinement. Finally, the social organization of the 1830s and 40s worked through
informal personal associations, the sustained, everyday contacts
between neighbors and kin, social networks which were especially
familiar and comfortable to women. Thus it is not surprising that
one in three of Utica's associations was a congregation of females.
Women's associations were formed, beginning in the first decade
of the nineteenth century, for a variety of purposes: to support
the frontier ministry, to educate poor children, to circulate religious tracts. Soon women began to organize in a more democratic
manner and in a spirit of mutuality rather than noblesse oblige.
Groups such as the Maternal Association, the Daughters of Temperance, and the Female Moral Reform Society were all dedicated
to serving the reciprocal needs of the members themselves, especially in rearing their children and ridding their homes of vice.
All these groups assumed a basic commonality between their members and those they might serve. The victims of alcohol or lechery
were all perceived as errant children of the same Protestant, native-
born, industrious and respectable culture. In sum women were
among the most active participants in the rich social life that trans-

pired within the voluntary associations, that American mode of antebellum social organization that so fascinated De Tocqueville. It could also be argued, in the case of Utica at least, that women played a formative role in creating the associational system. The region's first voluntary benevolent organization was the Female Charitable Society. The prototype of the more democratic associations was the Maternal Association which predated its male analogue, the Washingtonian Temperance Union, by over a decade. At any rate, the social order of antebellum Utica and environs was replete with women's organizations, of which the Female Moral Reform Society was only one special case.

The immediate antecedent of Female Moral Reform appeared in Oneida County early in the 1830s when John McDowall of New York City alerted the local population to the need to control seduction, prostitution, and obscenity. The very first issue of *McDowall's Journal*, appearing in 1833, recorded a ground swell of support in the city of Utica. The *Journal* reported individual donations from city residents as well as contributions from associated women, such as the "Female Benevolent Society of Utica." Moral as well as financial support soon followed. Mrs. Abigail Whitellsey, the editor of the *Mother's Magazine*, another offshoot of the women's organizations of Utica, also sent her appreciation and endorsement. Tokens of support also came from anonymous women, such as, "a Lady from Utica" who poignantly offered up "Two rings and a breast pin" to help finance the cause. The small towns outside Utica were the first to mobilize behind moral reform. Whitesboro had a chapter of the American Female Moral Reform Society as of 1835 which enrolled approximately 40 members. By 1837 when the Utica Society was formally established, the chapters in Clinton and Westmoreland had acquired a membership of 84 and 181, respectively. The 100-member Utica association pledged to wage a pious women's crusade: "we do feel dear sisters" announced the first annual report of the Utica Female Moral Reform Society, "that we have enlisted in the warfare for life and that we are not at liberty to lay down the armor till called upon by death to other services."[5]

The names of only a handful of the Utica reformers have been recorded on an occasional circular or newspaper account. These few identifiable members, however, represented a relatively wide range of women from the middling and upper classes. Wives of artisans joined those of merchants and prominent attorneys. Two seamstresses brought the interests of wage-earning women into the society. Although veterans of evangelical reform based in the Utica First Presbyterian Church formed the core of the Female Moral

Reform Society, women of Baptist affiliations also joined the
ranks. The single and the widowed, furthermore, joined with middle-aged wives and mothers in the moral crusade.[6] Finally, it
should be noted that the rural areas of Oneida County, including
both farming communities and industrial villages, displayed equal,
if not greater, enthusiasm for female moral reform than did the
city proper.

What then stimulated women from such a broad spectrum of
the population to take an interest in moral reform? It might be
expected that these women were simply reacting to a sudden up-
surge in the incidence of "adultery and seduction," the species of
vice which they were most determined to eradicate. Yet a survey
conducted by the Utica Society in 1843 uncovered a paltry record
of sexual offenses: nine cases of illegitimacy and two arrests for
prostitution. Although no more refined estimate of the frequency
of sexual relations outside of marriage is available for Oneida County, there are some indications that the rate of sexual license was
actually on the decline in the Northeastern United States. Analysis of vital statistics and church records suggest that the proportion
of births conceived before marriage had peaked in the late eighteenth century and actually reached its nadir in the era of moral
reform.[7] These statistics, however, hint at more complex changes
in sexual behavior than a simple decrease in premarital sexual relations. These cases of premarital sex were exposed by examining
genealogical records, proceeding, couple by couple, to simply sub-
tract the number of months between the date of marriage and the
date of first birth. Premarital sex which did not culminate in a
marriage record, then, is not recorded by these statistics. Hence,
it may be that the young women and men of Oneida County and
the Northeastern United States were engaging in sex outside of
marriage at the same, or even a higher rate than in previous decades,
but were now evading marriage to their sex partners. If this were
true then the decline in "early births" may indicate not a lower
incidence of premarital sex, but, rather, the breakdown of those
methods of social control which formerly insured that illicit intercourse and conception usually culminated in matrimony.

This second interpretation of changing sexual behavior in antebellum America is substantiated by evidence from Oneida County.
Although the actual level of premarital sex cannot be accurately
determined, it is quite clear that the community's ability to moni-
tor and regulate such behavior had eroded substantially. After
1830, neither the church nor the family retained its former control
over private sexual activity. Before then the local churches, Baptist,
Methodist, and Presbyterian alike, regularly called their members

to account for committing fornication and adultery. Seducers and adulterers were brought before the elders of the church to confess their sins, vow to change their ways or be excommunicated. Early in the 1830s, after heated ecclesiastical debates too complicated to recount here, the local churches discontinued this method of enforcing sexual morality.[8] At the same time, the rapid increase in the population of Utica and its increasing religious diversity prevented a single church (including the once-ruling Presbyterians) from overseeing the sexual behavior of the entire town.

At the same time parents' ability to restrict the sexual activity of their daughters and sons was being undermined by the extreme geographical mobility of the commercial era. The population of Utica quadrupled between 1820 and 1840, due in large part to the influx of young men and women unaccompanied by their parents. One-quarter of the city's population was between the ages of fifteen and thirty; as much as 30 percent of all those listed in the city directory called themselves boarders, most of whom were young men living apart from their kin. Many of these young urban dwellers were migrants from rural Oneida County where after the exhaustion of unimproved agricultural land in the 1820s, parents could no longer provide a livelihood for all their progeny on nearby farms. Thus Utica was inundated with young unsupervised men and women seeking jobs as clerks, canal boys, servants, and seamstresses. The industrial village of New York Mills, meanwhile, was filling up with unchaperoned factory girls of similar origins. Parents and the deacons of the church were not available then to control or protect these young migrants.

It was the Female Moral Reform Society that came to the aid of this peripatetic generation. Although the espoused goal of the society was to rout out seduction and adultery, the Utica chapter was most concerned about the former sexual transgression, the peculiar pitfall of the young and unmarried. The appearance of at least two seamstresses on the rolls of the Utica chapter represented a population of women who seldom enlisted in local reform groups. These working girls were especially vulnerable to seduction and the fateful consequences of becoming unwed mothers and may well have joined the Society for their own sexual self-protection. The bulk of the members of the Utica chapter, however, were married women who seemed to act more out of concern for their children than their own immediate self-defense. The brothels of the city, according to the reformers were the "known cause of ruin to multitudes of the rising generation" and were responsible for "rending the hearts of fathers and mothers." One mother from Clinton wrote the *Advocate of Moral Reform* describing the demographics of her interest in sexual control: "A daughter and a son have returned to their widowed mother from visiting distant cities and pined away victims of this sin" [of sexual indulgence]. The secretary of the New York Mills chapter explained the sources of maternal concern in this region as follows: "The state of society in this place is peculiar to manufacturing villages. Multitudes of youth are here collected who need light and instruction on this subject." The records of the female moral reform societies of Onieda County were most of all a repository of the anxieties of mothers. "Even our children are infested with [obscenity]," wrote the alarmed matrons. "Who amongst us have not had our hearts pained by the obscenity of little children? Who among us does not trouble at least if some who are dear to use should be led away by the thousand snares of the destroyer?" They feared for their sons as well as their daughters, whom they envisoned leaving home only to be enticed into brothels and descend therewith to the almshouse, prison, or the gallows. The female moral reformers, in sum, anticipated the dangers of unbridled sexuality in the fluid circumstances of commercial and early industrial capitalism; and they constituted themselves as a force to regulate and control such threatening behavior.[9]

Female moral reform, then, constituted a concrete, specific attempt to exert woman's power. Led and initiated by women, it was a direct, collective, organized effort, which aimed to control behavior and change values in the community at large. Because female moral reform entailed explicit social action it is possible to examine its origins, impact and limitations as an exercise of woman's power. Several manifestations of this power will be identified. First of all, the case of moral reform suggests how women could use their social position in a specific time and place as leverage with which to influence others, including males. Secondly, within the Female Moral Reform Society, women can be seen giving direction to the future of their sex. Specifically, it will be argued that the members of the Female Moral Reform Society helped to lay the groundwork for the Victorian sexual code which placed particular stock in the purity of females. Finally the case of female moral reform will illustrate the proposition that associated women were a force in history at large. In this instance women played a vital role in working out the ideology of sexual control which characterized the middle classes of the nineteenth-century city. Female moral reformers, it will be seen, clearly made history and reshaped aspects of the American sex/gender system. Yet their impact on the status of women was rife with ambiguities. In the end they used their social power to create a moral code which exacted particularly stringent sexual repression from their own sex.

How then did the women of the Female Moral Reform Society grasp the power to enact their program of purification? They began simply enough by activating the machinery of reform which had been operating in Oneida County for nearly a generation. One of the first endorsements of female moral reform was sent to *McDowall's Journal* by a matron calling herself "A Friend of my Species," who had arrived in Utica forty years before. For the benefit of her readers, McDowall described the correspondent as "a lady moving in the very first circle of society, a mother, a philanthropist, a Christian."[10] This writer, while anonymous to historians, was undoubtedly widely known among her Utica contemporaries. She might have been Sophia Clarke, founder of the city's Female Missionary Society and the Maternal Association, active abolitionist, and prominent member of the Presbyterian Church. Or, she may have been Mrs. Clarke's colleague, Sophia Bagg, the mistress of Bagg's Hotel who sat at the center of local society and founded the city's most august charitable institution, the Utica Orphan Asylum. Perhaps the identity of the "friend of the species" was the same as the unnamed woman who nearly rent apart the First Presbyterian church a few years previous when she censored a leading parishioner "on his political opinions." Regardless of individual identity, this matron, described as a "lady moving in the very first circle" was representative of a whole web of associations between women that had been growing and reinforcing itself since the first decade of the nineteenth century.

The oldest and strongest strand in this network linked together the members of the Presbyterian church. The female parishioners were assembled at the First Presbyterian Church of Utica in 1834 when Samuel Aiken, pastor and veteran revivalist, announced from the pulpit that "a whole tribe of libertines" was about to invade the city of Utica. Aiken then turned to the females of the congregation saying, "daughters of America! Why not marshall yourselves in bands and become a terror to evil doers."[11] It was not until three years later that the women of Utica put this plan into operation, forming their own chapter of the American Female Moral Reform Society. Two parishioners, Fanny Skinner and Paulina Wright, played the major leadership roles in the Utica chapter. Mrs. Skinner's ties to the local network of female associations went back to 1806 and the founding of the Female Charitable Society of Whitestown. The 1830s found her embroiled in abolitionism as well as moral reform, and exploiting her personal contacts in order to convince Angelina Grimké Weld to speak in Utica. Paulina Wright was a relative newcomer to Utica reform, yet she quickly found her way into the women's network as she peddled tracts and petitions for the Martha Washington Temperance Union as well as the Female Moral Reform Society. Her personal network of women's reform would also take her to the border of feminism. In 1836 she circulated petitions for the reform of married women's property rights in the company of Elizabeth Cady Stanton.[12] Again the trail of women's associations followed deeply rutted paths through local neighborhoods, churches, and reform circles.

Female moral reformers discovered a portal to public responsibility and power through the same social circle. Mrs. Whitellsey's letter to John McDowall in 1833 described a practice of moral reform which predated any formal association. Whenever she came in contact with defenseless young women, Mrs. Whitellsey resorted to this strategy: "I have either written a note or sent with them a messenger to such of my friends as might be able either to employ them themselves or direct them to others. Whether this course or some other equivalent is oftener pursued, many of the unfortunate victims of vice and wretchedness . . . would be greatly diminished." Mrs. Whitellsey was proposing that women could use the bonds of friendship which linked local households, that is, the existing female social network, as the mechanism of moral reform. The same device could be used to secure financial support for reform activity, as was inadvertently revealed by the editor of a local evangelical periodical. Charles Hastings wrote to the *Advocate of Moral Religion* (the periodical of the national organization) apologizing for his own inability to devote time to the worthy cause. He happily announced, however, that "A female in my family says she will go around among the families and see if she can't get something for your support." This door-to-door, woman-to-woman approach was also the means of expanding the ranks of reformers and influencing public opinion. The circulation of tracts and petitions was a routine of female organization in charities, temperance, and bible societies. In other words, female moral reform simply sent a new message, a new set of demands, through a familiar and personal network of comumnication.[13]

Faced with what they saw as an epidemic of vice, female moral reformers soon entertained the notion that more heroic measures were necessary; and they began to tread outside of their familiar social circles. They formed a visiting committee in 1841 which ventured into the more unseemly haunts of the town. Entering into some of the hovels of the poor, they met a sympathetic response among Utica's mothers and wives. Poor widows tearfully accepted their tracts and offered in return personal reports about sexual offenses and domestic crimes against women. The stories grew more lurid than a dime novel as these pious women of Utica encountered real-life cases of seduction and betrayal, of drunken and tyrannical husbands, and abused and battered wives. One of the visiting committee's informants told the sordid tale of her invalid neighbor. Night after night, the sick woman's husband took her nurse to his bed. This report like many others was accompanied by a remark which identified the offending man to his neighbors. "This man has the charge of a paper, the object of which is to uphold public morals," wrote the female reformer: "May we not ask how long shall men like this occupy responsible stations and be tolerated among Christian people?" Through the agency of the Female Moral Reform Society such stories transformed gossip into a public instrument of protest.[14]

The reports of the visiting committee also offered examples of militant assaults upon the forces of vice. One Utica matron became a heroine of moral reform after her unilateral attack on a local brothel. She told the following story. Her son had been keeping late hours night after night while she paced, prayed, and wept for his soul. Finally she could endure such passivity no longer: She marched straight to the nearby brothel, bounded up the stairs, pounded on the door of the chamber which harbored her son, and shouted that a constable was on his way. This enraged mother was hurled down the stairs by the brothel's owner, but she returned home to find a repentant son. It was stories like these that the officers of the Female Moral Reform Society had in mind when they reported that the monthly meeting had been "rendered highly useful and interesting from the reports of the visiting committee which have been replete with heart-stirring facts and appeals."[15]

Buoyed up by encounters such as these, the reformers became even more energetic and audacious. A committee of eight women secured between two and three thousand signatures on a petition to outlaw prostitution in 1841. Another woman visited twenty-two families, in a one-month period. Ultimately the membership of Utica's Female Moral Reform Society began to encroach upon the male centers of authority. One cadre of the movement marched to city hall and demanded statistics on sex offenders. Others accosted men of dubious character on the city streets and entered taverns to interrogate bartenders. The Female Moral Reform Society even took their cause into the courts. When a young servant woman came to the Society with a report of sexual exploitation by her employer, the members acted swiftly and de-

cisively in her defense. They brought the culprit to trial; provided
the victim with legal counsel, personal support, and a new job in a
respectable home. In this instance, the Utica Female Moral Reform
Society acted as a special police force and public prosecutor, whose
jurisdiction was sexual assaults on women. They had mobilized
not only to perform a community function once assigned to male
ministers and elders of the church, but they had also carried their
moral mission outside their own congregations and into the streets
and thoroughfares of Utica.[16]

In the process, the new female custodians of sexual morality also
altered the standards of propriety. Church trials were primarily
concerned with cases of adultery, that is the infidelity of married
men, and especially, women. The members of the Female Moral
Reform Society, however, were most concerned about the sexual
behavior of the young and unmarried and demanded stricter purity
from both their sons and daughters. Moral reformers repeatedly
lamented the lax standards of the recent past. For example, one
reformer noted that until recently a "young boy who was not
afraid to trifle with the most forward girls was esteemed above his
years and almost a man." Female moral reformers would not tolerate such permissive attitudes and attempted to purge local culture
of all suggestions of casual, lenient sexuality. The goal of moral
reform, as the minister of a largely female congregation put it, was
to eradicate all "unchaste feelings and licentious habits," not just
to condemn and punish sexual intercourse outside of marriage.
Toward this end, the Female Moral Reform Society instructed
women to "encourage both by precept and example, simplicity
with regard to dress and at their children's tables, that unseen
snares are not laid which shall lead to the vice we are striving to
exterminate."[17] They were, in other words, making connections
between a child's dress and diet and his or her disposition to sexual
indulgence in later life. The Female Moral Reform Society, as well
as the overlapping membership of the local maternal associations,
propounded methods of childcare which were designed to instill
sexual control in the very personalities of the rising generation.
They turned from external control of sexual behavior to an internalized repression of physical drives.

The women of the Female Moral Reform Society of Utica had
traveled a considerable ideological and social territory within a
few short years. They began simply by taking advantage of a
vacuum of moral authority in the commercial city and proceeded
to adapt traditional and previously male-directed methods of moral
surveillance to a new environment and their own interests (primarily
as mothers). By the early 1840s, they had revised the code of sexu-

al morality and created novel and forceful methods of circulating these revised standards. Coincidentally they had opened a new social space through which their sex could maneuver for power in the community.

The nature of their power is indicated by a major community conflict instigated by the female moral reformers of Utica in 1836 and 1837. The incident was one skirmish in a prolonged battle between the Female Moral Reform Society and the city's clerks. The moral reformers charged these youthful employees of stores and countinghouses with major responsibility for seduction in the city. When, for example, some members of the Society spotted the alleged perpetrators of some unnamed nocturnal infamy on a city thoroughfare, they jumped from their carriage and presented the offending clerks with a tract appropriately entitled "Run speak to that Young Man." In 1836 the Utica Society commissioned a Reverend Dodge to deliver a public lecture indicting the same class of young men on charges of licentiousness. The members of the Society were so pleased with Dodge's discourse that they published an endorsement of his remarks in the local newspaper. Suddenly they found themselves at the center of a raging local controversy. First a delegation of clerks held a public meeting and placed a newspaper advertisement to defend their good name. Then another group of citizens who also purported to represent the city's clerks rose to concur with Dodge's opinion.[18]

These two broadsides displayed a growing cleavage in antebellum sexual ideology. The supporters of female moral reform proposed an old-fashioned solution to the problem of sexual license in the commercial sector of the local economy. They recommended that employers assume the responsibility for overseeing the private behavior of their clerks; and they proposed that this obligation be written into a formal contract between the merchant and his young workers, just as in the ancient practices of indenture and apprenticeship, and on that same principle of paternal surveillance which once prevailed in stable farm households. In other words, these supporters of female moral reform seemed to hark back to more traditional methods of controlling sexual behavior. They had been compelled to announce their position, however, by the actions of a novel social organization, a band of reforming females who were considerably more sophisticated in their thinking about sexual questions. The clerk faction, on the other hand, rejected both paternal control of sexual behavior and the zealotry of the female reformers. As they saw it, "one of the first lessons to be learned by young men is to carry their lives and the regulator of their conduct in their own bosoms" independently of the commands of their superiors or the moral pressure of evangelizing women. Theirs was a highly individualistic and liberal position, which proclaimed the rights of private conscience.

Analysis of the signatories of these two lists reveals that these differences in sexual attitudes reflected the divergent social status of the two factions. The clerks who were appalled by Dodge's sermon garnered support from their employers and hence some of the city's largest and most influential merchants. The bulk of the signatories of the second resolution, that in support of female moral reform, turned out to be neither clerks nor the employers of clerks. In fact the largest single occupational group represented on this second document was that of artisans. The proponents and opponents of female moral reform also differed markedly in their family status. The opponents were not only clerks, but also boarders, and very often residents of the largest and most impersonal lodging houses and hotels of Utica. The allies of the Female Moral Reform Society, on the other hand, tended to reside with their biological families. Even among the minority who called themselves boarders, a significant proportion still shared a household with either their parents or their employers. In sum, the Utica Female Moral Reform Society had raised issues which divided the population by occupation as well as pattern of residence. It pitted artisans who favored a more traditional household structure against merchants and clerks who had chosen the residential pattern germane to a thriving commercial town, namely boarding.[19]

Still the fact remains that both factions and a substantial portion of the community's leadership, were forced to respond to issues that had been introduced into public debate by an organized group of women. The clerks in fact felt obliged to endorse many of the values expounded by the Female Moral Reform Society. They advertised their own chastity and proclaimed it a young man's "highest interest" and "most valuable capital." The financial establishment of Utica soon issued similar demands for sexual self-control. During the 1840s, the Mercantile Agency (forerunner of Dun & Bradstreet) sentenced many a young man to business failure by denying credit on the basis of a "bad reputation" or "running after the women."[20] In the risky enterprises of the aggressively capitalistic town of Utica, self-control was one predictor of financial prudence, and soon became a measure of middle-class respectability. It would become even more important as the city industrialized after 1845 and as more and more young men and women were permanently exiled from the farms and artisan workshops where fathers once enacted direct sanctions against the sexual irregularities of their children. The progeny of native-born artisans and farmers would increasingly find themselves in the more solitary and insecure circumstances represented by the city clerks of the 1830s. The ideology of individual internalized sexual control first formulated and most aggressively publicized by female moral reformers eased young women and men through this transition from farm to city, from the family economy to individualized occupations. In the end then, the history of the Utica Female Moral Reform Society suggests that women could play a central and initiating role in the transformation of class and ideology. They devised and implemented sexual standards and practices which would distinguish the urban middle class from their artisan and farming parents.

In sum, the events of 1837 provide a public illustration of how a few active, organized, well-situated women could exert power in history. They had a direct effect on the opinions of men and had found leverage that extended beyond their households, outside the women's networks and across the social and economic divisions within the city. In achieving their goals, the female moral reformers demonstrated a distinctive variety of women's power. This power did not take the covert and privatized form which nineteenth-century writers venerated as "women's influence." Rather the women of the Moral Reform Society set social standards, commanded public attention, and caused a major commotion right in the center of the local social system.

Their power is attributable not merely to the energy and ingenuity of the women involved, but also to the hospitable environment of a small commercial city in the antebellum period. These women were still located in relatively close proximity to the centers of public power. Fanny Skinner was particularly well-situated in relation to the male leadership of the youthful city. The instigator of the male defense of Utica Female Moral Reform in 1837 was Cyrus Hawley, a clerk who happened to reside in the boarding house full of young lawyers which Skinner had managed for over a decade. But women's influence was not limited to such domestic associations. Most importantly, it extended to a rich social network based in the long-term, habitual cooperation of women in church and reform activities. The collective power of these groups, finally, was situated in easy reach of the arenas in which the male leaders of the city jostled for authority. In the 1830s and early 40s, the polity of Utica was still composed largely of innumerable associations of men.

Informal networks not so different from the Utica Female Moral Reform Society, made decisions on everything from political candidates to the founding of factories. Accordingly, a well-organized women's network, operating parallel to these male associations, had at least a fighting chance of affecting the policies and opinions of the community at large. These historical conditions, as well as the social form of the voluntary association, confused the boundaries between public and private life, thus allowing women to form circles of influence outside their homes and put ideological and moral pressure on the male authorities of the public sphere. In Oneida County in the 1830s and 40s as in similar cases described by anthropologists, this muting of the barrier between private and public life seems to have enhanced the power of women within their communities.[20]

Neither these conditions nor the American Female Moral Reform Society would survive for very long. The last notice of an active local chapter of the Utica Society appeared in 1845, at about the same time that the city's first steam-powered cotton factory was put into operation, and just as the town was inundated with unskilled workers hailing from Ireland, Germany, and the British Isles. By mid-century, Utica had become a city of over twenty thousand inhabitants with a major industrial sector, and increasingly segregated pattern of residence. Once the old commercial community had become hopelessly fractured by ethnic and class differences, a band of Protestant women could no longer presume to make moral pronouncements for the city at large. Concomitantly, as Utica and Oneida County became more closely integrated into the national economic and political system, vital decisions were transferred from the neighborhood to a formidable city hall and then on to Washington and Wall Street, that is, to a remote, more formalized public sphere. The local conditions which allowed female moral reform to obtain this position of social power did not survive into a second generation.

This is not to say that the movement ended with a quiet failure in the backwaters of social history. Such a thesis can be rebutted by several arguments. First of all, the members of the female moral reform societies of Oneida County were willing participants in the destruction of their own organization. In fact the disappearance of the society can be interpreted as a measure of successful sex reform. The Utica association disbanded in the midst of a quarrel over whether or not to hold a convention in nearby Clinton. Some of the members deemed it improper to conduct a public discussion of sexual matters in a town full of young seminary and college students.[21] It would seem that the Female Moral Reform Society had become caught up in its own propaganda, converted by its own increasingly exacting standard of propriety, which in the end prescribed almost complete reticence about sexual questions. Furthermore, the sexual reform movement did not end even with the demise of the Society. The banners of purity which its members once hurled in the streets now paraded through popular culture. Wherever the young men and women of the 1850s might travel their path would be strewn with admonitions and expectations of sexual continence. The *Advocate of Moral Reform* itself survived the collapse of local chapters of the American Female Moral Reform Society and continued to propagate the ideology of sexual control.

That ideology had become increasingly detached from organized women's networks. The *Advocate of Moral Reform* soon presumed an alternative social mechanism through which women could control sexual behavior, that is, through the private relationships of wives and especially mothers. The *Advocate* was happy to announce that moral reform now took place "where it should begin, in the right instruction of children." The journal's editors embraced the same doctrine of women's domestic influence celebrated in the ladies' magazines of the era: "A mother's love will accomplish more than anything else except omnipotence."[22] From the first, female moral reformers had placed special emphasis on maternity. In fact they were among the first and most forceful exponents of women's glorified role as the socializers of children. With the dissipation of local associations after 1845, women were left stranded in this isolated private sphere which the reformers themselves had done so much to cultivate. In the last analysis, Victorian women were guided into domestic confinement by members of their own sex. Such is the convoluted and ironic history of this example of the power of women's networks.

This history can be instructive for contemporary feminists. It suggests, first of all, that women can find sources of organizational strength at the local level. The formal and national organizational structures which eluded the female moral reformers and which still have a fragile existence in today's women's movement can be strengthened and reinforced by connections with the everday associations and informal social networks of local and neighborhood women. In fact, such a bridge between local networks and national organization still exercises substantial social power. It is, however, the New Right which has proven particularly successful in utilizing such power, but for antifeminist purposes. Through neighborhood organization and affiliation with local and national churches, these women of the 1970s are conducting yet another campaign to control sexual mores: attacking homosexuality, fighting abortion and the ERA, and venerating the heterosexual nuclear family. Furthermore, like the moral reformers of the 1830s and 40s, the women of the New Right have come to public prominence at a time of major social and sexual change, when for example, the rising divorce rate threatens to sever the ties between husbands and wives nearly as frequently as children were separated from parents by the frenetic geographical mobility of the nineteenth century. Now, as then, some women are reacting to this crisis by defending the domestic institutions which seem to offer them security along with inequality. The rise of the New Right, like the power of female moral reform may omen yet another readjustment of the sex/gender system with dubious consequences for women. In fact, it prompts some skepticism as to whether women's culture and female networks, which continue to be rooted largely in the relations of housewives and mothers, can generate much more than reflexive and defensive, rather than critical, responses to social and familial change.[23]

It should be clear, at any rate, that not every incident and every species of women's social and historical power merits our applause. It is the use of that power which concerns feminists. In the case of female moral reform, the laudable ability to maneuver for social influence fell short of the feminist goal of subverting the restrictions and inequality delegated to women by the American sex/gender system. The power of women's networks, be it manifest in female moral reform or the New Right, deserves more than either congratulations or condemnation. It requires serious, critical attention to both its historical permutations and diverted feminist possibilities.

NOTES

I would like to thank Bert Hansen, the editors of *Feminist Studies*, and especially Judy Stacey for their help in revising this article.

[1] These ideas were raised and debated at the session "The Legacy of Mary Ritter Beard," chaired by Ann J. Lane, at the Fourth Berkshire Conference on the History of Women, Mount Holyoke, Mass., August 1978.

The concept of the sex/gender system is taken from Gayle Rubin, "The Traffic in Women: Notes on the 'Political Economy' of Sex," *Toward an Anthropology of Women*, ed. Rayna Reiter (New York: Monthly Review Press, 1975), pp. 157-211.

[2] Carroll Smith-Rosenberg, "Beauty and the Beast and the Militant Woman: A Case Study in Sex Roles and Social Stress in Jacksonian America," *American Quarterly* 23 (October 1971): 562-84; Barbara J. Berg, *The Remembered Gate: Origins of American Feminism* (New York: Oxford University Press, 1978).

[3] The exact population figures for Utica are as follows: 1820–2972; 1830–8323; 1840–12,782; 1850–17,565; 1860–22,529. The changing occupational structure of the city is represented in the following table:

	Merchants Manufacturers	Professionals	Shopkeepers	White Collar	Artisan	Unskilled/ Factory
1828	11.1%	4.8%	12.5%	4.8%	46.1%	14.1%
1845	2.7%	10.2%	11.9%	10.2%	45.4%	20.2%
1855	2.9%	8.6%	6.6%	8.6%	40.9%	24.1%

[4] Whitney Cross, *The Burned-Over District: The Social and Intellectual History of Enthusiastic Religion in Western New York* (Ithaca: Cornell University Press, 1950); Mary P. Ryan, "A Women's Awakening: Revivalistic Religion in Utica, New York, 1800 to 1840," *American Quarterly*, forthcoming.

[5] See *McDowall's Journal*, January, March, May, July and November, 1833, for correspondence from Utica.

[6] Only thirty-four female moral reformers were identified by name, and only nineteen of these could be traced to the city directories. Of this latter group, six were married to merchants or shopkeepers, five to professionals, two to artisans: two were seamstresses and four had neither occupations nor employed husbands. Seven single women, as well as wives and widows were found in the same group. This range of class and marital status is the widest of any of the reform groups studied.

[7] Daniel Scott Smith and Michael Hindus, "Premarital Pregnancy in America, 1640-1971: An Overview and Interpretation," *Journal of Interdisciplinary History* 5 (1974-75): 537-70.

[8] "The Session Records of the First Presbyterian Church," First Presbyterian Church Utica, New York, Volume 3, December 3, 1834; December 17, 1834; January 2, 1835; July 2, 1835.

[9] *Advocate of Moral Reform*, June 15, 1843; February 1, 1838; September 15, 1837.

[10] *McDowall's Journal*, November, 1833.

[11] Samuel C. Aiken, "Moral Reform" (Utica: R. R. Shepard, 1834), pp. 8-9.

[12] Information about Fanny Skinner is drawn from scattered references in local histories, church records, and reform society publications; for a biographical sketch of Paulina Wright see, Alice Felt Tyler, "Paulina Wright Davis," *Notable American Women 1607-1950: A Biographical Dictionary*, 3 vols. (Cambridge, Mass.: Harvard University Press, 1974), 1: 444-45.

[13] *McDowall's Journal*, June 1834; *Advocate of Moral Reform*, February 7, 1836; February 22, 1836.

[14] *Advocate of Moral Reform*, September 15, 1842.

[15] Ibid., July 1, 1842.

[16] Ibid., December 15, 1841; April 1, 1844.

[17] *McDowall's Journal*, June 1834; *Advocate of Moral Reform*, February 15, 1840; July 30, 1840.

[18] *Oneida Whig*, December 27, 1836; January 27, 1837; February 14, 1837.

[19] The occupations and residences of the parties to the Moral Reform Controversy of 1836 and 1837 are summarized in the following table:

	Supporters of Female Moral Reform	Opponents of Female Moral Reform
Total Number Identified	118	50
Occupations		
Merchants/ Manufacturers	22.9%	2%
Shopkeepers/ Farmers	13.6%	4%
Professionals	17.8%	12%
Clerks	9.3%	72%
Artisans	36.4%	10%

	Supporters of Female Moral Reform	Opponents of Female Moral Reform
Residence		
Home of Own	78.3%	11.8%
Boards with Relatives or Employers	3.3%	9.8%
Boards Alone	18.6%	78.4%

[20] Rayna Reiter, "Men and Women in the South of France, Public and Private Domains," *Toward an Anthropology of Women*, Rayna Reiter, ed., pp. 252-82; Michelle Zimbalist Rosaldo, "Woman, Culture, and Society: A Theoretical Overview," *Woman, Culture and Society*, Michelle Zimbalist Rosaldo and Louise Lamphere, eds. (Stanford, Calif.: Stanford Stanford University Press, 1974), pp. 17-42.

[21] *Advocate of Moral Reform,* September 15, 1845.

[22] Ibid., August 1838; August 1835.

[23] The parallels between female moral reform and the New Right were brought to my attention during the discussion of this paper at the Women and Power Conference.

6 "The Men Are as Bad as Their Masters...": Socialism, Feminism and Sexual Antagonism in the London Tailoring Trade in the 1830s

BARBARA TAYLOR

> "However loudly the men may bellow for their own
> liberties, they will never bestow what they obtain
> upon woman until she demands it from her masters,
> as they have done for theirs; and whenever that
> struggle arrives, the men will be as tenacious of
> giving up their absurd domination as is any other
> power of relinquishing its authority...."
>
> Editorial, *The Pioneer*, May 31, 1834

This essay tells the beginning of a long story, which hasn't come to an end, and most of a short one, which ended almost a century and a half ago. The unfinished story is the history of socialist-feminism in Britain, of which we have here the contribution of the Owenites, the "utopian" socialists of the 1830s and 40s. The short story is a tale of conflict between women and men workers in a trade riven by sexual competition. The two stories connect in London in the early 1830s, when the issue of female labor in the tailoring trade was fought out within a wider struggle over the role of women in the Owenite-inspired "general-union" movement. Voices were raised, demands formulated, analyses proferred which revealed key features of sexual subordination within the early nineteenth-century working class. The issues which resulted from that subordination were pushed into the middle of fledgling labor politics. At that moment, if only briefly, the "Woman Question" and

the class question were connected in ways which demanded new—
"utopian" solutions.

For too long the histories of socialism and feminism have been
written as if both were homogeneous traditions, each bearing little
or no relation to the other. Socialism as the historic march of the
male proletariat; feminism as the bourgeois-egalitarian protest of
middle-class women: small wonder that there appeared to have
been so few points of contact between them. With the recent work
of feminist historians, however, this picture has begun to shift and
alter.[1] Patterns of shared impulses, ideas, and strategies have begun
to emerge, revealing connections between class struggle and sex
struggle which must ultimately lead to the rewriting of both their
histories—and assist in the transformation of both their futures. It
is as a contribution to that collective political project that this essay
has been written.

Two final introductory points: first, unlike most accounts of the
early socialist movement in Britain, the figure of Robert Owen—
factory-reformer-turned-world-reformer, and so on—barely appears
in this essay. Individuals do not a movement make, and the movement which bore Owen's name had far less to do with his ideas or
activities than with the maturation of radical consciousness and
organization in the early nineteenth century working class. Second,
although Owenism was an extremely important force in class politics in the period which we are discussing, it was by no means a
majority strategy within the radical working class. Far more widespread was the support given to the campaigns for parliamentary
reform in the early 1830s, which developed into the Chartist movement in the later part of the decade. Inside and outside these other
struggles (for many Owenites were also democratic activists), socialism remained the ideology of a minority, albeit a very vocal and
influential minority. With this in mind, let us meet them, hear
their ideas, and witness their early struggles.

The history of the Owenite movement divides roughly into three
periods. The first was the early cooperative phase of 1829-32, when
small societies of workers all over Britain established trading and
manufacturing associations based on collectivist principles and
aimed at accumulating sufficient funds for the establishment of
rural Communities of Mutual Association. The second period included the militant trade union struggles of 1833-34, which culminated in the establishment and demise of the Grand National Consolidated Trades Union (G.N.C.T.U.) in mid-1834. The final decade included intense propagandistic and organizational activity
inaugurated by the establishment of the "Association of All Classes

of All Nations" (A.A.C.A.N.) shortly after the collapse of the
G.N.C.T.U. At the height of its strength, the A.A.C.A.N. (or Rational Society, as it was later called) had sixty-five branches in all
parts of the country; many with their own schools, libraries, and
"Halls of Science." The A.A.C.A.N. produced dozens of newspapers and millions of tracts, employed some twenty Social Missionaries, and sponsored lectures by hundreds of voluntary publi-
cists. It was also responsible, directly and indirectly, for the establishment of a number of "utopian" communities, the largest one
being Harmony, in Hampshire. "There is scarcely a town of any
magnitude in which Socialism has not taken root," the conservative *Liverpool Standard* told its readers gloomily in 1839, an exaggerated but not wholly improbable estimate of Owenite influence at the time.[2]

Although each of these phases of the movement produced different organizational emphases, they were linked not only by a
large and fairly continouus core membership, but also by a revolutionary socialist purpose which ran like an ideological backbone
down through all Owenism's practical developments. As one of
its advocates wrote in 1833, the movement embodied "a spirit of
combination . . . of which there has been no example in former
times. . . ."

The object of it is the sublimest that can be conceived, namely—to establish
for the productive classes a complete dominion over the fruits of their own
industry. . . . Reports show that an entire change in society—a change amount-
ing to a complete subversion of the existing 'order of the world'—is contem-
plated by the working classes. They aspire to be at the top instead of the
bottom of society—or rather that there should be no bottom or top at all.[3]

From the tiny cooperative shop to the most grandiose schemes
for Social Communities, this promise of a "world turned upside
down" fueled every Owenite venture, transforming even the most
prosaic activities into steps on the road to the New Moral World.
But it was not only the class system which was to be overturned
en route. For unlike many of the socialist organizations which
grew up after it, the Owenite strategy had at its center the abolition
of *all* relations of power and subordination: capitalist to worker,
but also parent to child, old to young, and, above all, man to woman. "Whatever affects the condition of one sex, must, I conceive,
affect the condition of the other," a socialist woman wrote in 1839:

But a woman has been the slave of a slave. . . . What is the result of [this] ? . . .
To create, by their arrangements, individual interest, till brothers and sisters,
husbands and wives, look on each other with jealousy . . . to set up one half

of the poor people against the other half, to subdue them and make them quiet. . . .

But . . . 'changes of no ordinary kind are at hand.' I perceive, now that through the circulation of truth we are progressing towards the mansion of happiness, which, when gained, will . . . give emancipation to every human being from one end of the earth to the other . . . my tears flow when I compare this scene of confusion and opposition to that tranquil state of existence. . . .[4]

This commitment to the "emancipation of every human being" both expressed and transcended an earlier style of democratic radicalism. The feminism of the Owenite movement was part of the ideological inheritance from eighteenth-century advocates of *egalité* who had rested their own case for women's emancipation on the abstract right of all "reasonable" creatures to self-determination. "Who made man the judge, if woman partake with him of the gift of reason?"[5] But along with this intellectual case for female equality, the early socialists had also inherited the political struggles in which feminist demands had been articulated, a context which had important implications for their own theories on the Woman Question. Let us move back a few decades to look at these developments.

Modern British feminism was born into an ideological climate in which even relatively modest political claims were tarred with the brush of Jacobin revolt. The publication of Mary Wollstonecraft's *Vindication of the Rights of Women* only shortly after her vigorous defense of the French Revolution immediately led to the equation of feminism with social insurrection, the heritage—in Burke's felicitous phrase—of the "revolutionary harpies of France, sprung from night and hell." As waves of counterrevolutionary anxiety swept through upper-class homes in England, they brought in their wake the Evangelical revival with all its conservative implications for women. Whatever bourgeois platform feminism had once had (and it had been a narrow and fragile one) now crumbled beneath the weight of religious dogmas of "domestic duty." Feminism moved well outside the pale of genteel opinion; or, as one popular woman's magazine told its middle-class readership in 1798:

The champions of female equality, who were as inimical to the happiness and interest of the sex, as those who preached up the doctrine of liberty and equality to the men, are no longer regarded as sincere and polite friends. . . .[6]

But with the loss of polite supporters, new advocates were acquired. The success of the Revolution had given new heart and muscle to growing working-class movement in England, and *The Vindication* was heralded as a major radical text. It was, according to working-class newspapers like the *Black Dwarf* and *The Republican*, the feminine equivalent of Tom Paine's *Rights of Man*, a libertarian manifesto which dared to extend the demands of the democatic Revolution into the very fabric of human relationships. "Spirit of . . . Mary Wolstonecraft [sic]," a "Citizen" wrote exultantly to one of these papers, "your varied brilliancies of genius . . . will alone rescue your sex! . . ."[7]

Of course, there were middle-class progressives who continued to support women's demands, notably many utilitarians. But even among them, this advocacy was so nervous and feeble that it actually served to radicalize the more militant feminists in their ranks. The first important text of socialist-feminism, for example, was William Thompson and Anna Wheeler's *Appeal of One-Half the Human Race* (1825), which was written in direct response to the failure of the Benthamites to support women's suffrage and then more generally against the weakness of their entire reformist program. No legal or political changes in women's position, Thompson and Wheeler argued, would substantially alter women's status until the underlying sources of inequality—private property and the patriarchal family—were abandoned, and Communities of Mutual Association established.[8] Or as one Owenite calling herself "W.W.P." wrote several years later:

Under the withering influence of competition for wealth, mammon worship and an aristocracy of birth . . . very little progress can be made in the attainment of true liberty for women. . . . The only way left . . . is to organize small societies on a better system, as examples and patterns to the rest of the world—so that men and women may meet in equal communion, having equal rights and returns for industry . . . and equal attention given to the cultivation of their whole nature, physical, moral and intellectual.[9]

The language was still that of the radical democrats, but where they had demanded social equality on the basis of abstract "natural rights," Owenite feminists substituted a far more concrete and revolutionary concept of equality based on the elimination of the material and ideological sources of social hierarchy. The ideological link between socialism and feminism was being forged.

In the 1830s and 1840s this link was strengthened in the hundreds of books, tracts, lectures, and newspapers published by the movement which discussed everything from collective childcare in the new communities to the phrenological evidence for women's innate mental superiority over men. Ideas which initially had been held by only a few radical intellectuals were taken out to mass audiences. In London in 1833, for example, up to three meetings a week were being held on "women's rights" with large audiences reported.[10] Outside London, the visit of a feminist Owenite lecturer was an occasion which could bring out several thousand people, including many women who were sometimes reported "carrying their small children in their arms."[11]   The largest meetings were those held in the late 1830s and 1840s to discuss the Owenites' opposition to Christian marriage doctrine (particularly to the church's views on divorce), and these often became vast arenas of public debate in which women fully participated: cheering the Owenite lecturer and jeering her/his opponent (or sometimes vice versa); voting on whether divorce should be legalized; and on one occasion, seizing the moment to denounce a philandering husband spotted across the hall.[12]   The scale of female enthusiasm for all this argumentation and propaganda horrified middle-class observers: "The humbler ranks of society lie open and exposed to the full effects of this most frightful malaria," wailed *The Christian Lady's Magazine*; "Hundreds of rooms re-echo every night . . . to such blasphemies as were never heard, while crowds of English females applaud them!"[13]

It is beyond the scope of this essay to trace all the threads which formed this feminist commitment, or to follow its fortunes—both theoretically and practically—throughout the entire history of the early socialist movement. I will introduce just a few essential points before going on to concentrate on the issues and struggles of one period, the general-union movement of the early 1830s.

If by "utopianism" one is referring to the grandiose scale of a strategy, rather than its viability, the feminism of the Owenites was a direct result of their utopianism. It was precisely because this was a movement committed to revolutionizing all aspects of social life—not only economic and political relations—that it was capable of nourishing existing feminist traditions, developing and transforming them into a wider radical vision. *Why* the movement developed in this way will become clearer in the second half of the essay, as we consider its roots in the social and economic upheavals of the early nineteenth century. But it is worth noting two preliminary points here. First, the scope of the Owenite solution was a necessary response to the scale of the problems faced by its advocates, including shifting boundaries of sexual roles at work and in family life. Second, in arguing for the reform of "human character" as well as human institutions, Owen himself served to reinforce concerns already current at a popular level. The making of a socialist society, he impressed upon his followers, depended as much on the creation of human beings who were fit to live "harmoniously" as it did on the material changes afforded by communal life.[14]   Or as one "Old Co-operator" reminded his brothers and sisters:

It cannot be too often impressed upon persons entering into co-operative associations, that . . . their disposition to perform a fair portion of . . . labour . . . is not all which is required. . . . The mind must undergo a corresponding change; perhaps I cannot express it better than in the language of Scripture, 'They must be borne again. . . .'[15]

What is more central to this "rebirth" than the reorganization of the most intimate areas of human existence, the family and sexual relations? Owen himself devoted a long series of lectures to discussing the need to replace existing family structures—and the sexual hierarchy embodied in them—with the new collective arrangements of the social communities.[16] Rules drawn up for these communities promised women not only an equal place in all revolutionized social institutions, but also the intellectual and moral emancipation which such equality would make possible. "To be a good wife, nowadays," one socialist told an Owenite congress, "means nothing more than to be a good drudge." All this was to change:

The Socialists want women to be educated equal to themselves; they want to place women in such a position, as that the lecture-room, the ball-room, the study of the stars and earth, might be to her as to others, a source of amusement and pleasure. [cheers] They wished her no longer to be the inhabitant of the cellar and the kitchen. [cheers] [17]

Endless schemes for the collectivization of housework were devised, although most assumed that the responsibility for this communalized domestic labor would still remain with the women of the communities. Occasionally a real iconoclast would attack the sexual division of labor itself; interestingly, however, it was usually children who were suggested as appropriate substitutes for mundane household tasks. (This was following a suggestion made by the French socialist, Fourier, who argued that in a society organized around human predispositions the pleasure that children take in dirt could be put to a social purpose.) At no point was male responsibility for childcare proposed. But if this most intractable of "women's duties" was to remain the female prerogative, at least the Owenites were determined that it should not imply female dependency. In a society in which each labored for the whole, they explained, the economic basis of sexual hierarchy would be swept away. In 1840, a government spy reported on a speech delivered by one of the leaders of the community in Hampshire "in the open air, close to a large pig stye" in which the audience of local farmworkers was told to:

look at the women in our community; they are as women ought to be; educated in such a manner as to make them equal with men. . . . We have none but married women, but they are not tyrannised over by their husbands; no, they are equal with them; they are not depending on them for support; they derive their subsistence from a community which they admire and to which they contribute. . . . See, my friends, how happy we live; and look at your own miserable condition. . . .[18]

As innovative and important as such ideas were, however, they must be considered carefully from the point of view of source and context. Before leaving these general themes, then, let us pause to consider this final point: the complex class location of feminist doctrines within the popular movement as a whole.

Like the early intellectuals who had introduced feminism into the movement, a number of the women who addressed audiences or wrote on women's issues to the socialist press were from the middle class, or more accurately, from that ambiguous region inhabited by respectable ladies of smallish means. Journalists, writers, actresses, "stipendiary lecturers": many of these were women who by choice or necessity found themselves struggling to forge out an independent living in a society where that was made acutely difficult both by lack of work opportunities and the middle-class's disapproving attitude toward female employment. The combined effect of this was often to make such women economically and socially marginal: once outside the walls of respectable married life it was all too easy for these women to find themselves on the slippery slope down into poverty, insecurity, and other unladylike difficulties. Far too many women throughout the nineteenth century went that route, and of these many became feminists.[19]

For some of these women, Owenism was no more than a platform from which to raise demands which the middle class—caught up in the new conservative sexual morality—no longer wished to hear. And even for those who, through a combination of their own ambiguous class status and a genuine conversion to socialist ideas, came to identify sexual emancipation with social emancipation, older ways of thinking remained. Poised as they were between the earlier "Rights of Women" debate and the new communist project of a largely working-class movement, their writings and lectures displayed all the strains and contradictions inherent in an ideology in transition: harkening back to Wollstonecraft and her eighteenth-century sisters for polemics against feminine "idleness" or bourgeois "property marriage," they would then publish these in journals read by women and men for whom idleness was an unknown luxury and "property" the wages one lives on.[20] Looking for solutions to economic dependence they would urge "industrial emancipation" on women for whom hard work was the only thing they had enough

of. And most important, faced with a movement whose female
contingent was largely working class, they frequently reiterated a
view of women's position which made gender the sole category of
analysis. Thompson and Wheeler's *Appeal* set the tone: women
were everywhere and at all times "the moveable property, and ever-
obedient servant to the bidding of man . . ."; "his involuntary breeding machine and household slave. . . ."[21] The analogy with black
slavery was made continuously. "Is not the world a vast prison,
and all women born slaves?" Wollstonecraft's fictional heroine,
Maria, had sighed, and Owenite feminists sighed with her five decades later.[22] But when they came to specify this slavery it was
often in terms of middle-class social relationships, universalized
into "women's condition."

This does not make the ideas less important, or the socialist solution less valid. But it does mean that in tracing the transmission of
those ideas into the popular movement, we must become sharply
aware of class context. The same words on a new platform could
acquire very different meanings: the language of sexual equality
used in a working-class context, for example, could challenge certain sexual boundaries which did not even exist within the middle
class, and vice versa. I am not suggesting, as will become obvious
in what follows, that it was any less meaningful a demand for
working-class women, only that it addressed specific forms of
sexual hierarchy, intervened in particular sorts of struggles.

The emergence of just such a working-class context can be seen
quite clearly in the Owenite movement in the early 1830s. As the
popular base of the movement expanded, new voices joined those
of the radical intellectuals who had initially introduced feminism into the movement. Advertisements for public lectures listed as speakers not only established feminists such as Anna Wheeler or Eliza Ma-
caulay but a "Female Operative" or a "London Mechanic's Wife."[23]
Letters from such women began to appear in the Owenite press,
usually in the awkward, elaborate prose of the slightly educated, always with the painful earnestness of those struggling to articulate
ideas which they had once hardly dared think, much less express. A
report of a meeting of Owenite workers in London described an inter-
ruption by a woman who rose and "in a kind of whisper" observed

that a great deal was said of the slavery of the working classes, and of the inad-
equate wages of the man, but never a word of the slavery of the poor women,
who were obliged to toil from dawn to midnight for seven or eight shillings a
week.[24]

"This is the still small voice of woman, which we fear must be suppressed for a season till man be served," commented *The Crisis*

condescendingly, adding "but yet it will speak like thunder and make even the male slaves blush to think they also have been tyrants."[25]

As the movement grew and new platforms for women developed, however, the suppression of that voice became impossible. In the rest of this essay we will look at the most important period in this development, the trade union phase of Owenism. I should emphasize here that in choosing this period I am not trying to suggest that only the issues surrounding work and wages were of interest to working-class women; certainly the rest of the Owenite story—with its campaigns over marriage, women's right to education, and so on—show this to be manifestly false. I have chosen to concentrate on the Owenite union involvement for two reasons. First, it was in this phase of the movement that the voices of working-class women discussing both sex and class oppression can be heard most clearly. Second, I suspect there is a sense in which "economic" struggles are always a sort of test of the feminism of a movement. It is one thing to add new issues concerning women—sex, marriage, and family—to an already-existing class strategy; it is quite another to transform even the most fundamental assumptions of that strategy on the basis of a feminist perspective. With that in mind, let us follow the Owenites into the general union movement of the early 1830s.

The class basis of the Owenite movement was the skilled working class: workers in the old hand trades or in the new skilled jobs created by industrialization (especially textile spinning). Tailors, shoemakers, coopers, silk-weavers, lace-makers, strawbonnet-makers—these were not the "laboring poor" but artisans and the wives of artisans, men and women with lively cultural and intellectual traditions as well as a history of political involvements. Like the men of this sector, most of the women had some small amount of education, worked in some gainful employment (either assisting their husbands or on their own), and shared in a culture which prided itself on sobriety, intellectualism, and—increasingly—political sophistication.[26]

Support for the Ownite strategy reached a high point among these working people in the period immediately after the enactment of the 1832 Reform Bill. As bitter disillusionment with the restricted franchise contained in the Bill spread among those working-class militants who had fought so hard for its introduction, increasing numbers of them shifted their hopes away from parliamentary reform toward the economic changes which, the Owenites promised, would undermine ruling-class power at its roots. Or as one movement ideologue put it,

The loud-mouthed Bill bestowed no vote upon us, but what of that? We have as large a suffrage as we care for, for if our employers vote against our interests, they shall not have our labour.[27]

It was as the "class of producers," not as the "citizenry," that working people had power, the socialists explained. What did they want with politicians and parliamentarians? It was out of this emerging class consciousness that workers in one industry after another began to look toward each other for the formation of "one big union," one mass expression of united class interest. Between 1818 and 1833 a number of attempts had been made to establish just such a General Union, but all had remained small and regionalized. Now, with conditions in the trades deteriorating and the failure of the Reform Bill, many believed the time had come: "All minds are now directed to the formation of one great National Union," one Owenite journalist told his readers in October 1833.[28]

The movement which did finally develop among these workers was based on an extraordinary blend of the defensive and the visionary. For many—probably the majority—who became involved, it ultimately represented no more than an attempt to move past isolated acts of militancy toward the wider network of solidarity and financial support necessary to sustain successful strike actions. Higher wages, shorter hours, and the right to organize to achieve them: these were the most many unionists sought. But alongside them stood an increasing number for whom the Owenites' greater hopes had acquired a new credibility and urgency. Through unity, the socialists argued, they would acquire not only higher wages and shorter hours but the capital with which cooperative workshops and factories could be established. Excess profits would be abolished, profiteering capitalists superseded or forced out by competition with worker-controlled enterprises, a new economic system built from the materials of the old. Or as one convert to this strategy expressed it:

The Trades Union will not only strike for less work and more wages, but they will ultimately ABOLISH WAGES, become their own masters, and work for each other; labour and capital will no longer be separate but they will be indissolubly joined together in the hands of the workmen and workwomen.[29]

In the Operative Builders' Union, it was claimed, "the opinion was definitely forming that [it] and the other unions which would grow up around it, would take over, in fact, the whole administration of the country,"[30] while the silk-workers at Derby announced the establishment of cooperative factories to the employers who had locked them out: "We have hitherto worked for you. . . . We shall henceforth work for ourselves."[31]   Owen himself saw the General Union as the industrial wing of a new world system—a scheme which was taken up and argued at length in the unionist press.[32] The leading newspaper of the movement, *The Pioneer*, told its readers excitedly at the height of the agitation that the unions would become embryos of the new world, each with its own government electing delegates to a central committee in turn forming "the Annual Parliament; and the King of England becomes President of the Trades' Union!"[33]

But alas for utopia: the general union which was finally established in 1834—the Grand National Consolidated Trades Union— was a short-lived conglomerate of both old and new unions, dominated by London craftsmen with tentacles of support spreading out into the Midlands, the Potteries, and the workshops of Lancashire. It was long on speeches, short on funds; different trades eyed each other with suspicion and soon accusations of misbehavior, short-sightedness, and stinginess began to occur. In the midst of this both employers and the government—who took the new union militancy very seriously indeed—began intensive persecution of known unionists and their supporters, culminating in the trial and transportation of six Dorchester laborers (the "Tolpuddle Martyrs") for taking a union oath. Intimidation and strikebreaking on this scale could not possibly be overcome by such a weak and divided organization, and the entire edifice crashed down only seven months after its inauguration.[34]

Women workers also participated in this brief and cataclysmic episode. At the height of the union movement, reports came in to the Owenite press of lodges of lace-makers, strawbonnet-makers, shoemakers, laundresses, milliners, stockingers and workers in other "female" trades. Regular women's union meetings were held at the Owenite center in London,[35] while metropolitan leaders traveled out to the provinces to report on progress among working women there. "I had the pleasure of opening a lodge of females at Worcester," ran one report from the glove-making district there, "and such had been the fright of the poor masters . . . that they had even endeavored to induce their servant-maids to sign a declaration against it; but they stated their inability to do this, inasmuch as they had previously signed a paper in favour of it."[36] Similar anxieties about growing union support among domestic servants were expressed by employers in other towns, while reports of successful strikes like that of the Kensington washerwomen ("they all demanded an advance of 1s. a day, with beer")[37] must have confirmed their worse fears of female insurrection.

One of the largest women's unions reported was that of the Lei-

cester stockingers, over one thousand strong. *The Pioneer* announced jubilantly that "the scandalous bye word of 'blue stock-
ing' which has been thrown at every intelligent woman who happened to have more sense than her stupid husband, has not deterred
the ladies of Leicester from uniting to obtain the advance of themselves and their kindred";[38] while a letter from a London workingwoman ("a member . . . of the vulgar mob") congratulated "the
ladies of Leicester" who "have set a noble example in commencing
so good a cause, in defiance of good or evil report, as I know that
women's opinions, generally speaking, are treated with contemptu-
ous ridicule by many men who thinking themselves infallible. . . ."[39]

But for all this proud rhetoric the number of female unions was
never very large. Nor would most have wielded much power, based
as they were in women who worked inside their own homes or in
small workshops and in trades which had never had the organizational strength of the old male "guilds." Nonetheless, for the wom-
en who became active in the unions, they obviously represented a
leap forward both in class consciousness and female self-assertion:
"You might as well think of hewing blocks of marble with a razor,
as think of preventing women from forming themselves in union,"
one wrote proudly.[40]

This militancy was based on a mixture of old traditions as well
as new styles of thought and action. Like the men, many of these
women would have been active in the parliamentary reform movement of only a few years before. Some also were in trades which
already had histories of union organization: the lace-makers of
Nottingham who joined the G.N.C.T.U., for example, had an impressive record of militant action,[41] as did the women glovemakers
of Worcester, whose violence in dealing with their opponents was
noted with awe by observers in the early years of the century.[42]
Violence, indeed, had been a common feature of female-dominated
mobilizations, and this too persisted into the general union: the
women who came out in the Derby silk-workers' strike, which
initiated the G.N.C.T.U., fought and stoned police and scabs. "A
poor woman is now in prison . . . for crying Ba! to a black sheep
. . . ," the Derby strikers reported.[43] But they also led mass marches
carrying banners inscribed "Union is Strength, Knowledge is
Power," joined the men in public meetings, and set up their own
union organization. A letter from one of these women appeared
in *The Pioneer*:

Be it known to the world that a female union is begun in Derby, and that the
tyrants have taken fright at it, and have brought forth a document for the
females to sign against union membership or *leave their employment*, not

only to those who are employed in the factory, but *to the servants in their
own* houses also. Here is a specimen of knavish tyranny; but, be it known
that we have refused to comply with their request. . . . In consequence of
this, there is a great number more added to the turn-out . . . Sisters! awake,
arise . . . form lodges in every town and hamlet. Mothers of families, and
maidens, come forward and join us in this our glorious cause, and we will
defy the power of our adversaries; and let the first lispings of your innocent
offspring be *union! union!*[44]

The style of militancy expressed here was also a mixture of old
and new. In particular, the appeal to the "mothers of families"
had been typical of women's mobilization throughout the eighteenth and early nineteenth centuries. In the Derby strike, as in
so many struggles throughout this period, it was not only workers
who fought the employers, but the entire community who came
out in their support. And it was then—as the mothers and wives
and sisters of strikers, as well as workers themselves—that women
went into the meetings and onto the streets, in a sort of militant
extension of women's duties. "I stand here as a woman, an *operative* and a *mother*," was the typical beginning of one speech delivered by a workingwoman in London in 1834,[45] while a letter
from a "London Mechanic's Wife" to the Owenite press in the
same year urged a full role for women in the "progressive march
of reform" on the grounds that "our natural and ardent attachment
to our tender young, would prompt us to use all our powers to obtain a far better state for the enslaved and degraded children of
labour. . . ."[46] Far from being a conservatizing influence, here the
responsibilities of motherhood drew women out of their homes to
act and speak in ways shocking to upper-class observers, used to
associating mothering with passivity and domestic confinement.
The "London Mechanic's Wife" went on to address such critics:

Shall the idiot-like, the stupid and usurious capitalists, tell us to look to our
domestic affairs, and say 'these we understand best'? We will retort on them
. . . that thousands of us have *scarce any domestic affairs to look after*, when
the want of employment on the one hand, or ill-requited toil on the other,
have left our habitations almost destitute. . . . Ah! fellow bondswoman . . .
may we live to see the whole of our sex exert themselves for their own, their
children's and their country's emancipation from the cruel bondage of physical and mental taskmasters![47]

It was impossible to "de-sexualize" the language of class oppression,
just as it was impossible for women to leave their sexual role behind
in order to enter struggles on identical terms with men. Sex and
class were inescapably interlocked, both in their lives and in their
thought.

This has always been (and remains) true of women workers; but its consequences for their consciousness have been far from uniform. Certainly working-class women in 1834 did not question the fundamental structure of sexual roles within the working class *per se*, nor could many find the words or even the ways of thinking with which to challenge the subordination embodied in those roles as well. But for others—a small but vocal group—sexual awareness had begun to connect with class militancy in new ways. In 1833, as the general-union agitation moved into high gear, *The Pioneer* opened a "Page for the Ladies" (which was later changed to "Women" when it was pointed out that "Ladies" was "too aristocratic"). The editor of the paper, a housepainter from Birmingham called James Morrison, was the husband of a feminist writer and lecturer in the movement. In starting the "Page" he urged women to use it as a medium through which to "express your grievances, air your wrongs, and plan your emancipation," while his wife Frances contributed letters which combined Wollstonecraftian views ("Maybe the time is not distant when the superiority of educated females will be acknowledged over those that are kept in blind and stupid ignorance. . . . The mother is the first to sow the seed of instruction . . . and if the seed is bad, what can we expect from the fruits?")[48] with protests like the following addressed to "The Women of the Working Classes":

Sir,—. . . It is time the working females of England began to demand their long-suppressed rights. . . . In manufacturing towns, look at the value that is set on woman's labour, whether it be skilful, whether it be laborious, so that woman can do it [sic]. The contemptible expression is, it is made by woman, and therefore cheap? Why, I ask, should woman's labour be thus undervalued? Why should the time and the ingenuity of the sex . . . be monopolized by cruel and greedy oppressors, being in the likeness of men, and calling themselves masters? Sisters, let us submit to it no longer. . . .[49]

It was as if a stopper had been lifted, allowing a sudden rush of words into the silence which surrounded the lives and consciousness of working-class women. Wages and conditions of work, the desire for education ("Men, in general, tremble at the idea of a reading wife. . . ."), the experiences of marriage and family life—all were raised in the "Woman's Page," often with timorous self-deprecation but sometimes with the force of long-suppressed anger. The Bible commanded husbands to love and honor their wives, wrote one old woman, "But how often is that pretended love converted into hatred . . ." and affection dissolved into recrimination and abuse: "What a bitter mixture for a poor woman to take! and if she offers the least resistance, it is thrust down her throat with his fist, possibly with the loss of a tooth or the spilling of a little of that blood which he thinks so inferior to his own. As he is lord of the castle, he is master and must be obeyed. . . ."[50]

In their editorials the Morrisons took up these and other issues, analyzing women's legal status, arguing for political rights, and quoting Wollstonecraft in favor of "educated motherhood." One long editorial analyzed economic relations within the working-class household:

If a working man should make thirty shillings a-week. [sic] He may drink [ten pints] if he pleases; go to a coffee-house every night, and read the papers, and bring in fifteen shillings a-week to keep home and pay the rent withal. *He has a right to do this*, for he makes the money. But what is the woman doing? She is working from morning till night at house-keeping; she is bearing children, and suffering all the pangs of labour, and all the exhaustion of suckling; she is cooking, and washing, and cleaning. . . . And all this is nothing; for she gets no wages. Her wages come from her husband; they are optional; he can give her either twenty shillings . . . or he can give her only ten. If she complain, he can damn and swear, and say, like the Duke of Newcastle, 'Have I not a right to do as I please with my own?' And it is high treason in women to re-sist such authority, and claim the privilege of a fair reward of their labour![51]

After centuries in which women's subordination had been des-cribed almost entirely in terms of bourgeois social relations, articles like these provided some of the first accounts of gender division within the working class. Owenism was like a bridge between that older tradition and a class-conscious feminism as yet only partially formulated, a tentative syntheses of the older views on sex-slavery with a new class specification of that oppression. Working-class women were, they quoted Shelley, the "slaves of slaves": depend-ent subordinates in marriage, secondary labor in the workplace, excluded or confined to a subordinate role in class organization. "The men educate us to obey them, and then make us slaves . . . and we shall find that we shall have to struggle as hard for our free-dom as they are struggling for theirs. . . ."[52]

Certainly the number of working-class women who found the words and courage in which to begin to make these connections remained very small. The "Women's Page" provides us only with a voluble handful; the Owenite movement as a whole with not very many more. And how many of these women then came to accept the Owenites' communist strategy as a solution, is impossible to judge. To look at other points in the history of the movement, particularly the huge controversy which blew up in the early 1840s over the future of marriage, would give a better chance to assess what such women thought of the whole utopian project; but here at least that is not the issue which immediately concerns us. For what we *can* see in the early 1830s is how women used the Owenite feminist presence within their own class movement to issue a challenge to the men in that movement. Standing on the platform provided by their Owenite supporters, using the language of militant unionism, they launched protests which took the "Woman Question" right across the central class issues of the day. "Allow me, Sir, to inform you, that there is a great number of men that cannot bear the idea of women's union, and yet they are unionists themselves," began one letter signed, "An Initiated Weaver's Wife":

Now, Sir, I will just ask those men one simple question; "do you know the fundamental principles of the noble cause you have embarked in?" You will surely say "yes;" well then, I say, act up to your professions, and if you can see that women stand in need of reform, extend your charity toward them, and do them justice. . . . We are only waiting for the signal to form our own lodges; and we will let them know, that woman, by her own exertions and intelligence will be free, and the very essence of freedom exhibit to the world; and her dastardly tyrants shall yet fall at her feet never more to triumph over her; therefore, they that are not for us are against us. . . .[53]

"There is a jealousy in the men against Female Unions," ran another letter, "What can be the cause of this but the tyrannical spirit of the male? . . . In these days, when servants are rising up against their masters . . . why should the spirit of tyranny still reside in the very servants themselves? . . . But it is clear enough from this whispering spirit of jealousy . . . that the men are as bad as their masters. . . ."[54]

The women's complaints were well-founded. Although the founding articles of the G.N.C.T.U. had contained a strong statement of support for female unionism, male unease or outright hostility was evident from the start. Many of the women's unions were completely segregated from the men's, even where they were employed in the same trade: a likely indication of the women's marginalization from decision making and the formulation of strategy. Certainly no woman emerged as a leader in a mixed context. At the same time, even these all-female unions were frowned upon by some male unionists: "It is not work for women, but for men," wrote one male glovemaker of the women's union in Worcester,[55] and accusations from men that attending meetings would automatically lead to other forms of unfeminine behavior were common. A letter from a union tailor claiming to support female unionism, yet arguing that "none but lazy, gossiping, drunken wives" would wish to go out to meetings,[56] elicited furious responses from several women:

I am neither a lazy, gossiping, drunken nor tattling wife, and yet I have been to meetings alone" [wrote a sixty-year-old woman who asked the editor to correct her writing errors "as I have not had a pen in my hand these seven years"], "what does he think women must be? . . . either stocks or stones? But I hope he will find himself mistaken, as I . . . believe we are . . . coequal with him. . . . If not, then down with the Union that is now amongst men![57]

"Do not say the unions are only for men," began another letter from a strawbonnet-maker busy organizing her sisters in Essex, " 'tis a wrong impression, forced on our minds to keep us slaves! . . . We have been foolishly taught to think it preposterous for woman to make herself in any way public; and even now . . . we are told unions of women would make us idlers and, some have the audacity to say, drunkards. Let us, sisters, banish the idea. . . ."[58]

What were the sources of this conflict? Most of the women who wrote to the Owenite press appear to have been married, often to husbands who saw female organization outside the home as a direct threat to male dominance inside the home. "Possibly this is the tailor's reason his wife should not go to meetings, for fear she should hear that he is in the wrong. . . ," one woman suggested of the reprehensible correspondent, adding however that she herself was persuaded that "a good wife . . . will not neglect business to seek that which is useless. . . ."[59]

But for many male unionists these general fears of female uppity- ness were further reinforced by the threat posed by female labor within their own trades. Our unfortunate tailor came, in fact, from just such a trade; and clearly a number of the women who respond- ed to his remarks suspected him of motives related as much to his work role as to his home comforts. In the early months of 1834, several letters from a tailoress appeared in the "Women's Page" asking anxiously if rumors she had heard of a planned strike of London tailors against the women in the trade were true. "Surely . . . [the men] will not turn oppressors themselves?" one letter asked, pointing out that many of the needlewomen were the widows of tailors who had no other source of livelihood than garment-making.[60] A second letter from this woman, a worker employed by a West End tailoring workshop for eighteen years, took up the issue again, this time raising specific demands for an alternative strategy for the union. This letter is worth looking at in some detail since the issues it raised—and the position which she adopted on those issues—were typical of the views expressed by a number of these militant workingwomen.

The letter began by thanking *The Pioneer* for "pressing the rec- ord of [women's] various wrongs upon the notice of our 'lords and masters'. . . ."

An ingenious commentator has observed that woman was made of a rib taken out of the side of a man—not out of his head, to rule him, not out of his feet, to be trampled upon by him; but out of his side, to be his equal—under his arm, to be protected; near his heart, to be beloved. Alas! Alas! that poverty and oppression have so hardened the hearts of *man*kind that, instead of regarding woman in the light . . . intended by their Maker . . . they should be found amongst her worst oppressors! nay, that they should have united . . . to deprive her of the means of subsistence![61]

For many of these women, she went on to insist, there was no alternative to these low-paid employments: "did the man do his duty as a husband and father . . . and procure the means wherewith to support his family," his wife would not have to find work in addition to her domestic duties, but in many homes this simply was not possible.

I myself know a woman whose husband was ill . . . for four months, and during that time . . . she supported him, herself and her three children, by the work of her own hands. That husband is now dead; and if the men succeed in their present diabolical purpose, this honest . . . woman and her children must starve, or *go to the workhouse*. This is but one . . . out of hundreds of similar cases. . . .[62]

Moreover, she went on, some men actually married in order to be supported by their working wives—"instead of working themselves, they can loiter away half the week in a pot-house"—leaving the entire burden of child support on the woman. The ideology of the male breadwinner disguised and reinforced a reality of female poverty. There was no question—at least for this woman, and, I suspect, for most of her working-class sisters—of challenging the notion of the male breadwinner *in principle*; but in practice, increasing numbers of women were forced into direct dependence on their own wage. There was, she concluded, only one just route by which the tailors' union could prevent these women from underselling their labor: "There are some few good men who from humanity and a fellow-feeling with the female labourer . . . would gladly join in raising the price of her labour to the male standard: to these men . . . my heartfelt thanks. . . ."[63]

By today's standards this was hardly a revolutionary position. But in the context of 1830s labor politics, the demand for women's right to work and equal pay implied far more for sexual relations than the claims themselves indicate. The material interests which had come to divide men and women within so many industries created antagonisms which were to reverberate down through the entire history of the trade union movement. "If women be prohibited from producing wealth . . . they will raise a sexual war. . . ,"

The Pioneer predicted,[64] and to a certain extent it was sexual war which went on in many trades in this period.

It was impossible for a socialist-feminist position to develop which did not confront these divisions within the working-class movement itself. Why and how the Owenites did this is the rest of our story. Let us begin by following our two protagonists—the tailor and tailoress—back into their trade and the origins of this sexual strife.

Tailoring provides a particularly useful case study for three reasons. First, tailors and tailoresses were absolutely typical of the Owenite movement as a whole both in terms of work and family patterns. Second, the London tailors' union was the largest affiliate of the Grand National Consolidated Trades Union. And third, it was in the London tailoring trade that the issue of female labor finally exploded into open controversy at the peak of the general-union agitation. By looking at this struggle and the background to it we can see not only the nature of the sexual division between workers in the old crafts, and the Owenite-feminist response to it, but also the roots of the Owenite "utopian" strategy as a whole.

The tailoring workshop of the eighteenth century had been a man's world of hard work, hard drinking, and tough union politics. Up to the end of the century the London journeymen tailors' union was one of the strongest in the country, with virtual control over prices, hours, and labor recruitment, including stringent restrictions on female employment. This had meant that while there had always been a few women apprenticed to some sectors of the trade, in general female labor was confined to the female wing of the garment industry: the lower-paid, unorganized trades of dressmaking, millinery, and so on.[65]

Unlike the situation of the home-based craftsman, such as a weaver or hatter, whose wife assisted him at his labors, the tailor's wife had no place in his working life. This did not mean, however, that she was without income-earning employment. Throughout the eighteenth century, tailors' wives worked as necklace-makers, embroiderers, mantua-makers, milk-sellers, and so on.[66] As in the other trades, only a master craftsman could afford to support a nonworking wife; and by the late eighteenth century very few journeymen could ever hope to attain such affluence. Nonetheless, a tailor and his wife could earn enough between them to maintain a "respectable" life-style, as measured by the employment of a single young servant, participation in local cultural and political life (at least for the tailor), and the little accoutrements of decent home life: brass plate, a few books and maybe a piano, "small statues of Shakespeare beneath glass shades."[67]

Labor, leisure, and social power were firmly divided along sexual lines within these artisan families. The wife's income was usually essential to the family economy, but it was also secondary to the husband's wage. Her primary responsibilities were domestic, and any other employments had to be fitted in around those duties. Moreover, for the top layer of these skilled men it was a mark of disgrace to have a wife working "away from home." Shopkeeping, laundressing, and taking in lodgers were, therefore, the only "respectable" alternatives to domestic trades for the wife of an experienced craftsman, just as the wives of the highly paid factory spinners rarely went into the mills themselves in the late eighteenth century, but left that for the wives and daughters of the truly poor: agricultural laborers, indigent hand-weavers.[68]

But by the early decades of the nineteenth century this entire life-style was under threat. As the old (and new) skilled occupations fell under the blows of the capitalist reorganization of industry, so also did traditional patterns of gender roles and gender authority begin to shift and break apart. Although the specific mechanisms of the process differed from trade to trade, the pattern of change which we see in tailoring was typical of a large sector of the skilled working class.

Tailoresses had entered the trade through waistcoat-making. "When I first began working at this branch," one man recalled to Henry Mayhew in the mid-century, "there were but very few females employed in it";

A few white waistcoats were given out to them, under the idea that women could make them cleaner than men. . . . But since the increase of the puffing and sweating system [subcontracting work out to "sweaters" who employed other workers in their homes or workshops], masters and sweaters have sought everywhere for such hands as would do the work below the regular ones. Hence the wife has been made to compete with the husband, and the daughter with the wife. . . . If the man will not reduce the price of his labour to that of the female, why he must remain unemployed. . . .[69]

The only way to prevent any extension of this process, the tailor's union had argued in the early decades of the century, was to prevent production outside the workshops which they controlled. Up to the late 1820s, the strength of their union had been such that several strikes fought on this issue had been won. "It will be found universally . . . where men have opposed the employment of women and children . . . their own wages are kept up to a point equal to

the maintenance of a family," the master tailor Francis Place reported in 1824, adding, "Tailors of London have not only kept up,
but forced up their wages in this way. . . ."[70]

But by the 1830s, escalating demand and the development of
new profitable production methods in the "slop" (ready-made)
clothing sector had drawn a new style of clothier onto the "quality" tailoring scene: the capitalist fabric merchant who expanded
into garment production and retailing. "Show-shops" displaying
garments at standard measurements were opened by these men,
and soon competitive pressure from them was driving many small
master tailors to the wall. Journeymen from the declining workshops found themselves forced to resort to the show-shops for
garments to be taken home and there completed by both himself
and his wife. Those staunch union men ("the Flints") who refused
to do homework were undercut by the unapprenticed or inferior
workmen previously excluded from the union ("the Dungs") who
were soon giving out work not only to their wives but to other
women outside their families as well. "This trade, like almost
every other, is divided against itself, one part rapidly undermining
the other," Morrison warned in 1833,[71] while a "public address"
from the union secretary bewailed the role of women in this savage
competition:

Have not women been unfairly driven from their proper sphere in the social
scale, unfeelingly torn from the maternal duties of a parent, and unjustly en-
couraged to compete with men in ruining the money value of labour?[72]

As in every major transformation in a mode of production, the
effects of these changes were not confined to the workplace itself.
Falling wages, underemployment, and overwork had profoundly
disruptive effects on social and cultural life, while the impact on
family life was particularly traumatic. Much has been written
about the restructuring of proletarian family life in the new textile
districts of the North; but far less attention has been paid to the
effects of capitalist development on the home life of groups like
the tailors, where the breakdown of male craft domination had
simultaneously led to the breakdown of the male breadwinning
role. Competition between female and male workers at the level
of the industry as a whole often translated into a new dependency
on the wife's labor in the industry at the family level: for the husband, loss of craft power became a loss of manly status, of sexual
authority.[73]

There is no sense in which this dislocation of the old patriarchal
arrangements could be called "liberating" for the women involved.
It happened at a terrible cost in terms of intensification of exploita-

tion and poverty. Hence the support from women themselves for
the male "family wage," as in the tailoress' letter. But at the same
time, by sharply imposing on women an economic role which weakened older gender divisions, these changes forced—or allowed— them
to challenge male dominance in other ways as well. "I do not wish
to take any power from man that he can with justice claim," wrote
one woman to *The Pioneer*, "only let us, who bear an equal share
of the evils of circumstance, unite to defend our own. . . ."

Are we not forced from home to labour, and may we not go from home to en-
deavour to lighten that labour, without the fear of an angry husband when we
return? . . . Then let us, sisterworkwomen, make a beginning in our own business; our number is great, our power equal. . . .[74]

A heightened class contradiction heightened an existing sexual
contradiction. There was nothing unique in this: the history of
British capitalism tells a similar story in one trade after another
from the mid-eighteenth century on. What was unusual, however,
was for this conflict to become the center of open controversy, as
it did in tailoring in the 1830s. In order to understand the reasons
for this we must turn from the specific conditions in tailoring back
to their meaning for Owenite socialism.

Early socialism, as we said above, was rooted in this crisis of
skilled labor. All over the country, in one trade after another, the
fate of the tailors was being repeated, as labor processes and labor
recruitment were wrenched from the control of workers and restruc-
tured according to the needs of expanding capitalist enterprise.
Whether the weapons employed by capital to do this were the
glossy new machines of factory industry (as in textiles) or the
far less glossy, but equally effective, ones of piecework and
sweated outwork (as in tailoring), the outcome was the same:
the displacement of skilled (usually male) labor by cheaper, unorganized (usually female) labor, and through this the establishment of a new level of capitalist command over the workforce as
a whole. There was nothing inherently more "modern" about the
machines than the sweated outwork: both were routes to a higher
level of profitability, the single "modernizing" imperative of capitalist development. Both were the making of the modern British
proletariat.[75]

The economic strategy of the Owenite movement was a self-
conscious struggle to resist this new level of capitalist command,
to short-circuit it at its source. *There was nothing "backward"
about this struggle*: the Owenites had no desire to abolish machinery or eliminate the new mass markets which had transformed the
old crafts. The new communities and cooperative production units

were planned to be as technically efficient as possible. But what the socialists would not accept were the class relations embodied in these economic developments. Rooted as these workers were in the power of craft, the capitalist road to economic growth appeared to them as not only undesirable but entirely unnecessary. They were the "skilled and industrious . . . whose labor is responsible for the wealth of this nation. . ."; the capitalists, on the other hand, were "mere parasites," profiteering middlemen who had somehow inserted themselves between these potentially self-managing craftsmen and their means of production and distribution. Who needed them? asked the tailors, shoemakers, cabinet-builders. "It is only ignorance which leaves a man to do so foolish a thing as to work for another instead of himself. . . ."[76] The answer, then, was simply to turn one's back on the bosses and let them wither away. "Many parts of London have for some days been covered with placards . . . maintaining the absolute independence of the working classes from those by whom they have hitherto been employed," it was reported at the climax of the G.N.C.T.U. in May 1834. "According to this profound doctrine, industry requires not the moving power of capital, and accumulation is altogether useless!"[77]

This was an ideology of transition: the consciousness of a class "in the making" struggling against the conditions of its own creation. Unlike later socialist movements, in which working people organized *as* the proletariat, the Owenites organized *against* proletarianization. It was this which made them "utopians": not yet fully enmeshed in capitalist social relations, they could readily imagine others; not yet fully subordinate to capital, they were determined to use what power remained to them to reestablish the material conditions of freedom.

Of course they had to fail; that is not the issue. Coming out of a history of artisanship, all their optimism flowed from a set of social relations which were fast disappearing. But while the grip of capital had yet to tighten completely, a space existed in which to plan and maneuver; and the socialist "New Science of Society"—with its demands for the "right to the whole produce of labour" and its blueprints for achieving it—was the weapon with which that space would be wrenched open to allow the new society through. All was plastic, all was possible; nothing was settled.

Here was the space in which all the elaborate schemes for the New Life were mooted: the social communities, the cooperative economy, the revolution in sexual and familial relations. And here was the "utopian" space where feminists found their platform, even in the midst of the very struggles in which sexual competition

figured so centrally. For once it was not merely the defense of old
craft privileges but the transformation of craft power into the basis
of a new order that was at stake, it was possible to think past existing divisions into a period when all divisions would dissolve. "Men
dread the competition of other men . . . in every line of industry,"
William Thompson addressed his female readers in the *Appeal*,
"How much more will they dread yours! . . . How much will this
dread . . . be aggravated by their previous contempt of your fabri-
cated impotence!" But . . . "not so under the system of Association of Labour by Mutual Co-operation . . . where individual property and competition are forever excluded. . . ."[78] Or as one "old
journeyman tailor" told his comrades in the tailoring union, the attempt to exclude women from the trade was the "very acme of tyranny," for "if women are equal in the state of human existence" then
the assertion of male craft privilege against them could only be a reactionary tactic: "Competition is the great, the only, the all-prevail-
ing evil. Competition must be destroyed, and associated labour raised
upon its ashes; all the rest . . . must end in disappointment."[79]

But as the succeeding events in the tailoring trade clearly showed,
the support which men such as these gave to the women workers
could not abolish the sexual contradiction in the trade—it could
only force it into the open. In November 1833, a meeting was held
of the London tailors' union in which the leadership managed to
convince their members that unless some of the crippling divisions
within the trade were overcome, all possibility of staving off the
employers was lost. The union adopted a policy of "equalization":
all workers of all grades and experience were to be admitted "without difference or distinction."[80] To many of the workers present,
the decision amounted to no more than a sophisticated defensive
tactic—better the "Dungs" be organized from within than under-
cutting from without. To the many Owenites there, however, it
was step one on the road to class emancipation. Urging the establishment of cooperative workshops, they hastened to support initia-
tives toward the creation of the G.N.C.T.U., the national network
from which the peaceful revolution would be launched. And in
the midst of all this, a tailor-poet (who had written articles on
sexual equality in the radical press) stood to remind his fellows,
"be not unjust to our sisters."

Remember, Equality is the order of the day; therefore, those who have learned
certain trades have an equal right to join the lodges of the trade to which they
belong. . . .[81]

But despite the rhetoric of worker-equality, it took a "utopian"
to defend women's rights to these men, for whom the threat of

unskilled male labor was simply not equatable with the far deeper and more complex threat posed by female labor. In May 1834, the London union came out on a strike whose demands included an end to piecework and homework . . . an end, in other words, to cheap tailoressing. Immediately there began a series of public attacks and counterattacks between employers and the union over the issue of female labor, with the employers shedding crocodile tears (through their mouthpiece, *The Times'* editorials) over the union's "dictatorial" attitude toward these "honest and industrious" (and cheap) females.[82] Women workers were brought in to scab; some were attacked, their materials taken. Garments made by these women for the employers were prominently displayed in marketplaces. "The masters seem resolved to feminize the whole trade, rather than yield . . . and to stir up an uncivil war between the sexes," one observer reported.[83]

The position taken by the union itself throughout this episode is not entirely clear, despite the initial demands. Contradictory statements were made, some claiming to support the women's right to employment while at the same time denouncing the shops which provided it. At one point the union accused the employers of lying about the issue in order to "turn our mothers and sisters against us": they were even willing to set up a women's union, another letter claimed.[84] The most obvious conclusion from all this was that the men were divided, with the socialist-unionists the most vehement supporters of a nonexclusionist strategy: the cooperative workshop which they opened during the course of the strike had women working in it alongside the men.[85] Certainly several of the leading Owenite ideologues across the country put pressure on the tailors to take the more progressive path. In an article comparing the situation of women in the cotton industry to the current struggle within tailoring, John Doherty, the Lancashire cotton spinners' leader, wrote that while it was true that the problem of women underpricing male labor was a very serious one, its solution was obvious: "What is the antidote? Why merely for you to acknowledge the natural equality of women . . . include them in all your schemes of improvement. . . ."[86] Other socialist papers agreed, while in *The Pioneer,* Morrison used the occasion to publish a long editorial on the entire issue of female labor. The arguments which he put forward there are worth quoting at length, for they are virtually unique in nineteenth-century trade unionism:

The women have always been worse paid for their labour than the men; and, by long habit . . . they have been taught to regard this inequality as justice. They are, therefore, content with merely a portion of a man's wages, even when their work is equally valuable. . . . If a woman makes a waistcoat for two-thirds of the sum which is charged by a man, she will . . . monopolize the waistcoat trade to herself, or compel him to lower his charges. It is to prevent this diminution of wages that the male tailors have declared war against the female tailors.[87]

The tailors claim, he went on, that they "do not want to deprive the women of their means of living, provided they do not prove prejudicial to the trade at large," and this he approved so long as it meant that equal pay was the strategy; "but where they wantonly throw out of employment a number of females, merely because they were women, we think this an encroachment on the liberties of humanity. . . ." He went on to suggest that the question divided itself into two: have male workers the right to undercut each others' wages—to which the answer is always no—and "has a woman a right to reduce the wages of man, by working for less than man?"

Certainly not, were woman considered equal to man, and did she enjoy the same rights and privileges; but since man has doomed her to inferiority, and stamped an inferior value upon all the productions of her industry, the low wages of woman are not so much the voluntary price she sets upon her labour, as the price which is fixed by the tyrannical influence of male supremacy. To make the two sexes equal, and to reward them equally, would settle the matter amicably; but any attempt to settle it otherwise will prove an act of gross tyranny.[88]

"Hear this, ye men!" wrote the West End tailoress in the following issue, "and when next you meet to proceed against the rights and liberties of the weaker part of the creation, may the still small voice of conscience whisper in your ears the words of *The Pioneer*. . . ."[89]

But whatever the men felt about these arguments, by late May it would have made no difference. The employers had presented the workers with their final ultimatum, and the strike slowly collapsed as the other G.N.C.T.U. affiliates refused further financial support. The tailors' union then pulled out of the general union, and it too came to an end. Sixteen years later when Henry Mayhew interviewed old London tailors, many remembered the strike and told him that their defeat then had been decisive in finally breaking craft controls: sweating, piecework and female labor had all increased dramatically in the succeeding years. So bad had their situation now become, they told him, that they would soon all "be reduced to the position of the lowest of the needlewomen."[90]

The development of capitalist production on the basis of gender division has meant that no workers' struggle has ever been free of these sexual politics. Choices like the ones posed for the tailors in 1834 are always there to be made; the fact that they usually remain unacknowledged has only meant that their suppression was part of the decision. Women marginalized, excluded, voiceless through lack of confidence or support: these are too often the basis on which strategies are determined. Those feminists who in 1834 raised the issue of women's interests were not being divisive; they were simply giving voice to divisions which were already there. "The working men complain that the masters exercise authority over them," Morrison wrote of the tailors, ". . . but speak of any project which will diminish the authority of the male . . . and then the spirit of Toryism awakes. . . ."[91]

The ability to recognize and fight this sexual Toryism even within the working-class movement itself: that was an important test of the strength of feminism among the Owenites; more important perhaps than even the most well thought-out schemes for family reorganization or collective housework. For as long as the sort of painful contradictions which I have outlined continue to exist, it has been all too easy for the emancipationist hopes of working-class women to be named "utopian" or "divisive" and then thrust aside. "I repudiate that there is any sex antagonism" one labor leader was to tell working-class suffragists in denying them his support for enfranchisement over a half-century later; the suffragists, he went on, had "placed sex first, but . . . we have to put Labour first in every case. . . ."[92]

There is a funny sense, then, in which one of the weaknesses of the early socialist movement was also one of its strengths: lacking any scientific theory of the historic role of the proletariat, they lacked also that principled basis from which to reject female claims, which was later to be developed with such verve by Marxist antifeminists. Deeply committed to a revolution which would dissolve all power relations, they had every reason to support women's claims: to free the "slaves of slaves" was, after all, integral to the abolition of social slavery as a whole.

But nostalgia is no substitute for analysis. Owenism was an ideology of a transition now long past. It is the Marxist inheritance—with all the enormous progress it represents over the earlier socialist theories, as well as all the sins it has committed against women in the name of that progress—which modern socialist-feminists must now develop and transform, forcing the issue of gender hierarchy into the very center of class analysis and class strategies. But as we begin to do that, it is encouraging to lean back and hear those earlier women's voices, telling us that this project also has a history.

NOTES

This essay appears, in a revised form, as Chapter 4 of my *Eve and the New Jerusalem: Socialism and Feminism in the Nineteenth Century* (London: Virago, and New York: Pantheon, 1983). Apart from background research into female employment, early trade unionism, and the tailoring trade, the major sources are radical publications of the period, particularly the short-lived Owenite-unionist newspaper, *The Pioneer; or Trades Union Magazine* (Birmingham, London: September 1833-September 1834) edited by James Morrison. At the height of the general-union movement, *The Pioneer* was one of the most widely read radical papers of the day, with a circulation of about 22,000 and a readership of perhaps ten times that. Other Owenite publications cited include: *The Crisis; or the Change from Error and Misery, to Truth and Happiness* (London, April 1832-August 1834) edited, in succession, by Robert Owen, Robert Dale Owen, and James E. Smith; *The New Moral World* (London, Manchester, Birmingham, Leeds, London, Harmony, Hants.: November 1834-November 1845), edited by George Fleming. A number of the other periodicals cited were more closely allied with the "parliamentary reform" wing of the working-class movement; these include the very influential *The Poor Man's Guardian* (London, January 1831-December 1835) edited by Henry Hetherington and James B. O'Brien; *The People's Conservative and Trades' Union Gazette* (a continuation of *The Destructive*; London, February 1833-February 1834). With the exception of the *New Moral World*, these sources are useful only for the early phase of Owenism.

[1] Sheila Rowbotham's contribution to this project is well known. See *Women, Resistance, and Revolution* (London: Allen Lane, Penguin Press, 1972); *Hidden from History* (London: Pluto Press, 1973); *A New World for Women: Stella Browne—Socialist Feminist* (London: Pluto Press, 1977) and her numerous other books and pamphlets exploring the connected histories of socialism and feminism. See also Jill Liddington and Jill Norris, *One Hand Tied Behind Us: the Rise of the Women's Suffrage Movement* (London: Virago Ltd., 1978), a study of working-class women's campaign for the vote in Northern England.

[2] *The Liverpool Standard*, September 7, 1839, quoted in Patricia Knight, "Owenite Socialism from 1817 to 1840" (M.A. diss., University of Manchester, 1965), p. 110.

[3] Editorial, *The Poor Man's Guardian*, no. 124 (October 19, 1833): 33.

[4] "A Candidate for the Association of All Classes of All Nations" (pseud.), "To the Editor," *The New Moral World, or Gazette of the Universal Community Society of Rational Religionists* (Leeds) 6, no. 39 (July 20, 1839): 614.

[5] Mary Wollstonecraft, *A Vindication of the Rights of Women* (London, 1792); reprint ed., London: J. M. Dent and Sons Ltd., 1970); p. 11.

[6] "The Old Woman—No. III," *The Ladies Monthly Museum* 1 (September 1798): 186; quoted in G. K. Malmgreen, "Women's Suffrage in England: Origins and Alternatives" (M.A. diss., Hull University, 1975), p. 26.

[7] John Beachcroft Dixon, "A Citizen," "To the Editor," *The Prompter*, no. 23 (April 16, 1831): 374.

[8] William Thompson, *Appeal of One-Half the Human Race, Women, Against the Pretensions of the Other Half, Men, to retain them in political, and thence in civil and domestic Slavery; in reply to . . . Mr. Mill's celebrated 'Article on Government'* (London: Longman, Hurst, Rees, Orme, Brown, and Green, 1825).

[9] "W.W.P." (pseud.), "Woman as She Is, and As She Ought to Be," *New Moral World* 5, no. 13 (January 26, 1839): 210.

[10] See *The Pioneer, The Crisis, The Poor Man's Guardian*, and *The People's Conservative* for reports of these meetings. A number of them were sponsored by the French socialists, the Saint-Simonians, busy proselytizing feminist ideas in England at the time

(see all the above newspapers for reports of their activities, and also Richard Keir Pethick Pankhurst, *The Saint Simonians, Mill and Carlyle* [London: Sidgwick and Jackson, 1957]).

[11] *New Moral World* 11, no. 33 (February 11, 1843): 267; *New Moral World* 12, no. 20 (November 11, 1843).

[12] "Marriage" (unsigned), *Social Pioneer* (Manchester), no. 2 (March 16, 1839): 16.

[13] C. E. Tonna, editorial, *The Christian Lady's Magazine* 13 (1840): 378. Hostility from the church toward the Owenites reached an hysterical pitch by the early 1840s. See the bibilography in J. F. C. Harrison, *Robert Owen and the Owenites in Britain and America* (London: Routledge and Kegan Paul Ltd., 1969) for the long list of anti-socialist tracts produced by churches and individual preachers in this period.

[14] For a good introduction to Owen's ideas, see Harrison, *Robert Owen*, esp. pp. 45-87. For a discussion of the Owenites' attempts to build a whole new way of life, see Eileen Yeo's excellent "Robert Owen and Radical Culture" in S. Pollard and J. Salt, *Robert Owen, Prophet of the Poor* (London: Macmillan Press Ltd., 1971), pp. 84-114.

[15] *Weekly Free Press* clipping, February 1830, in William Pare, "Scrapbook" (newspaper clippings related to the cooperative movement), Family Welfare Association Collection, University of London, f. 61.

[16] Robert Owen, *Lectures on the Marriages of the Priesthood of the Old Immoral World, delivered in the year 1835, before the Passing of the New Marriage Act* (Leeds: A. Heywood, 1835), and also his *The Book of the New Moral World, containing the Rational system of Society* (London, 1844).

[17] George Fleming, speech at Fifth Annual Congress, *New Moral World*, n.s. 7, no. 87 (June 13, 1840): 1323.

[18] Home Office 44/38, f. 209.

[19] One of the leading socialist-feminists in the later phase of the movement, for example, was Emma Martin, a Baptist evangelical who deserted both her church and her husband to join the Owenites. She scraped together a living for her daughters and herself by writing, lecturing, shopkeeping, and teaching, but finally had to resort to a public appeal for funds. Letters from women in similar economic circumstances, particularly teachers and women engaged in "literary activities" (journalists, essayists) cram the *New Moral World*, while reports of Owenite meetings occasionally note the presence of numbers of these women (see, for example, *New Moral World* 4, no. 27 (August 11, 1838): 330, for reports of large numbers of female teachers attending socialist meetings in Leicester).

[20] See, for example, "M.A.S.," "Female Education," *New Moral World* 11, no. 12 (October 14, 1843): 121.

[21] Thompson, *Appeal*, pp. 57, 63.

[22] Mary Wollstonecraft, *Maria, or the Wrongs of Woman* (London, 1798; reprint ed., New York: W. W. Norton and Co., 1975), p. 27.

[23] "Speech of a Female Operative, as taken by a Reporter" at the Charlotte St. Institution, London, *Official Gazette of the Trades' Unions*, no. 6 (July 12, 1834): 46. Report of meeting to be addressed by a "Mechanic's Wife" in London, *The Poor Man's Guardian*, no. 148 (April 5, 1834): 70.

[24] *The Crisis* 3, no. 16 (December 14, 1833): 124.

[25] Ibid.

[26] For an excellent account of the artisan base of Owenism, see E. P. Thompson, *The Making of the English Working Class* (Harmondsworth: Penguin Books Ltd., 1972), pp. 857-915.

[27] Editorial, *The Pioneer* 1, no. 27 (March 8, 1834): 237.

[28] Editorial, *The Pioneer* 1, no. 8 (October 26, 1833): 60.

[29] "A Member of the Builders' Union," "*The Poor Man's Guardian* vs. the Trades Unions," *The Man* 1, no. 24 (December 22, 1833): 191.

[30] R. W. Postgate, *The Builders' History* (London: Labour Publishing Co., 1953), p. 59.

[31] "Address of the Derby Unionists to the People of Derby," *The Poor Man's Guardian* (January 4, 1834), quoted in W. H. Oliver, "The Consolidated Trades' Union of 1834," *Economic History Review*, 2d ser. 17, no. 1 (August 1964): 79.

[32] Report of lecture by Robert Owen, *The Crisis* 3, no. 6 (October 12, 1833): 42.

[33] "To the Editor of the True Sun" (editorial), *The Pioneer* 1, no. 16 (December 28, 1833): 129.

[34] The most detailed account of the G.N.C.T.U. is W. H. Oliver, *Organizations and Ideas behind the Efforts to Achieve a General Union of the Working Classes in England in the early 1830s* (Ph.D. diss., Oxford University, 1957). The most interesting examination of the artisan base of the Union is I. J. Prothero, *London Working Class Movements, 1825-1848* (Ph.D. diss., Cambridge University, 1966). Other sources include: G. D. H. Cole, *Attempts at General Union* (London: Macmillan and Co., 1953); S. and B. Webb, *The History of Trade Unionism* (London: Longmans and Co., 1896), although both of these have been superseded by Oliver's work. For the role of women in the G.N.C.T.U., see S. Lewenhak, *Women and Trade Unions* (London: Ernest Benn Ltd., 1977), pp. 29-44.

[35] The Women's Grand Lodge of Operative Straw-Blatters, Servees, Bleachers and Blockers met at "The Griffin" in Red Lion Square every Monday at 7:00 during the first half of 1834 (*The Pioneer* 1, no. 37 (May 17, 1834): 353); the Grand Lodge of Operative Straw Bonnet Makers met during the same period at the Owenite Institution at Charlotte Street (*Official Gazette of the Trades Unions*, no. 3 [June 21, 1834]: 22), as did the Grand Lodge of Miscellaneous Operatives, which was organized by a Mrs. Brooks. Women shoemakers had their own London lodge, but they were also urged to attend meetings of the mixed lodge (*Official Gazette*, no. 6 [July 12, 1834]: 48).

[36] James Morrison addressing "Great Meeting of Productive Classes," London, February 12, 1834, *The Crisis* 3, no. 27 (March 1, 1834): 220.

[37] *The Pioneer* 1, no. 41 (June 14, 1834): 407.

[38] "To the Ladies in Union at Leicester" (editorial), *The Pioneer* 1, no. 8 (October 26, 1833): 57.

[39] "A Mechanic's Wife in London," "To the Editor," *The Pioneer* 1, no. 19 (January 18, 1834): 152.

[40] "An Initiated Weaver's Wife," "To the Editor," *The Pioneer* 1, no. 28 (March 15, 1834): 247.

[41] See Jo O'Brien, "Women's Liberation in Labour History: a Case Study from Nottingham" (London: Spokesman Pamphlets, Pamphlet no. 24, n.d.) for an account of the trade and the militant actions of the women employed in it. Lewenhak, *Women*, pp. 48-49, gives an account of an 1840 strike of these lace-makers.

[42] Dorothy Thompson, "Women and Nineteenth Century Radical Politics," in J. Mitchell and A. Oakley, eds., *The Rights and Wrongs of Women* (Harmondsworth: Penguin Books Ltd., 1976), p. 116.

[43] "Doings in Derby," *The People's Conservative* 2, no. 54 (February 8, 1834): 6.

[44] "An Everlasting Enemy to All Tyranny," "To the Editor," *The Pioneer* 1, no. 25 (February 22, 1834): 211.

[45] "Female Operative," *Official Gazette*, no. 6 (July 12, 1834): 46.

[46] "A London Mechanic's Wife," "To the Bondswoman of Birmingham," *The Pioneer* 1, no. 25 (February 22, 1834): 221.

[47] Ibid.

[48] "A Bondwoman" (Frances Morrison), "To the Women of the Working Classes," *The Pioneer* 1, no. 23 (February 8, 1834): 191.

[49] Ibid.

[50] "An English Woman," "To the Editor," *The Pioneer* 1, no. 32 (April 12, 1834): 295.

[51] "A Page for the Ladies" (editorial), *The Pioneer* 1, no. 29 (March 22, 1834): 262.

[52] "Vesta," "To the Editor," *The Pioneer* 1, no. 28 (March 15, 1834): 245-46.

[53]"An Initiated Weaver's Wife," "To the Editor," *The Pioneer* 1, no. 28 (March 15, 1834): 247.

[54]"A Woman," "To the Editor," *The Crisis* 3, no. 26 (March 8, 1834): 230.

[55]"Edgar," "To the Editor," *The Pioneer* 1, no. 32 (April 12, 1834): 302.

[56]"Initiated Tailor" (George Edmonds), "To the Editor," *The Pioneer* 1, no. 30 (March 29, 1834): 274.

[57]"An English Woman," "To the Editor," *The Pioneer* 1, no. 32 (April 12, 1834): 295.

[58]"P.A.S.," "To the Bonnet Makers of London, Hartford and Bedford," *The Pioneer* 1, no. 32 (April 12, 1834): 295.

[59]"An English Woman," "To the Editor," *The Pioneer* 1, no. 32 (April 12, 1834): 295.

[60]"A Woman," "To the Editor," *The Pioneer* 1, no. 30 (March 29, 1834): 274.

[61]"A Woman," "Second Letter to the Tailors," *The Pioneer* 1, no. 32 (April 12, 1834): 203.

[62]Ibid.

[63]Ibid.

[64]"Woman's Page" (editorial), *The Pioneer* 1, no. 37 (May 17, 1834): 358.

[65]The sources used for this account of the tailoring trade include: S. and B. Webb, Trade Union Mss. Collection (London School of Economics and Political Science), Section A: XIV (Clothing Trades); Francis Place, "Minutes of Evidence," *First Report from Select Committee on Artizans and Machinery* (London: House of Commons, February, 1834), pp. 44-46; E. P. Thompson and E. Yeo, *The Unknown Mayhew* (Harmondsworth: Penguin Books Ltd., 1973), pp. 217-73; I. Prothero, "London Working Class Movements"; Thomas Carter, *Memoirs of a Working Man* (London: Charles Knight and Co., 1845); F. W. Galton, ed., *Select Documents Illustrating the History of Trade Unionism: 1. The Tailoring Trade* (London: Longmans, Green and Co., 1896); Anon., "The War of the Purses, or the Tailors of London," in E. Jones, ed., *Notes to the People*, vol. 1 (1851), pp. 363-69; T. M. Parssinen and I. J. Prothero, "The London Tailors' Strike of 1834 and the Collapse of the Grand National Consolidated Trades Union: a Police Spy's Report," *International Review of Social History* 22 (Spring 1977): 119-42. For women in tailoring see S. Alexander, "Women's Work in Nineteenth Century London" in Mitchell and Oakley, *Rights*, pp. 59-111. Most of the newspapers used in this essay also carried material on conditions in the trade.

[66]M. D. George, *London Life in the Eighteenth Century* (Harmondsworth: Penguin Books Ltd., 1965), p. 425.

[67]Ibid., p. 212 for a fascinating account of artisan life-styles in London in the eighteenth century. See Mayhew's reports to the *Morning Chronicle* (Thompson and Yeo, *Unknown Mayhew*, pp. 217-73) for the effects of a half-century of decline in tailoring.

[68]For the working lives of wives of London artisans, see Alexander, "Women's Work," pp. 63-65; for the sources of female factory labor in the Northern mills, see Ivy Pinchbeck, *Women Workers and the Industrial Revolution, 1750-1850* (London, 1930; reprint ed., London: Frank Cass and Co., Ltd., 1969), pp. 184-85.

[69]Quoted in S. Alexander, "Women's Work," pp. 81-82.

[70]Pinchbeck, *Women Workers*, p. 179n.

[71]Editorial, *The Pioneer* 1, no. 35 (May 3, 1834): 330.

[72]John Browne, Secretary to the Grand Lodge of Operative Tailors, "The Address of the Journeymen Tailors of the Metropolis," *The Pioneer* 1, no. 36 (May 10, 1834): 342-43.

[73]See Mayhew's interviews with "elderly tailors" where they complain of the alterations in husband-wife relations: Thompson and Yeo, *Unknown Mayhew*, pp. 220, 225, 226, 251 and many others.

[74]"P.A.S.," "To the Bonnet Makers," *The Pioneer* 1, no. 32 (April 12, 1834): 295.

[75] In describing mechanization and sweated outwork as two routes to "proletarianization" I am assuming that the proletarianization process involves not only the commoditization of the workers' labor-power through the "freeing" of labor from ownership of means of production and subsistence (which had occurred in tailoring three centuries earlier), but also the extension of capitalist command over the production process: the transition from "formal" to "real" subordination (Karl Marx, "Results of the Immediate Process of Production," Appendix, *Capital* [Harmondsworth: Penguin Books Ltd. and *New Left Review*, 1976] vol. 1, pp. 995-1039). Owenite theory and ideology, I am here arguing, needs to be analysed in relation to this transition, both in the old craft sector and in the new industrial sector. For this interpretation of Owenite class-consciousness I am heavily indebted to Gareth Stedman Jones, "Class Struggle and the Industrial Revolution," *New Left Review*, no. 90 (March-April 1975): 35-69, and also to his "The Limits of Proletarian Theory in England, 1830-50" (unpublished ms. in author's possession). I am grateful to him for letting me read the latter.

[76] Editorial (W. King), *The Co-Operator* (Brighton Co-Operative Society), no. 8 (December, 1828): 3. For reasons of space, it has been impossible here to examine the relationship of Owenite anticapitalist economics to the general-unionist strategy. In particular, William Thompson's views on the restructuring of the working class through the erosion of craft were important in developing the general-union strategy, and particularly in the emphasis on "equalization" found in the G.N.C.T.U. and a number of its affiliates, including the tailors. For Thompson's arguments see his *Labour Rewarded* (London, 1827).

[77] *The Times*, no. 15,473 (May 9, 1834): 3.

[78] Thompson, *Appeal*, p. 197.

[79]"B. Handy, a Unionist Tailor," "To the Editor," *The Pioneer* 1, no. 36 (May 9, 1834): 335.

[80] *The Man* 1, no. 22 (December 8, 1833): 173.

[81] "Agrarius" (G. Petrie), "The last Shift of the Profit-Mongers," *The Man* 1, no. 15 (October 20, 1833): 114.

[82] *The True Sun* 2 (May 26, 1834): 229. There were a detailed series of spy reports sent to the Home Office on the strike and some of these have been reproduced in Prothero and Parssinen, "The London Tailors' Strike." In this article the authors mention the use of female scab labor during the strike but ignore the dispute over women's role in the trade in *The Pioneer*. But since the burden of their argument is that the strike need only be understood in terms of the immediate economic issues facing the tailors—and their entirely defensive response to them—it is not surprising that they do not explore the wider issues raised by the struggle. For, as I have suggested here, it was precisely at the point where Owenism transformed defensive, sectorial struggles into socialist ones that women were able to find a platform for their own egalitarian demands. In denying that such a transformation actually occurred, the authors of the article are left not only with the problem of why so many tailors thought it had, but also of accounting for the existence of Owenite ideology at all. The search for continuities often means one stops recognizing change.

[83]"Female Tailors," *The Crisis* 4, no. 6 (May 17, 1834): 45.

[84] Browne, "Address," p. 343.

[85] *The People's Conservative* 2, no. 68 (May 17, 1834): 114.

[86]"Trades Unions" (editorial), *Herald of the Rights of Industry* (Society for Promoting National Regeneration, Manchester) 1, no. 14 (May 10, 1834): 106. Since Doherty had been the leader of the National Spinners' Union which voted to exclude women in 1829, however, it would be interesting to know if this represented a reversal of his earlier views, an indication that he had dissented from the 1829 decision, or simply a case of proffering advice to others which one is reluctant to take oneself.

[87]"A Page for the Ladies" (editorial), *The Pioneer* 1, no. 31 (April 5, 1834): 286.

[88] Ibid. In common with a number of other Owenite leaders, however, Morrison was

also very critical of the tailors' strike on the grounds that such "partial" struggles were foredoomed; what was needed, he and others argued, was a "Grand National Holiday" (general strike).

[89] "A Woman," "Second Letter," *The Pioneer* 1, no. 32 (April 12, 1834): 203.

[90] Thompson and Yeo, *Unknown Mayhew*, p. 227.

[91] "A Page for the Ladies" (editorial), *The Pioneer* 1, no. 29 (March 22, 1834): 262.

[92] Liddington and Norris, *One Hand*, p. 186.

7 One Hand Tied Behind Us:
A Review Essay

CHRISTINE STANSELL

"One Hand Tied Behind Us": The Rise of the Women's Suffrage Movement.
By Jill Liddington and Jill Norris. London: Virago, 1978.

Feminism and Suffrage: The Emergence of an Independent Women's Movement in America. By Ellen Carol DuBois. Ithaca: Cornell University Press,
1978.

These two new books on suffragism are important attempts to
integrate the study of politics and ideology, traditional concerns
of male-dominated history, with the new women's history of the
1970s. Only ten years ago, the studies of nineteenth-century suffragism written by a previous generation of feminist scholars
constituted most of the women's history available for new feminists looking for a past. Having moved away from the older emphasis on "great women" and the movements they led, to a more
broadly based social history of women, we have now come full
circle with these new studies. DuBois, Liddington, and Norris
are historians and activists who have reassessed suffragism from
the perspective of the second wave of women's liberation. Liddington and Norris broaden the history of English suffrage by
tracing its origins past the Pankhursts to a mass movement of
textile workers at the turn of the century; DuBois deepens our
understanding of the women who led the movement for the
vote in the United States. Although both books are written from
a socialist feminist perspective, there are striking differences in the
authors' understanding of politics—differences that raise important problems and perplexities about the nature of feminist radicalism.

*"One Hand Tied Behind Us": The Rise of the Women's Suffrage
Movement* excavates a piece of the past that has literally been

hidden from history, unacknowledged or unknown by past historians of British suffragism. From 1893 to 1906, thousands of Manchester textile workers, the best organized female industrial workers in Britain, conducted a campaign to win the vote. The leadership of the movement was a coalition of women trade unionists,
socialists, and Women's Cooperative Guild organizers, with a
socialist perspective on women's rights and a coherent political
strategy for winning the franchise. Although conventional histories of the English campaign stress the genteel character of the
participants and the vanguard role of the Pankhursts, Liddington
and Norris show how the Pankhursts, Manchester residents themselves, derived the impetus for their own campaign from this
working-class initiative.

Radical suffragism attracted both younger women new to
activism and older women who had served their political appren-
ticeships in socialist groups, the labor parties, and the women's
trade unions. Cissy Foley was one example of the first. As a
teenager in the 1890s, her wages from the cotton mill were a
major source of income for her large family. Embittered early
by her father's drinking, the drudgery of her mother's life, and
her own subjugation to the factory regimen, she turned to politics
and the cultural milieu of Manchester socialism. She shopped in
the Cooperative store, worshipped at the Labour Church, took
her holidays with a cycling club sponsored by the socialist newspaper, and borrowed radical books from the Cooperative library.
Talk about women's rights, which first appeared in the socialist
press in the mid-1890s, only clarified what she knew first hand
from her own household; by the turn of the century she was a
radical suffragist. Selina Cooper fell into the second category.
Already married and a mother when radical suffragism picked
up momentum, she came to political activism through work in
her union and membership in socialist and left-wing labor organizations. Much loved in her community, she was one of the
most popular speakers for the Cooperative Guild and, in the late
decade, an indomitable radical presence on the Manchester poor
law board, one of the few municipal offices to which women
could be elected. Her experiences with women's lack of political
power in the unions, the Left, and the municipality pushed her
steadily toward suffragism, and she became one of the movement's
most gifted and valued organizers at the turn of the century.

"One Hand Tied Behind Us" creates a unique picture of working-
class women acting collectively on their own behalf: petitioning
Parliament, lobbying within the trade unions, arguing motions
before the Labour Party, developing strategy among themselves—

all without the aid of male mentors. Unlike so much American
scholarship, in which working-class women appear as statistical
aggregates or as "functions" of the family economy, Liddington
and Norris present intelligent, politicized, decisive women. They
demonstrate, moreover, how these largely poverty-stricken wom-
en managed to sustain their political activism independent of their
men and in the face of overwhelming domestic responsibilities.
These were not, after all, women who kept servants, and their
housework was all-encompassing: as one suffragist wrote (in a
passage from which the book's title comes), "No cause can be
won between dinner and tea, and most of us who were married
had to work with one hand tied behind us." How did they do it?
More than any other factor, it seems to have been female cooperation that gave these women the necessary freedom for politics.
When a woman went to London to present a petition, sympathetic
neighbors cared for her children; while a suffragist spoke at the
factory gates at the noon break, a friend cooked her husband's
dinner back home.

By focusing on the dynamics of an organized political movement,
Liddington and Norris restore to women's history a view of politics
that has been largely claimed by men. The salutary effects of this
turnabout are considerable, particularly for American scholarship,
which so emphasizes the structural position of working-class wom-
en while neglecting their role as intelligent historical agents. But
the British historians' perspective, a celebration of the efforts of
working-class women, also has serious limitations. The weaknesses
are most evident in their treatment of two problems: sexual antagonism within the working class and the political character of
middle-class feminism.

Much of the story told by Liddington and Norris consists of the
frustrating and unsuccessful attempts of the radical suffragists to
win support from the trade unions, the radical Independent Labour
Party, and the Labour Party itself. A laborist perspective, however,
prevents the authors from ever analyzing the social roots of the
opposition. Although there was support for women's rights, particularly within the ILP, the antisuffrage forces consistently prevailed, and Labour did not ultimately back the suffragists. By
withholding it, both parties contributed to the eventual appropriation of the campaign by the wealthy ladies of the Pankhurst organization. But because the authors posit a basically unified working
class in which gender could be a dividing factor but never an antagonistic one, they never explain exactly *why* working men opposed
the reform. The explanation they do advance is political in the
narrowest sense: the labor movement refused to support women's

suffrage before there was universal manhood suffrage. Why, then, did some working men and not others support women's suffrage? And why did the radical suffragists, committted socialists and trade unionists themselves, still see their demands as progressive? In the end, we are left with the impression of abstract organizations—rather than the working men who comprised them—as the sources of opposition.

What accounts for working-class antisuffragism? There are scraps of possible answers throughout the book, although the authors do not piece them together. Certainly the very participation of women in independent political activity seems to have threatened the highly patriarchal families of workers in northern England. Liddington and Norris recount how one Manchester husband slapped his wife's face in public when she came home from her first meeting. "Their husbands didn't agree with them, in nine cases out of ten," recalled an activist years later. "Speaking for myself—my husband smashed my—broke my badge, and tore my card up . . . and it took me a long, long time to get him to see my way, and to understand it." Families, particularly men in families, depended on wives and daughters for a multitude of services: clean clothes, fresh bread, hot meals every day. They could fiercely resent the intrusion of a woman's outside interests as interfering with their own perquisites. "Go home and wash the pots," hecklers cried at outdoor meetings. "What about the ole man's kippers?" One feminist summed up the price of political activism: "Public disapproval can be faced and borne, but domestic unhappiness, the price many of us paid for our opinions and activities, was a very bitter thing."

We need to know much, much more about the antagonisms of organized labor. To what extent did the labor parties' strategies enhance the privileged position of male workers over women in the name of the family wage? How much did their understanding of progress for the working class depend on reducing competition from women in the labor market? How would an organized voting bloc of unionized, highly politicized women have forced a reorientation in labor radicalism—toward a confrontation, for instance, of the issue of equal pay for equal work, raised sporadically in the trade union movement on both sides of the Atlantic throughout the late nineteenth century? There is no sustained analysis of these crucial questions. For all of the authors' awareness of the limitations of male-dominated organized labor, they still do not admit the theoretical possibility that anti-suffragists within the ILP and the Labour Party were not simply *unenlightened* on the woman question, but actively *opposed* to women's interests. To put it another way, there is no allowance that working-class men as well as capitalists might have had a material interest in the subordination of women.

Just as they are unwilling to confront the possibility that working-class men might be systematically opposed to emancipation, Liddington and Norris do not recognize the possibility that women outside the working class might make a real contribution to female liberation. The Pankhursts emerge in their account as self-indulgent, politically retrograde, manipulative, and man-hating, with no interest in the struggle for support from the labor movement: a struggle which the authors pose as the one real political concern of serious feminists at the time. Although this may not be a necessarily inaccurate description of the Pankhursts, particularly Emmeline and Christabel, there are serious limitations in a view that defines genuine socialist feminism as existing only within the structure of the labor movement, and dismisses the political content of a feminist movement simply because its participants were from the privileged classes.

An insistence that a true politics for women's advancement under capitalism can originate only in the working class constrains a probing socialist feminist analysis. Theoretically, this position denies the existence of a patriarchal system of exploitation that cuts across class lines; historically, it denies the genuine radical edge of many middle-class feminist movements and neglects many fruitful, if uneven, collaborations of women across class lines since the nineteenth century. In *"One Hand Tied Behind Us,"* for example, the radical suffragist leadership included two socialists from the privileged classes. Esther Roper, who, as secretary of the genteel Manchester Suffrage Society, initiated the working-class petition campaign, was a college graduate from a solidly bourgeois Manchester family; her companion Eva Gore-Booth, a minor literary figure, was the daughter of one of the largest landowners in the west of Ireland. Although the authors do not ignore the importance of these middle-class women to radical suffragism, they do not connect their radicalism to social causes, and we are left to assume that Roper and Gore-Booth took the road they did because of individual good will or enlightened social consciousness. Yet throughout the late nineteenth-century Western world, daughters of the bourgeoisie, middling classes, and lesser aristocracy were cutting their ties to their backgrounds and creating their own feminist vision, intimately tied to socialist and working-class movements in some cases, only loosely so in others. They were militant, far-seeing temperaments like Gore-Booth and her sister Constance Markievicz (imprisoned in Ireland for her role

in the Easter Rebellion); daughters of socialist families like Eleanor
Marx; self-supporting "odd women" like Sylvia Pankhurst; rebels
like Emma Goldman. These women and the problem of middle-
class feminism must be rescued from mainstream interpretations
and integrated into a Marxist feminist analysis.

One of the greatest strengths of Ellen DuBois's *Feminism and
Suffrage: The Emergence of an Independent Women's Movement
in America* is her treatment of this knotty question of feminism
and class. DuBois is willing to risk a departure from familiar Marxist biases. She confronts both the class basis of American suffragism—with all the limitations it entailed—and the radicalism of early
women's rights politics. Although she never drifts from an insistence on the primacy of class relations in history, she combines her
Marxism with the clarifying perspective of sexual politics. Like
much political history, *Feminism and Suffrage* may seem dry to
readers whose tastes lie with the more vivid details of social history.
The author's mastery of political issues, however, and her ability
to vivify those issues within the context of women's history, make
the book rewarding reading, particularly as a model of how to
analyze the interaction of the politics of patriarchy with those
of the state.

The subject is the development of suffragism within the American antislavery movement, the rift after the Civil War within the
antislavery ranks over the issue of suffragism, and the subsequent
split within the women's rights movement. The first American
feminist leaders came from the antislavery movement: Lucy Stone,
Lucretia Mott, and Elizabeth Cady Stanton were all abolitionists
before they were feminists. Although the Seneca Falls Convention
of 1848 opened an era of independent organizing for women, the
personal, political, and ideological ties between the two movements
remained strong throughout the antebellum period. The implicit
bond of their association was a mutual commitment to the enfranchisement of women. When the radical abolitionists moved to take
power in the Republican Party after the war, however, they pared
down their political program to what they believed was a more
feasible package for the electorate. As early as 1865, the abolitionist Wendell Phillips informed women's rights activists that he
thought it best to set aside female suffrage for the moment in
order to ensure enfranchisement for the newly emancipated blacks:
"I hope in time to be as bold as Stuart Mill and add to that last
clause 'sex'!! But this hour belongs to the negro."

As the radicals divorced themselves from woman suffrage, the
suffragists split into two camps. The "moderates," whose most

prominent woman associate was Lucy Stone, were supporters of
the radical Republican strategy; the radical opposition was led by
Stanton and Susan B. Anthony and organized around their New
York journal, *The Revolution*. The moderates argued that woman's suffrage would be won in some indeterminate future, after the
enfranchisement of the more precariously placed freedmen; Stanton
and Anthony believed that the right could only be won while con-
gressional Reconstruction was underway and there was still momentum for constitutional revision. Years later, a Wisconsin suffragist remembered how Stanton and Anthony had warned "that
the debate once closed on negro suffrage, and the amendments
passed, the question would not be opened again for another generation." The *Revolution* faction altogether disassociated themselves from the radical Republicans and refused to support the
Fifteenth Amendment which enfranchised black men, formula-
ting in the process an anti-Republican position that often shaded
into elitism and racism. Stanton, for example, argued that it was
an outrage for "refined" white women to be governed by men
from "the lower orders of Chinese, Africans, Germans and Irish,
with their low ideas of womanhood." The split within the reform
coalition was acrimonious (still arousing the passions of historians
who write about it today); historians of feminism have generally
agreed that, by weakening the women's movement, it became a
major reason why women did not win the vote for another half-
century.

The political dilemmas were knotty: in the seemingly antagonistic needs of women and black men, they still seem problematic
today. In a period of racial crisis, did Lucy Stone, indeed, choose
the better part? Were Stanton and Anthony, in their insistence
on the urgency of women's demands, politically shortsighted, even
selfish? These are questions that have run through all previous
accounts of suffragism. DuBois does not so much take sides—
although when she does, it is with Stanton and Anthony; rather,
she cuts through the entire debate to another level of understanding. She argues that the radical Republicans, by narrowing their
vision of a democratic America, forfeited their claims to the leadership of postwar reform and ultimately paved the way for their own
defeat in Reconstruction. But DuBois is ultimately interested in
another point altogether, a dialectical interpretation of events: it
was this very failure of radical Republicanism, she argues, which
gave rise to an independent women's movement in America. In
defending their break with former allies, in answering those who
attacked them for their supposed betrayal of radical principles,
Stanton and Anthony deepened their comprehension of women's

special and peculiar political position and articulated a more far-reaching feminism. In their need to find a new constituency, they shifted from a strategy of agitating to one of organizing and thereby reached beyond the internal ranks of the antislavery movement to thousands of women with little or no previous political experience.

Where others have simply described a debacle, then, DuBois, looking at events in terms of sexual politics, sees some kind of victory: "The political conflict of the late 1860s significantly advanced the movement, liberated it from its subservience to abolitionism, and propelled it into political independence." And what, precisely, was the value of independence? "Just this: that suffragists were no longer able to look to other reform movements to enact measures of benefit to women; therefore, they had to look to women themselves not only to articulate the problem, but to provide the solution to women's oppression." The changes which hundreds of newly politicized women experienced in engaging in deliberate collective action created the basis for new social relations between women and men: exactly what antebellum women's rights leaders had expected that possession of the vote would do.

DuBois's style is spare and elegant, which makes her often brilliant reversals of well-worn questions all the more striking. The most dramatic of these reversals, the key to her arugment, is her analysis of the response of Stanton and Anthony to the Fifteenth Amendment. Without whitewashing their racism, DuBois shows the legitimate basis for their consternation. From the viewpoint of the amendment's supporters, it was a partial step toward universal democracy which would make the next step, female suffrage, all the easier. But from a feminist perspective, the amendment represented a step back rather than forward, because it made sex the *only* basis for exclusion from enfranchisement. Never one to mince words, Stanton declared that its only benefit would be a deepened sexual antagonism across the country: "Woman will then know with what power she has to contend. It will be male vs. female, the land over."

The women who appear in these pages, most notably Stanton and Anthony, are different from the women worthies who populate the older suffrage histories. DuBois creates a sense of women on the move: canny, shrewd, gifted political beings, intensely involved in the day-to-day tedium, wrong-headed choices and defeats of their movement as well as its great public moments. It is so easy to assume that these women, our foremothers, were born of more heroic stuff than we; but against the temptation to idealize them, DuBois shows instead how their remarkable commitment to feminism was formed in struggle, how it grew and strengthened over the course of a long, bitter, and discouraging fight which lasted the entirety of their adult lives. In our own difficult times, these women still strengthen the spirit. There were casualties as well as survivors. DuBois tells the poignant story of Letitia Holmes, who as a student at Oberlin in the 1840s was part of its circle of young women abolitionists and feminists. On graduating, she married a minister and moved to a small New Hampshire town, where her neighbors looked with hostility on both her advanced ideas about women and her ambition to use her education in some work other than that of a pastor's wife. Completely isolated from like-minded women, Holmes confessed in letters to her college friends that she lacked the strength and knowledge to argue her ideas. She wanted to take up the women's cause and "go forth" into public life but she found herself "long in beginning"; in the end, she faded into obscurity as a minister's wife.

What saved many others from Holmes's fate was the companion-ship of sympathetic women. As in the lives of the working-class suffragists of Manchester years later, the "bonds of womanhood" allowed these women to be political activists. They visited and carried on massive correspondences; although they had servants, they still needed help from each other with their children and lessons from each other in scarce political skills. In a typical episode in the long friendship of Stanton and Anthony, the most durable of these ties, Anthony sent her friend an urgent appeal for help with a speech for a teachers' convention: "For the love of me and for the saving of the reputation of womanhood, I beg you, with one baby on your knee, . . . and four boys whistling, buzzing, hallooing, 'Ma, Ma,' set yourself about the work, . . . I must not and will not allow these schoolmasters to say, 'See, these women can't or won't do anything when we do give them a chance.' "

The importance of sisterly relations to feminism should not be surprising, as so much recent scholarship has shown the importance of women's networks in resisting and opposing patriarchal demands. In her own analysis of sisterhood and politics, however, DuBois introduces some important distinctions. Against a strong tendency in American feminist scholarship, she insists on the separation of women's politics and their culture. The levels of activity can overlap, but they are not synonymous; to see how women either accommodate themselves to or transform existing power relations, we must be able to separate the two. The women of *Feminism and Suffrage*, in DuBois's eyes, were not, in the end, radical feminists because they drew constantly on the resources of women's sphere, but because they thought about their position in society, developed a strategy for changing it, and tried to organize others to do the same. Feminism, in this view, involves a politics that directly challenges patriarchal power as it is institutionalized, finally, in the state. Such challenges do not arise simply from a collective sense of sisterhood; they do not grow automatically from women's everyday relations with each other. They involve conscious organization, collective changes in consciousness, and a shared set of ideas about the nature of power and how to seize it.[1]

Only by drawing a distinction between the political lives of women and their lives with each other can we understand why they so passionately wanted the vote—a reform which, in hindsight, seems the merest legal palliative. In both situations under consideration in this review, it was women already involved in political activity who, in raising the demand, sought to broaden their lives outside their customary sphere. Enfranchisement had some immediate practical value: clout within the trade union coalitions and labor parties for the textile workers; strength in the great electoral battles of the 1850s and the Reconstruction period for radical women reformers. Beyond the practicalities, however, the vote had symbolic resonance. It represented an entrée to public life, to the political community. Winning enfranchisement involved winning from the male electorate the acknowledgment, at least in theory, that women's social duties outside their households were as great as those of men. In an illuminating passage, DuBois shows just how radical an ideological break such an acknowledgment would have represented in the nineteenth century. The political theory of republicanism in which antebellum American democracy was grounded located a man's capacity for citizenship in his "self-ownership": that is, in his freedom from the will of others. Women's position thus constituted the essence of dependence. Their interests in government, then, were in theory adequately represented by their husbands and fathers.

The demand for woman suffrage directly challenged these notions of dependency and male authority; it voiced the claim that women's interests were not identical to, or perhaps even compatible with, those of men. The demand represented the aspiration to public life, to a sphere with wider connections, more provocative challenges than those of women's cultural milieu. To be sure, nineteenth-century women collectivized, widened, and in some sense made public their own sphere through their relations with each other. But public life was something more, something different from the female world of social ritual, religious groups, and charity work of the Americans or the rich neighborhood life of the working women of Manchester. The strongest-minded women of the nineteenth century never devalued the comforts and necessities of woman's sphere, but neither did they feel it supported them in their ambitions for fully developed lives.

On this count, the analysis of DuBois converges with that of Liddington and Norris. If the British historians are unnecessarily rigid in their view of feminism, they nonetheless maintain, for feminist radicals, a crucial sense of how women mount politically effective attacks to change their position: by organizing themselves, petitioning door-to-door, bringing, in general, a vision of an altered world to the women around them. DuBois restores this more rigorous view of politics to the American context; her book opens the way for work on the order of *"One Hand Tied Behind Us"* exploring American suffragism on the local level. In a time requiring the most serious thought about defending and advancing women's political position, these histories and the controversies they will hopefully provoke are most welcome.

NOTES

My thanks to Sean Wilentz for his help.

[1] DuBois has elaborated this distinction between women's sphere and feminism in her essay in this issue.

8 Examining Family History

RAYNA RAPP, ELLEN ROSS
and RENATE BRIDENTHAL

INTRODUCTION

This article consists of three separate pieces jointly presented as a workshop at an international conference in women's history entitled "Women and Power: Dimensions of Women's Historical Experience" held at the University of Maryland in November, 1977. The workshop had the title, "Family History: A Critique." What we want to offer here is not a criticism of family history which would abolish it or lead to its replacement, but rather a critical examination of its underlying assumptions which should lead to its more fruitful expansion. We, like many others, have found the theory and data of the last decade of family history enormously valuable. What we want to argue, however, is that much of the field is complicated by the conceptual problem of relating the family to the larger world. Each of our three pieces examines the theories which historians have used to situate families in their social environments; and each piece suggests some of the pitfalls involved in the use of those theories. Rayna Rapp argues that the notion of family has been overly objectified and should be seen instead as a cultural device, an ideology, for a larger social purpose: recruitment into household and class. Ellen Ross peels the history of women out of family history in which it has too often been hidden. To do so, she challenges the assumptions of role theory, of consensus within families, and of the emotional isolation of families. Renate Bridenthal suggests a broader synthesis, "the mode of social reproduction," which shows the family to be only one agent among many, continuously transformed by the dialectical processes of capitalism itself.

In these papers, we employ a Marxist-Feminist perspective, which points toward an alternative vision of social relations, although we do not claim to arrive at it here or even to have resolved the disparities between our separate presentations. For example, we all agree that the assumptions of naturalness surrounding "the family" must be penetrated; but each of us focuses on a different set of contradictions which have been reproduced inside of families, both historically and in the present. We offer this discussion collectively as a contribution toward a recognition of the enormous weight—both positive and pejorative—that families have had in our history, in our present, and in our conscious constructions of the future. We feel that a Marxist-Feminist methodology not only clarifies the history of women and families, but also unmasks the intimate connections between the seemingly separate domains of personal and social life.

HOUSEHOLD AND FAMILY: RAYNA RAPP

A great many scholars have argued persuasively that the family has been not simply a passive recipient, but also an active agent of both its own changing form and content, and that of the "modernizing" world in which it has been situated.[1] Their methodological perspectives fall into two dominant schools: those who use quantitative techniques to discuss the role of the family in underwriting or responding to economic and social change; and those who focus more closely on the *mentalités*, or cultural practices and values which families both express and utilize in their interaction with larger social domains.[2] Yet whatever the mix of quantitative and qualitative methods, much of the work on the history of the family is conceptually wedded to an acceptance of the distinction between the family itself, and the larger world.[3] I will argue that it is this acceptance of "the family" as a natural unit existing in separation from the total social formation which *creates* the problem of its insertion into that world, at least at the level of theory. I will further argue that unless we develop a more critical awareness of the family as a social, not a natural unit, we run the risk of mechanically assigning it to either "cause" or "effect" in the study of social change. As a social (and not a natural) construction, the family's boundaries are always decomposing and recomposing in continuous interaction with larger domains. Without a more self-consciously social perspective on family history, we also run the risk of succumbing to a piece of dominant, postcapitalist ideology: we replicate the splits between public and private, workplace and household, economy and family. In short, we reproduce the notion of "the home as a haven in a heartless world."[4]

The methodological tools that we need in order to examine families in continuous interaction and interpenetration with larger domains are, in part, already provided in the family history literature. They may need some sharpening if we are to use them to dissect the very object they were created to build. One such tool is the distinction between household and family which appears in the demographically oriented literature of family history. I will be using that distinction in a slightly different way than it is usually presented. The household is usually defined as a coresident domestic group, while the family consists of those household members who also share kinship relations to one another.[5] I will focus on the household as a locus of shared activities, and the family as a unit providing normative recruitment to those household activities. I will argue that household activities are continuously part of the "larger" processes of production, reproduction, and consumption; as such, they vary by class. Household activities cannot be analyzed as separate from the socioeconomic relations of the societies in which they are embedded.

Households are material units within which people pool resources and perform certain tasks. It is within households that people enter into relations of production, reproduction, and consumption with one another, and on one another's account. Households are residential units within which people and resources are produced, connected, and distributed. The activities of households reveal the material links that connect them to the social formation. This can be seen in productive relations. An example would be in the contrast between households which send out labor power in exchange for wages, and those households that have access to farm land and sell cash crops. Links to larger domains are seen in reproductive relations as well, in both the narrower and the broader sense of the term. More narrowly construed, reproductive relations organize a social context for biology—different patterns of sexuality, of marriage, of fertility produce not only human beings; but they also produce participants in relations between the genders and the generations. In its broader sense, reproduction refers to all the activities in which households recreate themselves and in the process, contribute to the reproduction of the total society. Patterns of inheritance, domestic cycles, strategies for migration and employment are simultaneously part of household and of general social reproduction. It is through these relations of production and reproduction that conditions originating in larger arenas of society are internalized and experienced (and sometimes inverted or resisted) within households. Because household activities link members directly into the relations which continuously produce and reproduce the whole society, households can be seen to vary systematically by class in their ability to gain access to, accumulate, and transmit resources.

The concept of a family is a bit harder to define than is that of a household. In the family history literature, family usually means a grouping of kinsfolk minus servants, boarders, etc., who *should* be living together inside of households. I want to argue that we need to focus on the "should" portion of that definition (i.e., the idea of kin-based families as normative) in order to reveal a key structure crucial for the understanding of ideology. It is through their commitment to the concept of family that people are recruited to the material relations of households. Because people accept the meaningfulness of family, they enter into relations of production, reproduction, and consumption with one another—they marry, beget children, work to support dependents, transmit and inherit cultural and material resources. In all of these activities, the concept of family both reflects and masks the realities of household formation and sustenance. It also glosses over the variety of experiences that social categories of persons have within households. These experiences alter radically depending on gender, generation, and class. Women and men, the old and the young officially participate in the same families, but their experiences of them may be quite different. For example, Wolf contrasts the patrilineal, patrilocal kinship patterns conventionally described for China with the uterine families of a women's community that organizes female-centered reproduction and production in rural Taiwan. Women and men in this analysis have different families on which they can depend. Reiter argues similarly that in contemporary rural Provence, the men and women of a small agricultural village actually have two different (but overlapping) families: men's families are more nucleated; women's more extended, given the way in which work relations separate and reconnect households in the division of labor by gender.[6]

The meaning of family experiences differs significantly among different classes. For example, recent work on the history of children and of domestic cycles reveal that being a child is a highly variable social relation. I would argue that a great deal of that variation reflects recruitment and socialization to class. A young apprentice placed in an artisanal household had a different experience of his adolescence than did peasant children redistributed amongst neighboring households as surplus laborers and consumers, or childminding girls exchanged among related households of West African traders at different moments in their domestic cycles.[7] All three were culturally "youths" being recruited to class relations as they moved between households under the aegis of families.

To use a more contemporary example, a debate in the U.S. women's movement focuses on the future of the family as it constrains and sustains women. Yet not all women have the same experiences in their families, so they do not enter that debate with similar understandings of what the family provides and denies. Many very poor women use their relatives to form extended, flexible networks within which money, goods, food, furniture, and sometimes children are passed around.[8] The families of the middle class often seem to substitute commodity forms for the social processes in which poorer people participate as kinsfolk. "Women's work" is mediated in middle-class America by access to health plans, credit cards, bank loans, or welcome wagons at times of family tension in which poorer people turn to one another. Such experiences are intimately linked to relations of production, reproduction, and consumption which translate the abstractions of "class" directly into households. These relations are then experienced as "private" by the family members who occupy and connect those households. But to the extent that people enter the world of the family as socially defined members of more general categories, their experiences are not simply private. Nor are they uniform between genders, generations, or classes.

Yet those different experiences are not the subject of most social science analyses of the family. Social scientists, like everyone else, are participants as well as observers in families; and they tend rather easily to universalize experiences which reflect their own gender and class relations. As feminists, we must be particularly careful not to fall into the same trap by assuming that "the politics of family life" occur within a uniform entity. To do so is to incorporate a middle-class bias into our strategies of transformation, even when we attempt to build coalitions across ethnic and class lines. The problem of false universalization is deeply embedded in our culture; concepts which have class- and gender-specific referents are often used *as if* they described a single, uniform experience. People from radically different backgrounds may all believe in the family, but the social relations they are referring to are not necessarily the same. Their families are intimately conditioned by relations their households hold to processes of production, reproduction, and consumption. Belief in the family acts as a kind of ideological shock absorber which keeps people functioning and diminishes the tensions often generated by those continuous economic processes.

Of course, the ideological shock absorber which the concept of family provides is not used merely internally by different family members, or even by different classes. It is also used by the state to regulate relations between family members and classes. The nature of state organization and power is historically very variable. Nonetheless, I think it is fair to say that all states promulgate, enforce, and depend on a "family policy." The juridical realm has both defined legitimate family forms and relied on the notion of family to reproduce state authority. It is a long way from the first decipherable Mesopotamian law which specifies monogamy for women, not for men, to the welfare policies of the contemporary United States, which continue to award Aid to Families with Dependent Children payments to poor mothers only if there is no father contributing to the household.[9] In both cases, however, the power of the state to reorganize relations of reproduction is clear. Sometimes, states actively create the family form they need as part of political legitimation; this was the case in the sixteenth- and seventeenth-century concept of patriarchy in English political history.[10] The distinction between the household as material relations and the family as normative recruitment to those relations should allow us to examine both the creation of and resistance to political policies. Taxation, conscription, work, and welfare laws all govern relations of authority, and the extraction of surplus between genders, generations, and classes organized within households.

Using the distinction between household and family in the manner outlined above might allow us to penetrate the ideological assumptions of naturalness that permeate both the family history literature and modern social science theory about families. This perspective frees us to consider problematic topics such as the ideological power which attaches to notions of the family, and the potential for transformations inherent in family forms.

Once we make a theoretical distinction between households and families, we begin to understand how ideology penetrates our most *intimate* social relations, and conditions our acceptance of or resistance to dominant values in the larger society. For example, in the history of the United States, poor people have often been blamed for their own poverty. Middle-class family norms have sometimes provided the vocabulary in which the poor were held responsible for their own situation. The struggle over domestic education, schooling, male and female roles, and what "an American family" was supposed to be was fierce during the second wave of immigration which brought much of the industrial working class to the cities of the United States.[11] Of course, the labeling of Black families as pathological in twentieth-century social science and government policy is another example of the same process, all the more harsh for its racial as well as class discrimination. Given the contributions of Black studies, we now can see that out of the oppressive circumstances of slavery and impoverished freedom on which the shifting bases of household formation rested, black women and men invented family forms (including adoption, and fictive kinship) that wove a kinship network where none was permitted to exist.[12] Out of their belief in families, they inverted the social reality of fragmentation and enforced mobility which undercut household stability, and made next-to-nothing go a very long way. Dominant ideology inverts those struggles, and labels Black families (and especially Black mothers) as faulty; what is faulty is rather the economic arrangements of society that preclude their households from forming stable bases. Such use of the concept of family to blame people in intimate terms for "failures" that are socially constructed is an instance of ideological domination along the simultaneous lines of race, class, and sex.

Once the ideological power of the concept of family is examined, we may have a better handle on an analysis of the transformatory potentials which different family forms might hold. Instead of arguing rather abstractly over whether the family is falling apart or sustaining itself, we may be able to examine more precisely which kinds of families both change and resist change in light of household links to larger domains. Such analysis will help us not only to understand better the different histories of family forms, but also to think more concretely in theory and practice about the experiments in alternative households that many progressive movements have attempted. With such an analysis, it becomes possible to see the defense of the working-class family during British industrialization as a form of collective resistance to proletarianization, bought, in part, by the strengthening of patriarchal relations within it. The implications for relations between men and women within households are very different than in some of the more female-centered households and families which have been analyzed in the Third World. For example, Moyo's autobiographical study of the Matabele of Rhodesia describes a tremendous struggle in defense of extended families waged by communities linked through "little mothers" and "big mothers." The indigenous meaning of motherhood extended kinship throughout the society, and all adult females were participants. When British missionaries attempted to identify families, they were confused by the fluid and complex extended relations they saw. They expropriated "orphans" because the tribal children didn't fall into the family forms the British were attempting to produce. Extended kinship groups, organized around big and little mothers, struggled to liberate the "orphans" as part of a resistance to state-imposed family forms which accom-

panied colonialism. Such female-centered extended kinship networks have been identified in the Caribbean as well, and Caulfield
sees them as a core feature of cultures of resistance.[13]   Although
the analogy is premature, it seems to me that we have the possibility to do in family history what anthropology has done in the
analysis of peasant rebellions and revolutions: delineate which
microforms are particularly well-situated for resistance, guerrilla
warfare, co-optation and the like.[14] We also need to think concretely about the different resources and resistances that categories of families bring to rapid social change.

In sum, I am obviously not against the study of family history—
I'm in favor of it. What I am against is doing it *as if* we had a uniform, and presumably natural unit with which to work. I believe
we have to deconstruct the family as a natural unit, and reconstruct
it as a social one. In the process, I think we'll find that one very
important aspect of the family is ideological. As such, its very
meaning becomes a terrain of struggle. It reflects and shapes the
material forces which link people inside of households to relations
we understand as gender and class.

WOMEN AND FAMILY: ELLEN ROSS[15]

Until recently, women's historians were less likely to study wom-
en as family members than as organized groups, distinguished individuals, or as a caste with shared concerns and collective demands.
Like other feminists, we saw families as oppressive and controlling
for wives and daughters and concluded that it was not in these roles
that women could ever "make history." Yet all of us are now
extremely interested in the historical development of family forms,
and, to judge from our fruitful use of earlier studies by Olwen Hufton, Laura Oren, Joan Scott, and Louise Tilly,[16] we are convinced
that work on women in their family context points in a positive
direction.

What has crystallized our desire to understand the family and
those experiences of women which are embedded in it? It seems
to me that we have only recently begun to appreciate the overwhelming power of family feeling and ties. The pull of motherhood, for example, did not disappear with the resurgence of feminism in the 1960s; it was only temporarily relaxed as millions of
women discovered the pleasure and significance of the nonfamily
worlds of job satisfaction, work relationships, group membership,
politics, and friendship. In the past four or five years, though,
feminists have faced up to the continuing importance of family
in our own lives. We have also begun to see the growth of right-

wing movements against abortion rights, the Equal Rights Amendment, and feminism in general which draw on and exploit widespread popular fears of family breakdown.[17]

A new feminist analysis of the family is emerging which goes
beyond earlier work on the economics of women's place in the
home to a conceptualization of the family's power in creating
and reproducing the core of our being as women, our feminine
identity. We have engaged Freud's and other theories of personality, as well as Marx, in our search for an understanding of the
continued strength of the "sex/gender system."[18]

This sharpened grasp of the significance of family in our own
generation's life histories has focused our attention on the fact
that motherhood, domesticity, and kin have formed the center
of life for the majority of women in Western and other societies.
To understand the historical parameters of women's lives, then,
we need to know more about them as mothers, daughters, and
sisters.

In the generation or so since Jules Henry and the Cambridge
Group structured their discipline in its modern form, family and
demographic historians have provided us with a wealth of information about the kin-related experiences of millions of otherwise
invisible women. Techniques of collecting and interpreting data
on marriage ages, fertility rates, household size, and patterns of
family residence and migration have provided knowledge about
women's situations which even half a generation ago was mostly
unavailable. Our appreciation of the historical dimensions of
womanhood has enormously deepened as a result. Today, for
example, it is quite well known that American and European
women spend about one-seventh of their seventy-five year expected lifespan as "mothers" in the physical sense—either pregnant,
nursing, or caring for preschool children—compared with about
one-third of their much shorter life expectancy as recently as
1900.[19] Thus the actual physical, material experience of motherhood has diminished in significance, to be compensated for, perhaps, by a greater emphasis on its psychological aspects.

But scholars whose central focus is women's history are likely
to encounter methodological problems as they hunt for women's
experiences in existing family history and demographic literature.
For much of it makes assumptions which obscure rather than uncover the actual historical experiences of women as well as the
forces determining the limits of their lives.

I am singling out four assumptions which run through both sociological treatments of the contemporary family based on structural-
functionalist methodology[20] and much family history which is also
roughly based on it: (1) that families are "natural," that is biological, units whose form can be understood in terms of blood ties
and in relative isolation from social forces and institutions such as
churches, state governments, the availability of employment, and
access to land; (2) that families are the only areas in which significant emotional contact takes place; (3) that the sexes and generations experience families in the same way, and that their needs and
interests are identical regardless of their position in the family, thus
obscuring the concerns of children and wives which are often un-
critically absorbed into those of the male "head of household"
(demographers, especially, make this assumption); and (4) that the
best way to conceptualize relationships among family members is
under the rubric of "role," with its implications of harmony and
of a process of simple "training" in how to fill them. In what follows I want to challenge these assumptions, showing how recent
historical work has already undermined them. Although we certainly do not yet have a new understanding of the historical process, we have come further than we know toward piecing together
a broader framework for the family history of women which rescues
wives and daughters from the conceptual "coverture" that has so
often been their fate.

The family as a biological entity. As Rayna Rapp has already
noted, the fact that there are indeed biological relationships within families obscures the extent to which "family" is defined by
purely social forces. Over two decades ago, Philippe Ariès showed
that childhood is not a biological but a social category. This should
have alerted us to the question of the "naturalness" of other such
definitions, but it is only lately that some historians have tried to
separate the social from the biological in the family.

Blood relationship is differently understood from society to
society. Even in European history, as Natalie Davis shows, there
has been a great deal of variation in church teachings about degrees
of consanguinity and prohibited marriages. Before the thirteenth
century, marriage within the seventh degree was prohibited, at least
in theory; later it was within the fourth degree. Godparents were
always considered blood relations in medieval Europe, though we
would consider them only "friends" today.[21] Today consanguinity
is so narrowly designated that first cousins may marry in many
Western cultures.

Concepts of significant kin relations have undergone similarly dramatic changes, expanding and contracting as support by kin was more or less needed. Family identity in the early Middle Ages tended to extend horizontally out to third and fourth cousins; and it included not only illegitimate children, but also retainers of various kinds. To members of this large network people turned for protection or revenge; they might also be punished for each other's crimes.[22] By the Renaissance in Italy, somewhat later in England, the more familiar "longitudinal" concept of family, as a name and property transferred from father to son had developed; sixteenth-century English genealogies now paid scanty attention to tracing any but the male line.[23]

In the intervening centuries, a constellation of social changes had taken shape which made the latter definition more common. State governments had taken over many of the protective functions of the earlier kin networks and clans; and indeed, as Stone demonstrates, in England the government had deliberately set out to weaken kinship as a rival system of power, and to launch a barrage of propaganda in favor of loyalty to state and sovereign.[24] True private property in land, capital, or offices which could easily be left to heirs, had also developed, while the power of fellow villagers, town governments, guilds, feudal lords, the church, and monarchs to determine what parents did with their children and property had decreased as well.[25] The Protestant stress on the value and dignity of conjugal love also had a place in this contraction of the family. If love is a powerful emotional bond between a newly married couple, it is also a way of separating them from their parents and other kin and establishing a new and distinct family unit.[26]

In the early modern era, legal changes also fostered this redefinition of family relationships. Coverture laws in England enhanced the material power of husbands over wives; the weakening of entail in sixteenth-century England "greatly strengthened the ability of the current head of the family to dispose of the property as he chose," Stone notes. Stone and David Hunt show that the desire of fathers to control their sons' occupational and marriage choices under these circumstances led to the harsh discipline in school and at home which upper-class children, especially boys, had to endure.[27] Law also increased the responsibilities of husbands and fathers, especially in the higher strata. An Elizabethan law (35 Eliz. cap. 1) required household heads to see that their children and apprentices went to church under penalty of a fine. Under Henry VIII (34 and 35 Hen. VIII cap.1), merchant, noble, and gentlemen householders were permitted to read the Bible with their families, but the privilege was expressly withdrawn from women and from men below the designation of "artificers."[28]

Seeing the family as a unit held together biologically makes some facts about its functioning unnecessarily puzzling; family historians sometimes find themselves having to account for the penetration of the family barrier—a barrier we are saying does not really exist—by forces outside it. In *The Making of the Modern Family*, Edward Shorter shows us many ways in which preindustrial village society in Europe interpenetrated family life through courtship, wedding, and funeral customs, and the absence of any popular belief about the privacy of the home.[29] He begins, however, with the "natural" image of the family, and sees community as intruding all too frequently on family privacy. As Christopher Lasch and Kenneth Keniston have recently argued persuasively, privacy—the sense of intimacy and retreat from the world which we associate with today's family—is both an illusion and a piece of twentieth-century ideology.[30] Our "private" families are as much social products and as closely intertwined with the public sphere as the more diluted or extended family relations Shorter describes. A more fruitful starting point might be a different question: Under what economic and social circumstances are nuclear and nonnuclear kin relationships strong, and when are community, neighborhood, or peer ties more important?[31]

Ties beyond the family. We do not have a clear understanding of historical changes in human emotional life. The sheer difficulty of getting at feelings and personality structures is one reason for our ignorance. Another reason is the failure to look beyond the family to other emotional contacts, which, in fact, might be more fully documented, thus forming a more complete and complex picture of emotionality. We may be emotionally engaged in clubs and civic groups; in visiting and sharing services with neighbors; in cooperating, socializing, or quarreling with work companions; and in sustaining same-sex friendships or love relationships. But the ideal of family exclusiveness, especially as formulated in twentieth-century Freudian terms, tends to downgrade the importance of all nonfamilial interactions.

Recent work based on diaries and correspondence has reconstructed and reinterpreted the emotional patterns of nineteenth-century middle-class American women. If we confined our picture to relations between these wives and their husbands, looking only within the family, we would find these relationships stiff and formal; and we would make judgments about personality and affective life accordingly. Yet the diaries and letters show that in attachments to women friends and kin, the same women are passionate, sensual, and devoted. The rigid separation of the female from the male sphere in middle-class American society; the designation of women as the more compassionate, sensitive, and religious of the sexes; and their shared experiences in schools and churches, as well as in the family, were the historical ground in which such intimate friendships grew and were honored.[32] In the last decades of the century, though, these attachments seem to decline in power, as married love became a more central emotional focus and social preoccupation.[33]

Parallel networks have linked poor and working-class women kin and neighbors in ways whose emotional, economic, and political significance we are only starting to understand. Women whose families moved too often for them to participate in neighborhood networks, but who were far from kin could be especially lonely and vulnerable. Nineteenth- and twentieth-century British sources show neighbors exchanging food; childcare; and other major services, such as shelter and comfort during domestic crises; help during sickness; even assistance in feeding or bathing each other's husbands.[34] Prostitutes in Plymouth and Southampton, harassed under the Contagious Diseases Acts in the 1860s through 1880s; established a subculture providing companionship and mutual aid; they were also sufficiently part of their female communities to get financial help and support in court from their landladies, from female kin, and from "poor but respectable neighbors."[35]

Such friendship and support networks have likely also provided the crucibles in which collective acts of rebellion were formed. In the 1800s, groups of Worcester leather glovemakers attacked ladies wearing the silk gloves that were causing their unemployment; in the 1830s, groups of working-class women supported Chartist candidates by collectively patronizing merchants who had voted for them. Neighborhood women harassed police trying to make arrests under the Contagious Diseases Acts in the 1860s and 1870s and were active in organizing demonstrations against the Acts. The middle-class organizers for repeal of the Acts seemed quite comfortable with these popular forms. As long as working-class political strategies were compatible with female collective traditions, women were also active in radical politics in Britain. But by the 1850s, Dorothy Thompson suggests, women began to be left behind by more structured unions and the new interest of skilled workers in exercising the local franchise.[36] In the more formal politics that emerged, the transition from personal contact to political action could less easily be made.

E. P. Thompson's "Time, Work-Discipline, and Industrial Capitalism" may be read as a picture of the effects of industrialization on the emotional as well as work life of men, in particular, because it describes the segregation of friendship and sociability from work exacted by factory discipline.[37] A very differently organized male social world emerged in response, in which friendship and conviviality were part of the cluster of "leisure" institutions—clubs, sports events, and pubs—which grew up as the industrial workday in England decreased to ten, then eight hours.[38]

Family harmony. The danger of assuming unity or complete harmony of interests among members of the same family is a problem which all three of our essays address. Because contemporary observers and official statistics often use fathers to represent their families (in assigning class and assessing standards of living, for example) the households are absorbed into their "heads." Differences in the situations of generations or sexes within families are obscured. When tensions do appear in the literature, they are usually between fathers and sons, as in Platt and Weinstein's *The Wish to be Free*, Richard Sennett's study of middle-class Chicago families in the 1880s, or Lutz Berkner's work on the "stem family" in eighteenth-century Austria.[39]

Demographic historians have a tendency to assume that decisions about limiting family size are made by both members of a couple; contraception is usually called a "family decision." But in their discussions of "domestic feminism" in nineteenth-century America, Daniel Scott Smith and Linda Gordon have suggested that contraception has to be seen not only as a "family matter," but also as an arena contested between the sexes, parts of the struggle occurring within families, and parts in more public political forms.[40] Looked at from women's vantage, families indeed become areas in which power has a concrete, daily meaning. Johnny Faragher and Christine Stansell's account of American women on the overland trail focuses on the suffering and loss of wives in particular that was part of what is often blandly labeled "migration." Families may have been the units which migrated and worked together, but Faragher and Stansell's research revealed widespread resentment among women whose husbands had forced them to leave behind beloved homes, kin, and friends; and they document wives' repeated attempts to recreate their lost women's world.[41] When Laura Oren looked behind the mystique of family unity in budget studies of pre-World War I British families, she found that it was incorrect to use this evidence to establish a family standard of living. Instead, she discovered two distinct standards, one for husbands, a second for wives and children. The amount of meat eaten per week, the quality of health care, and availability of recreation—all differed dramatically between husbands and wives within the same family.[42] So far historians know too little about life inside the household to grasp many of the concrete historical variations of the sex/gender system; unwillingness to break families down into their constituent parts has surely slowed us down.

Role theory. The use of the terms "role" and "women's role" presents a most elusive problem; all of us will continue to use these terms because it is hard to find substitutes. Wording describing the actual activities of women avoids the misleading implications of "role"; but its connotation of socially defined expectation is a valuable conceptual element which we lose this way.[43] We may continue to speak of roles but I think we should use the term carefully and critically.

For one thing, roles are an important part of functionalist theory and provide the building blocks of the harmonious families and societies which functionalism posits; they are thus pieces of a static and conflict-free social picture. Using this framework, it is hard to think about power or to examine strategies that women, for example, have used to increase theirs. Tension and conflict cannot be explained by role theory except as a product of multiple roles which are out of phase, as in Viola Klein and Alva Myrdal's study of employed wives in England, *Women's Two Roles: Work and Family.*[44] The existence of roles that fail to mesh is simply a concession in functionalist theory to the undeniable reality of dysfunction and struggle as permanent, not sporadic, parts of social life.

Role theory further ignores the reality of the unconscious reproduction of sex and gender—just that reality feminists have begun to face and explore. In its implications about personality formation, role theory is behaviorist, assuming that we are simply trained to fill appropriate social slots. In different ways, Juliet Mitchell, Nancy Chodorow, Adrienne Rich, Dorothy Dinnerstein, and others have shown that changes in gender role are far more difficult to bring about than role theory implies.[45] Such changes require more than better "role models" or "positive reinforcement" for new behavior. The strength of psychological ties to family—especially to mothers—helps explain the magnitude of the task required to reorganize sex and gender relations. For the family is not only the main arena in which girls and boys are "trained" to assume appropriate roles. It also provides a nexus of personal relationships which condition our sexuality and bind us to some form of "femininity." Mothering by women, as Chodorow argues, means that personality structures and emotional needs and strengths for boys and girls, men and women, inevitably diverge, as the mother-child dyad has different emotional content for boys and girls through early infancy as well as into the oedipal stage.[46] Thus femininity and masculinity are not only a series of behaviors we are taught, but also integral parts of human personality formed through the different ways each sex experiences the historical fact of mothering.

As disciplines, women's and family history cover much of the same historical turf. What distinguishes them are not so much their objects of study as their own histories and ideological origins: women's history in feminism, family history in a social-science tradition often strongly influenced by functionalism. Historians of women would reach a dead end without learning much more about this central human social arrangement, the family. It would be equally unproductive though if women in history were to be once more silent, absorbed into the category of family from which they have only recently and precariously been rescued. The understanding we have achieved so far about the ways families operate ought to make this impossible once and for all.

FAMILY AND REPRODUCTION: RENATE BRIDENTHAL

Family history, like its progenitor, the sociology of the family, emerged in the nineteenth century in the context of social dislocation caused by rapid industrialization and the attendant disintegration of working-class families. From Engels's *Origin of the Family, Private Property and the State* (1884) on, politically charged scholarship has traced the impact of changes in the economy on the family and vice versa.[47] Mainstream family history, by definition, has been non- or anti-Marxist, across a spectrum of increasingly sophisticated methodologies. Within that conceptual limitation, it has provided a wide array of rich descriptions focusing on the size, form, and composition of the family and/or its functions in society at large. However, such studies usually reflect their structuralist-functionalist heritage, whose main weakness is a lack of theory about what generates change. They tend to see social change as the product of individuals and families coping with their life circumstances. What is left out is an understanding of the continually changing, wider context in which these lives and their circumstances are shaped. Patterns are usually not sought.

It is as if family historians viewed their subject through a kaleidoscope. They shake up the pieces to create new combinations, but few have questioned the validity of the pieces themselves. The terms structure and function recur as an agreed-upon language.

The language does indeed serve a purpose: it permits a level of analysis which simple humanistic narrative would not. Yet it has severe limitations.[48] The most serious of these is the loss of *process*. Structuralism is a method derived from linguistics and has been most successfully applied to anthropology. It sees social relations as coded like language, each relation analogous to a phoneme, an element within a larger system whose syntax can be diagramed. Functionalism adds a circular teleology: the structures exist to perform certain functions and the functions create certain structures. The static nature of the model is immediately discernible. When historians try to adopt it, its anticausal bias becomes a problem. If the system works to reproduce itself—and that is a structural/functionalist assumption—then how do new social formations emerge? In other words, if elements gear into one another successfully, how and why does change occur? It is the historian's old problem of continuity and discontinuity made more difficult by the systemic equilibrium of the structuralist model.[49]

All in all, structural functionalism which has dominated family history, by its very architecturalism denies the complexity of relations between individuals and classes.[50] Individuals relate to one another through several institutions. The family is only one; and its membership and reciprocal obligations have varied greatly over time and space; so much so, that the term "family" itself can be questioned. In fact, the field of home economics, created precisely to conserve the family, has recently signaled defeat by omitting biological relationship completely from its definition:

The focus of home economics is family in its various forms. Family is defined as a unit of intimate, transacting, and interdependent persons who share some values and goals, resources, responsibility for decisions, and have commitment to one another over time.[51]

Rather than argue over a definition of the family, however, I propose we place familial relations within a larger analytic category, the mode of social reproduction. This takes into account the *several* institutions that create and shape us as particular social beings; and it stresses relationship over structure, thereby introducing more flexibility into the notion of reproduction. With this approach, we gain the opportunity to see individual relationships reflecting larger social relationships and to see the contradictions that compel change.

In capitalist society, the relations to be reproduced are those of hierarchy, of contract (market relations), and of the private ownership of collectively created products. Families, interacting with other institutions, reproduce all of these, though differently in different classes. In the process, however, conflicts are aroused, which in turn threaten to dissolve the families themselves. Thus, like the capitalist society in which they are embedded, families carry the seeds of their own transformation.

To begin with, social relations in contemporary capitalist society are hierarchical, specifically they are class relations. The capital-owning class keeps power in its own hands by transmitting its private ownership of collectively produced social wealth to its heirs. The obvious advantages of wealth and the implicit threat of disinheritance are forms of social control which recreate class mores and weed out those considered not fit to rule. On the other hand, limited opportunities for social advancement through education and intermarriage also admit some outsiders into the capitalist class. Thus, the class reproduces itself with personnel, interests, and skills, primarily, but not only, through family relations. The daily physical reproduction of class members is usually assigned to paid personnel such as nurses, servants, etc.

The working class, defined here very broadly as that class which sells its labor power for wages, also must be reproduced not only physically, but as a group with particular skills. These vary according to the historical situation and so, therefore, does their reproduction. Thus, a craftsperson may teach trade arts to her or his child or to an apprentice from another family of the same social class in one period, a school may do it in another. At still another time, the number of training institutions may diminish as the demand for skilled labor decreases. Physically, the class may be reproduced by the unpaid domestic labor of the women of that class supplemented by paid labor in restaurants, laundries, childcare centers, health clinics, and state services. The working class too, then, reproduces itself only partly through family relations. In fact, over time the working-class family controls its own reproduction less and less. Increasingly, the state has assumed some of those functions through policies of health, education, and social insurance. And its more recent interventions in childcare, through the back door of concern about child abuse and neglect, indicate a continuing trend. As *public* services they mask control over working-class reproduction. Public services also incorporate an interesting contradiction: they claim to support family structure; yet, as often, they actually undermine it. For example, a common condition for receiving aid in the United States today is family breakdown, specifically an absent male "head of household." This prerequisite reinforces, by rewarding, precisely such breakdown and increases the need for more state help. On the other hand, endemic and epidemic unemployment and underemployment leave no other option. Relations of dependency and hierarchy tend to be reproduced by this mode of social reproduction, in which families are partly functional, but are also made dysfunctional by the state.[52]

There is also a contradiction between family ideology and the actual practice of real families. The ideology maintains that families are privately responsible for the socialization and maintenance of their members, whether they are actually able to be so or not. To the extent that people internalize this value, they experience shame in the event of failure. Acceptance of some social services then appears to be a sign of family weakness, rather than as the necessary mediation of business cycles by an advanced political state. This internalization shields the system from analysis and allows state responsibility for social care to be conveniently flexible. Aid may be given or withheld, depending on other needs of capital for investment and on demands raised by social unrest. Thus, in a period of fiscal crisis, social services are cut. The burden is felt directly in the family, which must pick up the slack. The added pressure may further disintegrate it; conflict over money is a leading cause of divorce.[53]

A second set of relations socially reproduced under capitalism are market relations. Like relations of hierarchy, these are reproduced in and by families as well as other institutions. One sociological school has construed family relations in the language of the market, with members having "resources," with which they "bargain" for a greater share in "decision making." According to this point of view, women move toward greater equality in the family when they become wage earners because income gives them more clout to wield at home.[54] This theory at least acknowledges the individual interests of women in the family. However, its proponents do not comment on the ideological contradiction between such contractual relations and the sentiment of love, considered priceless (without a money value) and altruistic. Bargaining presupposes calculated, rational self-interest on the part of a freely contracting individual. In fact, family members are not absolutely free, any more than are other contracting individuals in the capitalist market in which economic coercion reigns. And the incursion of contractual models to explain family relations reveals the encroachment of capitalist relations into what has been seen as supposedly a refuge from social atomization.

Market relations also transform the family by creating new needs, which arise out of traditional family needs, but come into conflict with them. This is a dialectical development which works in the following way: new needs for consumer goods and services are created and the cost of old ones is raised as capitalist development proceeds. These needs can be met only by the addition of more wage earners in the working-class family because unemployment among primary wage earners tends to recur and inflation tends to erode real wages over time. Thus, not only new consumer goods, but old ones like schooling of the young, now prolonged well into adulthood, propel increasing numbers of married women into the labor force.[55] This social development, in turn, creates new needs for women as workers: for education, training, clothing, ready-made foods, transportation, etc. The reproduction of women workers, as well as of their husbands and children, is accomplished increasingly by other-than-familial institutions: schools, manu-facturers and distributors of food and clothing, childcare services, laundries, restaurants, and so on. The very attempt of the working-class family to reproduce and maintain its members and their skills by sending out more wage earners then undermines the family's ability to do so by itself. The process changes the structure of the household and moves its functions increasingly out of the private and into the public sphere.[56] If these social processes generate tensions within the household itself, the household's stability may be threatened. This is perceived as "the breakup of the family" and is often attributed simply to working wives and mothers, rather than to a stage in the development of capitalism. By looking at the *overall* mode of social reproduction with the family as only one agent of it, we can observe the dynamics of the larger society in the contradictions of the family and household relations. The dialectic that emerges in microcosm is that families reproduce market relations and, by responding to them, become transformed.

A larger contradiction looms: if capitalism dissolves the working-class family, it thereby undermines an important ideological foun-dation of class rule, that is, the importance of family for the trans-mission of socially created, but privately owned wealth. However, not only the owning class, but also the working class defends the notion of family. The latter resist the encroachment of market relations and try to preserve the family as a refuge from them. Working-class resistance through conservation of family forms is beyond the scope of this paper, but it is an important topic for further research.

Finally, the concept of social reproduction allows us to examine a third set of social relations under capitalism: the contradiction of collectivity and individualism. In social production, collective work relations are masked by their opposite, the private appropria-tion of products. People create a common product through special-ized labor in factories and offices, but both profit and wages are private. This specialized hierarchically ranked labor is paralleled in the family. Here, too, there is both collectivity and its opposite, individualism. The contradiction creates painful tensions in the lives of most people, but especially of women, who have been emotionally "specialized" to live for a collective, the family. In historical practice, this has translated into women living for their families and men individuating out of their families. Fred Weinstein's and Gerald Platt's *The Wish to Be Free* makes this ideology clear. In it, a Parsonian nuclear family is described as the matrix within which nurturant women provide love and security, and gently and with proper timing, release men and boys into the world as freely interacting individuals. The women themselves remain totally embedded; indeed, they *are* the matrix.

But what happens when women also move out into the world? Is there a matrix left? Or should we find another, less literal and less static metaphor for family? Perhaps that of network is more apt, as it suggests connection and communication of a group, without the necessary centrality of any given individual. It also suggests a plaiting and replaiting of skeins, allowing us to visualize more flexible living arrangements without imputing pathology.[57]

The final contradiction we should note is that between socially produced alienation and the private experience of it. Divisions between and within families, resulting from exploitation and competition, reinforce the social alienation already produced by divisions in the workplace. On the one hand, family loyalty protectively encloses past and present problems and intimacies; but the lid of secrecy becomes stifling and enhances feelings of shame. Thus families become both havens and traps. Expectations of intimacy run high but often crash against walls of alienation. A mutually dependent but atomized society is reproduced in family relations, as it is in work relations, where people create together but take away vastly different shares of their product.

In sum, family as an analytical category has only limited value for historical explanation. A broader approach, using the concept of mode of social reproduction may yield more. If we consider that human beings are created by a complex set of social relations of which family relations are only one, then we must acknowledge a total mode of reproduction appropriate to any society at a particular time in its history. In the contemporary West, the relations under which people are reproduced extend far beyond the family. In order to analyze them, we must begin to ask both quantitative and qualitative questions about the social processes that go into such reproduction. For example: how much medical care and technology is embodied in different individuals? How much training of hand and mind and, regrettably, of will? How much nourishment of body and psyche? Such an approach would allow the historian to trace how reproduction has become increasingly socialized, that is, performed by the many for pay—rather than private, that is, performed by a housewife for love and subsistence. It would put the role of the family as an historical social construct in perspective and relate it to the larger dialectical process.[58]

NOTES

The collective planning and writing of this article was very valuable to us all, and we are pleased to acknowledge our intellectual debts to one another. We also want to thank the participants of the conference at which the ideas which led to this article were first presented. Their comments, criticisms, and enthusiasm contributed concretely to this work and helped us to understand its relevance to an ongoing, interdisciplinary feminist studies.

[1] The active participation of families in large-scale social change is discussed in Peter Laslett, *The World We Have Lost* (New York: Charles Scribner's Sons, 1965); Tamara K. Hareven, "Family Time and Historical Time," *Daedalus* 106 (Spring 1977): 57-70; and Natalie Zemon Davis, "Ghosts, Kin and Progeny: Some Features of Family Life in Early Modern France," *Daedalus* 106 (Spring 1977): 87-114.

[2] A distinction between quantitative and qualitative perspectives is implicit in much of the family history literature, for example, Lutz K. Berkner, "Recent Research on the History of the Family in Western Europe," *Journal of Marriage and the Family* 35 (August 1973): 395-406; and E. Anthony Wrigley, "Reflections on the History of the Family," *Daedalus* 106 (Spring 1977): 71-86. It is made explicit in Lynn Hollen Lees, "Alternative Approaches to the History of the Family," unpublished paper presented at the Conference on Social Theory and Social History, Columbia University, February 19, 1977. Examples of demographically oriented, quantitative analyses include: *Household and Family in Past Time*, ed. Peter Laslett (Cambridge, England: Cambridge University Press, 1972); Lutz K. Berkner, "The Stem Family and the Developmental Cycle of the Peasant Household: an Eighteenth Century Austrian Example," *American Historical Review* 77, no. 2 (April 1972): 398-418; E. Anthony Wrigley, *Population and History* (New York and Toronto: World University Library, McGraw-Hill, 1969); and J. Hajnal, "European Marriage Patterns in Perspective" in *Population in History*, eds. D. V. Glass and D. E. C. Eversley (Chicago: Aldine Publishing, 1965). Examples of a more qualitative orientation include works by psychohistorians, e.g., *The History of Childhood*, ed. Lloyd de Mause (New York: Harper & Row, 1974) and cultural or *mentalites* works such as Philippe Ariès, *Centuries of Childhood*, trans. Robert Baldick (New York: Vintage Books, 1962); Lawrence Stone, "The Rise of the Nuclear Family in Early Modern England: the Patriarchal Stage," in *The Family in History*, ed. Charles Rosenberg (Philadelphia: University of Pennsylvania Press, 1975); Lawrence Stone, *The Family, Sex and Marriage in England, 1500-1800* (New York: Harper & Row, 1977); and Natalie Davis, "Ghosts, Kin and Progeny." Both perspectives, of course, are generally considered important, and scholars increasingly attempt to integrate the two, e.g., Louise Tilly and Joan Scott, *Women, Work, and Family* (New York: Holt, Rinehart & Winston, 1978); Tamara K. Hareven, "Modernization and Family History: Perspectives on Social Change," *Signs* 2 (Autumn 1976): 190-206.

[3] Elizabeth H. Pleck, "Two Worlds in One: Work and Family," *Journal of Social History* 10, no. 2 (Winter 1976): 178-95, presents an excellent review of this position in recent social historical writings, but still leaves us with two separate worlds, rather than a single more complex one.

[4] Christopher Lasch, *Haven in a Heartless World* (New York: Basic Books, 1977). While we are sympathetic toward Lasch's attempt to pursue a dialectical analysis based in both the psychoanalytic and Marxist perspectives, we rapidly lose patience with his querulous blaming of social science and the feminist movement for what he takes to be the disintegration of the contemporary family. Such a target short-circuits both the analysis of advanced capitalism, and of the real struggles—notably, in the black, feminist and gay movements—which have surrounded changing family forms. It leaves us with a politics of despair, insufficient for building theory or practice toward a nonsexist and noncapitalist future.

[5] This distinction is presented in much of the quantitatively oriented literature listed in n. 2; it is specifically stated in Laslett, ed., *Household and Family in Past Time*, p. 1.

[6] Margery Wolf, *Women and the Family in Rural Taiwan* (Stanford: Stanford University Press, 1972) and Randy B. Reiter, *Sexual Domains and Family in Two Communes in Southeastern France* (Ann Arbor: University Microfilms, 1974).

[7] European apprentices are discussed in Laslett, *The World We Have Lost*; peasant exchange of children as laborers and consumers is discussed in Berkner, "The Stem Family and the Developmental Cycle of the Peasant Household"; and West African child-minders are discussed in Gloria Marshall, *Where Women Work* (Ann Arbor: University Museum Publications, 1975).

[8] For examples, see studies such as Carol B. Stack, *All Our Kin: Survival Strategies in a Black Community* (New York: Harper & Row; 1974); Joyce A. Ladner, *Tomorrow's Tomorrow: The Black Woman* (Garden City, N.Y.: Anchor Doubleday); and Molly Dougherty, *Becoming a Woman in Rural Black Culture* (New York: Holt, Rinehart & Winston, 1978).

[9] Mesopotamian legal codes are discussed by Ruby Rohrlich-Leavitt, "Women in Transition: Crete and Sumer" in *Becoming Visible: Women in European History*, eds. Renate Bridenthal and Claudia Koonz (Boston: Houghton Mifflin Co., 1977). Current A.F.D.C. policies and their implications for families are discussed by Colin C. Blaydon and Carol B. Stack, "Income Support Policies and the Family," *Daedalus* 106 (Spring 1977): 147-62, and Kenneth Kenniston and the Carnegie Council on Children, *All Our Children: the American Family Under Pressure* (New York: Harcourt Brace Jovanovich, 1977).

[10] Stone, "The Rise of the Nuclear Family in Early Modern England: the Patriarchal Stage."

[11] The family reforms proposed for working-class migrants are discussed by Barbara Ehrenreich and Deirdre English, "The Manufacture of Housework," *Socialist Revolution* 5, no. 26 (October-December, 1975) and Carole Lopate, "The Irony of the Home Economics Movement," *Edcentric*, nos. 31/32 (November 1974): 40; and Samuel Bowles and Herbert Gintis, *Schooling in Capitalist America: Educational Reform and the Contradictions of Economic Life* (New York: Basic Books, 1976). Elements of both the moral reform movement and the progressive movement can be seen as addressing the issues surrounding changing relations between genders and generations as American capitalism underwent the dual processes of proletarianization and urbanization.

[12] Recent analysis of Black families both historically and in the present includes work such as Herbert Gutmann, *The Black Family in Slavery and Freedom, 1750-1925* (New York: Pantheon, 1976), Eugene Genovese, *Roll, Jordan, Roll: The World the Slaves Made* (New York: Basic Books, 1974); Ladner, *Tomorrow's Tomorrow*, Stack, *All Our Kin*, and Robert Staples, "The Black Family Revisited: a Review and a Preview," *Journal of Social and Behavioral Sciences* 20, no. 2 (1974): 65-78.

[13] My interpretation of working-class family relations is in part based on Heidi Hartman, "Capitalism, Patriarchy and Job Segregation by Sex," *Signs* 1, no. 3, part 2 (Spring 1976): 137-70, and Jane Humphries, "Class Struggle and the Persistence of the Working-Class Family," *Cambridge Journal of Economics* 1 (1977): 241-58. My Third World examples are interpretations of Edgar Moyo, *Big Mother and Little Mother in Matabeleland* (Oxford, England, Ruskin College History Workshop Pamphlets, no. 3, 1973), and Mina Davis Caulfield, "Imperialism, the Family, and Cultures of Resistance," *Socialist Revolution*, no. 20 (October 1974): 67-85.

[14] Fine-grained analysis of peasant social structure as it contributes to political mobilization is found in Eric Wolf, *Peasant Wars of the Twentieth Century* (New York: Harper & Row, 1969), in Hamza Alavi, "Peasants and Revolution," in *The Socialist Register*, eds. Ralph Miliband and John Saville (London: Merlin, 1968); Alavi, "Peasant Classes and Primordial Loyalties," *Journal of Peasant Studies* 1, no. 1 (October 1973): 23-62; and Eric Hobsbawm, "Peasants and Politics," *Journal of Peasant Studies* 1, no. 1 (October 1973): 3-22.

[15] Ellen Ross wants to thank Christine Stansell for her helpful reading of an early version of this essay.

[16] Olwen Hufton, "Women in Revolution, 1787-1796," *Past and Present*, no. 53 (November 1971): 90-108; Laura Oren, "The Welfare of Women in Laboring Families: England, 1860-1950," *Feminist Studies* 1, nos. 3-4 (Winter-Spring 1973): 107-25; Joan W. Scott and Louise Tilly, "Women's Work and the Family in Nineteenth-Century Europe," in Rosenberg, ed., *The Family in History*, pp. 145-78; Louise Tilly, Joan W. Scott and Miriam Cohen, "Women's Work and Fertility Patterns," *Journal of Interdisciplinary History* 6, no. 3 (Winter 1976): 447-76.

[17] See Linda Gordon and Allen Hunter, "Sex, Family and the New Left: Anti-Feminism as a Political Force," *Radical America* 11, no. 6; 12, no. 1 (November 1977-February 1978): 9-25.

[18] The term is used by Gayle Rubin in her important synthetic article, "The Traffic in Women: Notes on the 'Political Economy' of Sex," in *Toward an Anthropology of Women*, ed. Rayna R. Reiter (New York and London: Monthly Review Press, 1975), pp. 157-210.

[19] Evelyne Sullerot, *Women, Society and Change* (New York and Toronto: McGraw-Hill, 1971), pp. 74-75.

[20] See pp. 189-190.

[21] Davis, "Ghosts, Kin and Progeny," pp. 101 ff. See also Stone's discussion of sixteenth- and seventeenth-century English conceptions of "friendship," in *The Family, Sex and Marriage*, pp. 97-98.

[22] Davis, "Ghosts, Kin and Progeny," p. 88; Stone, *The Family, Sex and Marriage*, pp. 132-35; Joan Kelly-Gadol, "Did Women have a Renaissance?" in *Becoming Visible*, pp. 137-64; p. 146.

[23] Stone, *The Family, Sex and Marriage*, p. 135.

[24] Ibid., pp. 132-33.

[25] Davis, "Ghosts, Kin and Progeny," p. 88; Stone, "The Rise of the Nuclear Family," p. 32.

[26] W. J. Goode, "The Theoretical Importance of Love," in *The Family: Its Structure and Functions*, ed. Rose L. Coser; 2nd ed. (New York: St. Martin's Press, 1974), pp. 143-56.

[27] Stone, "Rise of the Nuclear Family," pp. 35, 36-49; David Hunt, *Parents and Children in History* (New York: Harper Torchbooks, 1972), pp. 133-39; 152-58.

[28] Christopher Hill, *Society and Puritanism in Pre-Revolutionary England*, 2nd ed. (New York: Schocken Books, 1967), pp. 446-47.

[29] Edward Shorter, *The Making of the Modern Family* (New York: Basic Books, 1975), pp. 39-53; 121-38, 213-26; on "privacy" in the American colonies, see Nancy Cott,

"Eighteenth-Century Family and Social Life Revealed in Massachusetts Divorce Records," *Journal of Social History* 10 (Fall 1976): 20-43; see esp. pp. 21-24.

[30] Lasch, *Haven in a Heartless World*; Kenneth Keniston and the Carnegie Council on Children, *All Our Children*.

[31] See, for example, David Sabean, "Aspects of Kinship Behavior and Property in Rural Western Europe Before 1800," in *Family and Inheritance: Rural Society in Western Europe 1200-1800*, eds. Jack Goody, Joan Thirsk, and E. P. Thompson; paperback ed. (Cambridge and London: Cambridge University Press, 1976): 96-111.

[32] Carroll Smith-Rosenberg, "The Female World of Love and Ritual: Relations Between Women in Nineteenth-Century America," *Signs* 1, no. 1 (Autumn 1975): 1-29; Nancy Cott, *The Bonds of Womanhood, "Woman's Sphere" in New England, 1780-1835* (New Haven: Yale University Press, 1977), chaps. 2 and 5; Nancy Sahli, "Changing Patterns of Sexuality and Female Interaction in Late Nineteenth-Century America," paper presented at Third Berkshire Conference on the History of Women, Bryn Mawr College, June 11, 1966.

[33] Sahli, "Changing Patterns of Sexuality."

[34] Michael Young and Peter Willmot, *Family and Kinship in East London* (Harmondsworth, England: Penguin Books, 1957) and Robert Roberts, *The Classic Slum* (Harmondsworth, England: Penguin Books, 1973) are rich in neighborhood detail. See also Standish Meachem, *A Life Apart. The English Working Class 1890-1914* (Cambridge: Harvard University Press, 1977), chap. 2; Nancy Tomes, " 'A Torrent of Abuse': Crimes of Violence Between Working Class Men and Women in London, 1840-1875," *Journal of Social History* 11, no. 3 (Spring 1978): 329-45; 335-38; and Paul Thompson, *The Edwardians: The Remaking of British Society*, paperback ed. (St. Albans, England: Paladin Books, 1977), pp. 52-53; 88; 119-20; 144.

[35] Judith Walkowitz, "The Making of an Outcast Group," in *A Widening Sphere*, ed. Martha Vicinus (Bloomington: Indiana University Press, 1977): 72-93; 85-87.

[36] Dorothy Thompson, "Women and Nineteenth-Century Radical Politics: A Lost Dimension," in *The Rights and Wrongs of Women*, eds. Juliet Mitchell and Ann Oakley, (Harmondsworth, England: Penguin Books, 1976): 112-38; 116-20; 125-26; 136-38; Walkowitz, "The Making of an Outcast Group; see also her "The Common Prostitute, 1840-1914: An Overview," paper delivered at the National Conference of British Studies, New York University, April 1, 1978.

[37] E. P. Thompson, "Time, Work-Discipline and Industrial Capitalism," in *Essays in Social History*, eds. M. W. Flinn and T. C. Smout (Oxford, England: The Clarendon Press, 1974), pp. 39-77.

[38] Gareth Stedman-Jones, "Working-Class Culture and Working-Class Politics in London, 1870-1900: Notes on the Remaking of a Working Class," *Journal of Social History* 7, no. 4 (Summer 1974): 460-508.

[39] Berkner, "The Stem Family in the Developmental Cycle of the Peasant Household"; Richard Sennett, "Middle-Class Families and Urban Violence: The Experience of a Chicago Community in the Nineteenth Century," in *Anonymous Americans*, ed. Tamara Hareven (Englewood Cliffs, N.J.: Prentice-Hall, 1971), pp. 280-305; Fred Weinstein and Gerald M. Platt, *The Wish to be Free. Society, Psyche, and Value Change* (Berkeley: University of California Press, 1973).

[40] Linda Gordon, "Voluntary Motherhood; The Beginnings of Feminist Birth Control Ideas in the United States," *Feminist Studies* 1, nos. 3-4 (Winter-Spring 1973): 5-22; Daniel Scott Smith, "Family Limitation, Sexual Control, and Domestic Feminism in Nineteenth-Century America," *Feminist Studies* 1, nos. 3-4 (Winter-Spring 1973): 40-57.

[41] Johnny Faragher and Christine Stansell, "Women and their Families on the Overland Trail 1842-67," *Feminist Studies* 2, nos. 2-3 (1975): 150-66. Faragher's forthcoming

book on the same subject (Yale University Press), however, tends to lose sight of this perception.

[42] Laura Oren, "The Welfare of Women in Laboring Families: England 1860-1950," *passim*; see also Meacham, *A Life Apart*, chap. 3.

[43] I owe this observation to Joan Scott (conversation, November 1977). This section on the implications of role theory was a part of a talk prepared jointly with Rosalind Petchesky for a workshop on "Teaching about the Family," East Coast Regional Women's Studies Conference, Livingston College, November, 1976.

[44] Viola Klein and Alva Myrdal, *Women's Two Roles: Home and Work*, 2nd ed. (London: Routledge and Kegan Paul, 1968).

[45] Nancy Chodorow, "Family Structure and Feminine Personality," in *Women, Culture and Society*, eds. Michelle Rosaldo and Louise Lamphere (Stanford: Stanford University Press, 1974), pp. 43-66; and *The Reproduction of Mothering* (Berkeley: The University of California Press, 1978); Dorothy Dinnerstein, *The Mermaid and the Minotaur: Sexual Arrangements and Human Malaise* (New York: Harper Colophon Books, 1977); Juliet Mitchell, *Psychoanalysis and Feminism: Freud, Reich, Laing, and Women* (New York: Pantheon Books, 1973); Adrienne Rich, *Of Woman Born: Motherhood as Experience and Institution* (New York: W. W. Norton & Company, 1976); Jane Flax, "The Conflict Between Nurturance and Autonomy in Mother-Daughter Relationships and Within Feminism," *Feminist Studies* 4, no. 2 (June 1978): 171-89; addressing the same issues but using a different psychological framework is Jessica Benjamin, "Authority and the Family Revisited; or, A World Without Fathers," *New German Critique* 13 (Winter 1978): 35-57.

[46] Chodorow, "Family Structure and Feminine Personality," pp. 43-54.

[47] Toward both ends of the spectrum there has been acknowledgment of the political nature of this debate. See Peter Laslett, *Household and Family in Past Time*, pp. 4, 7; Elizabeth Fox-Genovese and Eugene D. Genovese, "The Political Crisis of Social History: A Marxian Perspective," *Journal of Social History* 10, no. 2 (Winter 1976): 205-20.

[48] To the best of my knowledge, these were first pointed out by Tamara K. Hareven in "The History of the Family as an Interdisciplinary Field," *Journal of Interdisciplinary History* 2, no. 2 (Autumn 1971): 300-414; reprinted in *The Family in History*, ed. Theodore K. Rabb and Robert I. Rotberg (New York: Harper Torchbooks, 1973).

[49] I wish to thank Wolf Heydebrand of the Department of Sociology at New York University for calling my attention to my own difficulties with this problem in an earlier work.

[50] There is a school of structuralist Marxism which does try to come to grips with the dynamic of change through class struggle as manifested in various social structures and ideologies. It has not, however, been applied to family history, as far as I know, and therefore falls outside the scope of this paper.

[51] "New Directions," *Journal of Home Economics* (May 1975): 26.

[52] Kenneth Keniston, *All Our Children*; Robert M. Moroney, *The Family and the State: Considerations for Social Policy* (London and New York: Longman, 1976).

[53] Bert N. Adams, *The American Family* (Chicago: Markham Publishing Co., 1971), p. 265; Mary Jo Bane, *Here to Stay: American Families in the Twentieth Century* (New York: Basic Books, 1976), pp. 32-33 suggests this more indirectly.

[54] Robert Blood and Donald Wolfe, *Husbands and Wives* (New York: The Free Press, 1960).

[55] Gabriel Kolko, "Working Wives: Their Effects on the Structure of the Working Class," *Science and Society* 42, no. 3 (Fall 1978): 257-77.

[56] Leonard I. Pearlin, *Class Context and Family Relations: A Cross-National Study* (Boston: Little, Brown & Co., 1974).

[57] Stack, *All Our Kin*.

[58] Renate Bridenthal, "The Dialectics of Production and Reproduction in History," *Radical America* 10, no. 2 (March-April 1976): 3-11. The present article has evolved out of this earlier one. I am grateful for the thoughtful readings and helpful suggestions of not only my co-panelists, but also of Martha Gimenz, Wolf and Sarah Heydebrand, Gerda Lerner, Hobart A. Spalding, Jr., and Philip Dawson. I owe a special debt to Deborah Hertz and Joan Scott, whose trenchant questions at the original workshop forced me to re-examine and refine some of my concepts. Finally, the editorial board of *Feminist Studies* made this a better piece by their penetrating criticism.

9   The Doubled Vision
of Feminist Theory

JOAN KELLY

Feminist theory is today bringing about a major advance in social vision. If we take as an index of the reemergence of feminist theory Juliet Mitchell's 1966 essay on the four structures by which to assess "woman's estate,"[1] we can appreciate how our understanding of women and society has developed. For more than a decade, the women's movement has been confronting sex oppression in the domains she helped name for us—production, reproduction, sexuality, and socialization. Since 1966 we have struggled personally, intellectually, and politically against the socializing of girls/women into the servicing, mother role, and against the socializing of boys/ men into requiring it. We have moved in thought, feeling, and action against the restriction of female sexuality to phallus and family. We have struggled to understand how and why male-dominant institutions control biological and social reproduction, and we have been fighting that control. And we have moved in several ways against an organization of work that fosters and profits from the sexual division of labor and the unequal relation of the sexes that flows from it. In practice and consciousness, this phase of the women's movement is no longer where it was when Juliet Mitchell marked out the paths along which we did indeed move; and our theoretical understanding has developed accordingly.

Responding to women's changed, and rapidly changing social situation and consciousness, feminist theory is now at a point where a significant transformation in social vision is both called for and being accomplished. What I propose to do here is characterize an aspect of this advance in theoretical outlook that I see emerging out of the several schools and strands of feminist thought and scholarship. It consists of what I call a unified, "doubled" view of the social order, and it promises to overcome certain conflicts in theory and practice that stem from earlier notions of sex oppression and social change.

TWO SOCIOSEXUAL SPHERES

In examining the sex order (or sex/gender system) of our society, recent feminist theory has shown how the industrial world of the nineteenth and early twentieth centuries construed society as divided into two sociosexual spheres. The bourgeois conception of a private and a public domain, a domain of work and one of leisure, also separated the sexes. Settling women and men into their respective spheres of home and work, it defined the place and roles of the sexes as separate and "complementary."

Our understanding of this view, and its impliactions for women, has been clarified by virtually all feminist scholarship. Feminist thinkers in the Marxist tradition[2] have traced the divided sociosexual order to the organization of capitalist production outside the home. They have shown how the separation of work (production) from leisure (consumption) really exists for men only. As a conception of society, the notion of home as a refuge from the world of work masks a sexual division of labor. It mystifies women's work in the home, obscuring the fact that this domestic labor helps "reproduce" capitalist and patriarchal society. I.e., procreation and the daily work that goes into consumption (housework) and socialization (childrearing) in the private family sustains the working population; trains people to know and keep their place; and provides for their replacement. At the same time, this unwaged and unacknowledged work of women in the home keeps women dependent on men and bound to a subordinate, servicing role.

Radical feminists,[3] concerned more with sexuality and socialization than with labor, have supplemented this analysis. Focusing upon consciousness and culture on the one hand, as well as the obscure levels of the unconscious, they have analyzed the psychic, sexual, and ideological structures that differentiate the sexes, setting up an antagonistic relation of dominance and subjection between them. We owe to this tradition our understanding of gender, of the lived inequalities of the "complementary"sex order, and how those inequalities are perpetuated by casting all women into the role of Mother.

With different emphases, one on societal structures, the other on psychic-sexual ones, both the radical and socialist currents of feminist thought thus point to the centrality of *reproduction* in women's lives. The defining of women as reproductive beings—as housewives and mothers—is seen as shaping women's self-image and sense of worth; sexual preference and expression; and women's relations with other women, with children, and men. In the Marxist inspired analysis, women's work of biological and social reproduction in the home (procreation and domestic labor) is seen as supporting an economic, social, and political order dominated by men, while at the same time preventing women from participating directly in that order. Industrial society made women marginal to the realm of production as it developed. It excluded women from the modern state. And "official" thought and culture, shaped by the male-dominant institutions of Church and Academy, sought to legitimate this sociosexual division by justifying the confinement of women to their separate sphere.[4]

To define the present state of feminist theory, it is important to note that in the nineteenth and early twentieth centuries, even opponents of the prevailing social order accepted in certain ways its establishment of two sexual social domains. This limited feminist and socialist theories of sex oppression, putting them in conflict with each other at certain points, and in internal conflict as well. To be sure, the different experience of middle-class and working women is reflected in the emphasis one theory put on gender and the other placed on class. But that feminists in the liberal/radical line of thought (as set forth by Harriet Taylor, for example) should generally ascribe the subjection of women to the "personal" satisfactions of male privilege,[5] while socialists saw it rooted in the property arrangements of class society, also points to conceptual difficulties in arriving at a view that would encompass the situation of all women.

This difficulty is especially evident in nineteenth-century socialist theory, which sought to be genuinely comprehensive on the Woman Question. It attempted an analysis of sex and class, and of the public and private domains. But it was never able to "see" sex/class operating simultaneously in both realms. Marxist thought on women, as developed by Engels and Bebel, found in the propertyless condition of the modern wage-earning family *the* material basis (and not just a basis) for the liberation of women. Once the productive property that was now held privately by the families of the bourgeoisie was publicly owned, there would be no patrimony to bind middle-class women to reproduction of the patrilineage. Nor would there be poverty that was forcing working women into sexual service to men. Although this view covered the different situation of both groups of women, it was not adequate to explain either the nature of sex oppression or its causes. Sex oppression was taken to be "private," as having to do only with sexuality and procreation, while causes were all in the "public" domain of capitalism's productive relations. Many socialist feminists developed more complex views. Crystal Eastman, for example, was sharply aware of sex hierarchy in the work force and of male domination in the socialist movement.[6] But the mainstream of Marxist views

on the "Woman Question" did not become responsive to the issue
of sex hierarchy in social production and social organization, and
it continued to regard male interest in the subordination of women
(independent of property) as vestigial only.[7]

In addition to differences between socialists and feminists, and
between the claims of sex and class, other currents of feminist
thought expressed other versions of the divided sociosexual world.
Many feminists came in different ways to defend and prize the so-
called female realm and its values. In the voluntary motherhood
circles, e.g., and even among suffragists and free lovers, as Linda
Gordon has shown, traditional sex roles were generally accepted.[8]
While resisting male control over sexuality and reproduction, over
what they themselves took to be their "natural" domain, many of
these women sought to deepen appreciation of family, motherhood,
and/or the particular virtues of Woman. Even some socialist wom-
en held similar notions, maintaining that socialism would simply
make it possible for all women to lead domestic, mothering lives.[9]

In somewhat different form, these conflicting tendencies still
divide the contemporary women's movement and feminist theory.
In the United States, we oscillate between participating in, and
separating from, organizations and institutions that remain alienat-
ing and stubbornly male dominant. We are pulled in one direction
by a Marxist-feminist analysis of the socioeconomic bases of wom-
en's oppression, and in another direction by a radical feminist focus
on male control of women's bodies as the key to patriarchy. Our
differences have not hampered the ad hoc coalitions formed around
struggles for abortion and protection against sterilization abuse; for
affirmative action, maternity leave, and daycare; for the Equal Rights
Rights Amendment and the right of sexual preference. But differences in theoretical position do affect our broader social commit-
ments and political alliances. They affect our conception of the
scope of the women's movement; its relation to issues of race and
class; and specifically, whether or how to join with what are still
male-dominant movements of resistance to inequities stemming
from an imperialist organization of the world economy and society.

Women will not forget how this phase of the women's movement
was forced to repeat the first wave in its inception. Women's groups
developed out of the radical movements of the 1960s much as they
did in the 1840s and 50s when women from the abolition and peace
movements came to form their own organizations because men, in
those very movements against oppression, retained sex-oppressive
structures and behavior. It is when we remember this that we feel
the strongest temptation to stay within the supportive network of
our women's groups, to restructure our own relationships along

nonhierarchical lines, to live our own women's culture. The tension between the need for separation and the will to create social change runs deep in the women's movement and in each of our lives, as do the related tensions between the claims of class, race, and sex.[10] It is my belief that we will live with these tensions for a long time. We will live with them perhaps as long as there is race, class, and sex oppression. For the truth is that the women's movement encompasses all these positions. We need both separation and full social participation to liberate ourselves from our several forms of sex oppression; and sex oppression will not itself be overcome without liberation from all forms of domination and hierarchy.

To say this does not resolve these oppositions. But it may urge us toward other ways of conceiving them. It helps us feel in practical terms the course that feminist theory needs to take and, I believe, is taking. Indeed, the argument I want to make here is that these oppositions stem in part from a social order, and a conception of society, that we have already moved somewhat beyond. Conceived as antagonistic ways of explaining and dealing with sex hierarchy, the conflicts between separation and social participation, and between the claims of sex on the one hand, and race and class on the other, are themselves expressions of the nineteenth-century conception of two sociosexual spheres. It is this conception that feminist social theory is at the point of overcoming—not by suppressing such oppositions, but by understanding the systematic connections between them.

SUPERIMPOSING THE SPHERES

One of the new and striking features of contemporary feminist thought, and of the objectives of the women's movement, is how, despite such tensions, certain differences are being superseded. In thought and practice, neat distinctions we once made between sex and class, family and society, reproduction and production, even between women and men seem not to fit the social reality with which we are coping.[11]

Studies such as Adrienne Rich's on the institutionalizing of motherhood, and those of Dorothy Dinnerstein and Nancy Chodorow on the psychic and social effects of female care of infants, demonstrate how sexual/reproductive arrangements, for example, shape men as well as women—as fathers and husbands, and also as policymakers, as the male gender in whatever role. Those arrangements, societal as well as affective in origin, shape public life and policy in the very attitudes toward nature, life, and power borne by the gender that must overcome the Mother. Similar to this appreciation of the public import of personal relations, is our recognition of the role of social agencies in the childrearing once ascribed to women and private families. In addition to families—and even assuming many of their former functions—nurseries, daycare centers, schools, and the media all participate in the so-called domestic work of social reproduction.[12] And finally, just as the entire economy and society works to reproduce itself, so we have come to realize that women produce, and always have produced, goods and services for society at large as well as for their families. Woman the gatherer may have sustained hunting-gathering societies even more than man the hunter did, and in every age women as well as men have engaged in the basic production of their societies.[13]

These new perceptions are emerging out of a newly complex social experience. With more of the work originally done at home becoming socially organized, and women following their work into the domain of socially organized production, women in increasing numbers are living in both the woman's and the man's world. We are living in the sphere of the family and of social production, and as we do so, we become increasingly aware of how the social relations arising from each sphere structure experience in the other. To be a mother in one domain deeply affects one's position, tasks, and rewards in the other domain. Mothering determines where and at what hours women work, and thus the jobs for which they are available. Conversely, the inferior pay and benefits of women's work in a sex-segregated labor market perpetuate women's economic dependence upon men. They pressure women to form sexual and/or familial attachments to men; and in the family ensure that the man's position will determine the place of residence and the unbalanced allotment of responsibility for domestic work and childcare to women.

Experiences such as these increasingly make us aware that *woman's place is not a separate sphere or domain of existence but a position within social existence generally.* It is a subordinate position, and it supports our social institutions at the same time that it serves and services men. Woman's place is to do women's work— at home and in the labor force. And it is to experience sex hierarchy—in work relations and personal ones, in our public and our private lives. Hence our analyses, regardless of the tradition they originate in, increasingly treat the family in relation to society; treat sexual and reproductive experience in terms of political economy; and treat productive relations of class in connection with sex hierarchy.[14]

In establishing these connections, feminist thought is moving

beyond the split vision of social reality it inherited from the recent past. Our actual vantage point has shifted, giving rise to a new
consciousness of women's "place" in family and society. From today's more advanced social situation, what we see are not two
spheres of social reality, but two (or three) sets of social relations.
For now, I would call them relations of work and sex (or class and
race, and sex/gender). In a Marxist analysis, they would be termed
relations of production, reproduction, and consumption. In either
case, they are seen as socially formed relations. They are seen to
obtain for women and men, and to do so *at the same time* in any
particular experience—be that work or leisure, familial or social,
personal or public. Relations of work and sex (or production,
reproduction, and consumption) affect women and men differently,
making "women" and "men" social categories, just as worker and
bourgeois are, and black and white. Relations of work and sex
combine so as to give women and men different relative positions
in society and the family, different powers, hence different sexual,
affective, and social experience. And such relations also affect
women differently by race and class. Thus female sexuality is
subject to male control by the welfare relation as well as by the
marital one. Class and race determine access to contraception and
abortion on the one hand, and sterilization on the other.[15] And
similarly, with regard to work and class position, women's subordinate position in the sex/gender system is expressed in super-
exploited sex-typed jobs for the majority, but also in the discrim-
inatory pay and advancement of more privileged women who do
find equal work.

From this perspective, our personal, social, and historical experience is seen to be shaped by *the simultaneous operation* of relations of work and sex, relations that are systematically bound to
each other—and always have been so bound. That is, we are moving beyond a nineteenth-century conception of society because
our actual vantage point has shifted. But just as the earth and
planets revolved around the sun long before Copernicus "saw"
that those were the relations of the solar system, so this dialectical
(or relational) unifying of our vision of the social order gives us a
sounder basis for understanding society—even society of the nineteenth and early twentieth centuries. The conception of two social
spheres existing side by side simply masked this more complex
social reality. It did not describe the society in which it arose so
much as reflect it ideologically. Wittingly or unwittingly, it served
to legitimate certain of the bourgeois patriarchal practices of that
society. At worst, by separating women out of production and
making them "the Sex," it drew a veil of Motherhood over the

forms of women's oppression that bourgeois society intensified: the economic super-exploitation of working women; gross abuse of the sexual advantage this gave middle-class men; subordination of bourgeois women to the property and personal interests of men of their class; and subjection of women to the demand for ever-increasing population to meet the needs of war and production.

Even in feminist and socialist thought, formed in opposition to capitalism and patriarchy, the theoretical outlook of two socio-sexual spheres led to partial theories of social change, and to partial theories of women's oppression and liberation. From today's position, we have already begun to see how earlier feminist and socialist thought itself partakes of the bourgeois and patriarchal outlook insofar as it subscribes to the dualities that society established.[16] We can no longer focus upon productive relations of class, suppressing those of consumption (sexuality/family) as Marx did, or focus on sex and familial arrangements (Freud, and Juliet Mitchell in *Psychoanalysis and Feminism*) without those of class, any more than we can place one sex in the category of sexuality/family and the other in that of society. To do so violates our social experience and the new consciousness that is emerging out of it. A more complex pattern of sociosexual arrangements is called for—and is appearing in feminist social thought. Feminist thought regards the sexual/familial organization of society as integral to any conception of social structure or social change. And conversely, it sees the relation of the sexes as formed by both socioeconomic and sexual-familial structures *in their systematic connectedness.*

The current political goals of the women's movement also indicate how the earlier, split vision of bourgeois patriarchal society is fading. These goals are neither to participate as equals in man's world, nor to restore to woman's realm and values their dignity and worth. Conceptions such as these are superseded in the present will to extirpate gender and sex hierarchy altogether, and with them all forms of domination.[17] To aim at this, as almost all parties (at least within the women's movement in the United States) now seem to do, is to make a program out of the essential feminist perception, that the personal is political. It is a program that penetrates both to the core of self and to the heart, or heartless center, of the male domain, for it will require a restructuring of all social institutions to change our subjective experience in this way. To restructure how we come to know self and others in our birthing, growing up, loving and working, feminist politics must reach the institutions that fatefully bear upon sexuality, family, and community. Schools and all socializing agencies will have to be rid of sex and sexual bias. Work and welfare will have to be transformed, placed in the humane context of the basic right of all to live, work, and love in dignity. And there will have to be genuine participation by all in shaping the modes and purposes of our labor and distributing its returns. A feminist politics that aims at abolishing all forms of hierarchy so as to restructure personal relations as relations among peers has to reach and transform the social organization of work, property, and power.

The theoretical outlook is just forming in which these several relations between sex and society will be examined. Feminist social thought is just beginning to overcome the dualisms it inherited; to account satisfactorily for sex, class, and race oppositions within a unified social theory. It is difficult, therefore, to describe this project clearly, because we are not yet in a position to look back and reflect upon a development that is not yet completed. Yet there is no doubt that most contemporary feminist thought adopts such a unified social outlook; and even at this early stage, certain consequences can be seen to flow from the redirection of thought it entails. I should like to conclude by mentioning three of them.

(1) Understanding women in such systematically unified terms should resolve those conflicts in feminist theory and practice that result from attempts to reduce sex oppression to class interests, or to see the relation of the sexes as always and ever the same, regardless of race, class, or society. Oppositions of this kind are no longer possible in a view that acknowledges the combined power of sexual-familial and productive relations in our lives, and the fact that these relations serve male and socioeconomic interests at one and the same time.

That is, a sharpened sense of particularity results from this vantage point; but the perspective itself unifies what is at once an economically and a sexually based social reality. Just as we see women and men in this perspective experiencing work and personal situations differently because of their respective sex (or gender) position, so women, because of our different class and race positions, experience sex oppression differently. The relation of the sexes operates in accordance with, and through, socioeconomic structures, as well as sex/gender ones. Hence, it operates differently in every society, and in the class and racial groupings of each.

(2) This unified view should enable us to understand better the persistence of patriarchy. In any of the historical forms that patriarchal society takes (feudal, capitalist, socialist, etc.), a sex/gender system and a system of productive relations operate simultaneously. They operate simultaneously to reproduce the socioeconomic and male-dominant structures of that particular social order. The labors of women that support societal life and foster its values are

thereby perennially harnessed to sustain and reproduce male dominance. And to men oppressed by the organization of labor and maldistribution of social wealth and power in society after society, the dual order of patriarchal society provides in many (but not all) instances the satisfaction of dominion over women.

(3) While our social understanding becomes more complex as the earlier, split vision of society merges into this unified, "doubled" view, the fact that we have such a view indicates that we are in a new social and political position with regard to patriarchy. It has been a strength of patriarchy in all its historic forms to assimilate itself so perfectly to socioeconomic, political, and cultural structures as to be virtually invisible. It could even couch demands for female subordination in terms of the prevailing social and cultural values: Athenian civilization, bourgeois equality (separate but equal), socialist priority of class struggle. If we are now in a position to see—as I believe we are now seeing—how the sexual/reproductive and the economic productive/reproductive orders operate together, our historical moment must be such that there is no longer that perfect mesh between the two that allowed us to see only one order or the other, but never the combined operation of the two. We must be at some distance from a social order that made one sphere, and one set of relations, fade from view as we looked at the other, so that at best we could establish only a few of the social connections between them. Now, conscious of women's subordinate place in the "private" (sexual/reproductive) and "public" (socioeconomic) domain; conscious of how relations of production, reproduction, and consumption operate to make women, as well as men, support a patriarchal social order; ours may be an historical moment when those relations are in sufficient conflict for us not only to "see" how the patriarchal system works, but also to act with that vision—so as to put an end to it.

NOTES

[1] Juliet Mitchell's article, "Women: The Longest Revolution," first appeared in 1966 in *The New Left Review*, no. 40. She revised it somewhat and incorporated it in her first book, *Woman's Estate* (New York: Vintage, 1973).

[2] What follows is not a comprehensive list, but rather examples of contemporary Marxist-Feminist analyses of women's work, in the home and in the work force: Charnie Guettel, *Marxism and Feminism* (Toronto: Canadian Women's Educational Press, 1974), and Dorothy E. Smith, *Feminism & Marxism—A Place to Begin, A Way to Go* (Vancouver: New Star Books, 1977) for general statements of position. For the special analyses of domestic labor and women's work, Margaret Benston, "The Political Economy of Women's Liberation," *Monthly Review* 24, no. 1 (September

1969); Mariarosa dalla Costa, *The Power of Women and the Subversion of the Community* (Bristol: Falling Wall Press, 1972); the English studies in *The New Left Review* (particularly Jean Gardiner in no. 89 [January-February 1975], "The Role of Domestic Labour"); the United States studies by Lise Vogel, "The Earthly Family," *Radical America* 7 (July-October 1973); and the issues of *Radical America* on women's work (7, nos. 4 and 5 [July-October 1973], 8, no. 4 [July-August 1974]; as well as the three issues or URPE's *Review of Radical Political Economics* on women (July 1972, Spring 1976, Fall 1977). The finest synthesis of much of this thinking is Sheila Rowbotham's *Woman's Consciousness, Man's World* (Middlesex, England: Pelican, 1973). All these studies are contemporary but find their forerunner in Mary Inman, *The Two Forms of Production Under Capitalism* (Long Beach, Calif.: Mary Inman, P.O. Box 507, Long Beach, Calif. 90801, 1964), originally in the *Daily People's World*, 1939.

[3] Outstanding examples are Adrienne Rich, *Of Woman Born* (New York: W. W. Norton & Company, 1976), Mary Daly, *Beyond God the Father* (Boston: Beacon Press, 1973), Shulamith Firestone, *The Dialectic of Sex*, rev. ed. (New York: Bantam, 1971), Dorothy Dinnerstein, *The Mermaid and the Minotaur* (New York: Harper & Row, 1977).

[4] There are several historical studies of this development. See, e.g., Nancy Cott, *The Bonds of Womanhood: "Woman's Sphere" in New England, 1780-1835* (New Haven: Yale University Press, 1977).

[5] "When . . . we ask why the existence of one-half the species should be merely ancillary to that of the other . . . the only reason which can be given is, that men like it." Harriet Taylor Mill, "Enfranchisement of Women" (1851) in John Stuart Mill and Harriet Taylor Mill, *Essays on Sex Equality*, ed. Alice Rossi (Chicago: University of Chicago Press, 1970), p. 107.

[6] Because of her sensitivity to sex discrimination in the work force, she was one of the few women committed to the labor movement and socialism who was an active advocate of the Equal Rights Amendment; and, although a socialist and probably a communist in the 1920s, she saw "the woman's battle as distinct in its objects and different in its methods from the workers' battle for industrial freedom." "Now We Can Begin," in *Crystal Eastman on Woman & Revolution*, ed. Blanche Wiesen Cook (Oxford: Oxford University Press, 1978), p. 53 *et passim.*

[7] E.g., ". . . the economic dominance of man over woman which long ago led to her dependency and subjection, does not exist any longer for the modern proletarian. The consequences in other spheres which also flowed from that dependency are now obviated." Henriette Roland-Holst, "Feminism, Working Women, and Social Democracy" (1903), reprinted in *Green Mountain Quarterly*, no. 2 (February 1976): 24. Sometimes called the Dutch Rosa Luxemburg, Roland-Holst was a leading Marxist at roughly the same time Crystal Eastman was active, although she lived until 1952.

[8] Linda Gordon, *Woman's Body, Woman's Right: A Social History of Birth Control in America* (New York: Viking, 1976), p. 114 *et passim.*

[9] Ibid., pp. 240-44.

[10] For the ways race, class, and sex (including heterosexis.   )ression are experienced in their combination, and the need for a theoretical position that will respect each and encompass all, see Audre Lorde, "Scratching the Surface: Some Notes on Barriers to Woman and Loving," *The Black Scholar* 9, no. 7 (April 1978): 31-35; Barbara Smith, "Toward a Black Feminist Criticism," *Radical Teacher*, no. 7 (March 1978): 20-27; and and "The Combahee River Collective: A Black Feminist Statement," in *Capitalist Patriarchy and the Case for Socialist Feminism*, ed. Zillah Eisenstein (New York: Monthly Review Press, 1978), pp. 362-72.

[11] For new work systematically connecting sex and class analysis, see Zillah Eisenstein, "Developing a Theory of Capitalist Patriarchy and Socialist Feminism" and "Some Notes on the Relations of Capitalist Patriarchy," in *Capitalist Patriarchy*, ed. Eisenstein. For connections between family, sex, and society, Eli Zaretsky, *Capitalism, the Family, and*

Personal Life (San Francisco: Agenda Publishing Co., 1973); Gayle Rubin, "The Traffic in Women: Notes on the 'Political Economy' of Sex," in *Toward an Anthropology of Women*, ed. Rayna Rapp Reiter (New York: Monthly Review Press, 1975), pp. 157-210; and Rayna Rapp, "Family and Class in Contemporary America: Notes Toward an Understanding of Ideology," *Science and Society* 42, no. 3 (Fall 1978): 278-300. For systematic and historical connections between production and reproduction, Linda Gordon, *Woman's Body, Woman's Right,* and for the social/psychic formation of gender, male and female, the works by Dinnerstein and Rich in n. 3 above, and Nancy Chodorow's several studies which have now led to *The Reproduction of Mothering: Psychoanalysis and the Sociology of Gender* (Berkeley: University of California Press, 1978).

[12] Renate Bridenthal, "The Dialectics of Production and Reproduction," in *Conceptual Frameworks for Studying Women's History* (Bronxville, N.Y.: Sarah Lawrence Publications, 1975). Rosalind Petchesky and Kate Ellis, "Children of the Corporate Dream. An Analysis of Daycare as a Political Issue under Capitalism," *Socialist Revolution* 2, no. 6 (November-December 1972): 8-28.

[13] Traditional Marxist thought regards the relations of production, reproduction, and consumption as forming one systematic social totality. Reproduction is not a separate "mode" of activity; it *is* the social process of production viewed "as a connected whole, and as flowing on with incessant renewal," (*Capital* I, chap. 23). Hence for Marxists, the idea of reproduction includes the notion of procreation and socialization, but applies to the reproducing of the productive system as well. It was chiefly the Frankfurt School and Wilhelm Reich in the twenties who began to work out the distinctive role of the family and sexuality in this reproductive work. Contemporary Marxist-Feminist analysis (in n. 2 above) distinguished women's work within the family. The role of "women's work" in the productive system as a whole has been worked out in the studies by Jean Gardiner, Batya Weinbaum and Amy Bridges, and Heidi Hartmann in *Capitalist Patriarchy*, ed., Eisenstein, and for hunter/gatherer societies by Sally Slocum, "Woman the Gatherer" in *Toward an Anthropology of Women*, ed., R. Rapp Reiter, pp. 36-50; Jane Lancaster, "Carrying and Sharing in Human Evolution," *Human Nature* 1, no. 2 (February 1978): 82-89; Adrienne Zihlmann, "Women in Evolution, part 2: Subsistence and Social Organization Among Early Hominids," *Signs* 3, no. 4 (Fall 1978): 4-20.

[14] On the old model of separate spheres, and the new one see Rosalind Petchesky, "Dissolving the Hyphen: A Report on Marxist-Feminist Groups, 1-5" in *Capitalist Patriarchy*, ed., Eisenstein, pp. 373-90. All the contemporary works cited in notes 10-13 above—and many others not cited here—are establishing these connections.

[15] *Workbook on Sterilization and Sterilization Abuse* (Bronxville, N.Y.: Sarah Lawrence Publications, 1978); Helen Rodriguez-Trias, M.D., "Sterilization Abuse," *Reid Lectures* (New York: Barnard College, 1976).

[16] It was in critiquing Juliet Mitchell that this became especially evident. See Eli Zaretsky, "Male Supremacy and the Unconscious," *Socialist Revolution,* nos. 21-22 (January 1975).

[17] Two major exponents of this view (and there are many, many others) are Mary Daly and Sheila Rowbotham, nn. 1 and 2 above.